MANN OF HIS TIME

Ed Youngblood

Whitehorse Press
North Conway, New Hampshire

Cover photo by Rick Kocks. Back cover photo by John Gola

Whitehorse Press books are also available at discounts in bulk quantity for sales and promotional use. For details about special sales or for a catalog of motorcycling books and videos, write to the publisher:

Whitehorse Press
P.O. Box 60
North Conway, New Hampshire 03860–0060
Phone: 603-356-6556 or 800-531-1133
E-mail: Orders@WhitehorsePress.com
Internet: www.WhitehorsePress.com

ISBN 1-884313-40-X

5 4 3 2

Printed in the United States

Contents

APPENDIX

Foreword

Someone once defined the word "wisdom" as "applied knowledge." If that brief, succinct definition is accurate—and I personally believe it is—Dick Mann is one of the wisest people I've ever known. That's not faint praise, either; I've been privileged to know quite a few exceptionally wise individuals during my six decades on this planet, and Mann ranks right up there with the very best of them.

My assessment of Mann's wisdom is not based on any criteria involving sheer intellect or a commanding grasp of global affairs. I'm sure, if you asked him, he couldn't tell you much about quantum physics or recite the key points of the North American Fair Trade Agreement. I would venture to guess, however, that if he were to get involved in such matters, he soon would be offering the leaders in those fields some of the most practical advice they'd ever heard.

Mann's wisdom, you see, is and always has been rooted in a commodity that seems to be in ever-dwindling supply in today's complex world: good old common sense. He has an uncanny ability to look at difficult problems and see through the stumbling blocks as though they were utterly transparent. He bypasses all the usually ancillary matters—political haggles, financial barriers, management dysfunctions, cultural anxieties, fragile egos, and any other sacred cows that might stand in the way of progress—and gets right to the very core of the matter. His observations are usually contained in short, brief statements, sometimes no more than just a few words. And if you choose to engage him in a debate, you'd better know of what you speak and be prepared to hear the truth—politely presented, but bare-naked and uncompromised. He doesn't always tell you what you want to hear, but far more often than not, it's precisely what you *need* to hear.

Mann is, of course, most widely known as a motorcycle racer of unparalleled versatility, a rider who competed successfully at the highest levels in more forms of the sport than anyone before or since. But his qualifications for greatness transcend mere on-track accomplishments. He also is a master mechanic, a skilled fabricator, a creative designer, an unsung inventor, a selfless promoter, and a clear-thinking visionary, all rolled into one. His keen insight has not been limited just to the hands-on, nuts-and-bolts aspects of the sport, either; his understanding of the intricate workings of motorcycle racing, as well as of the people in it, has always driven him to make the sport better, more exciting, and more enjoyable for everyone involved. There were times when the system that governed the races broke down more often than the machines that competed in them, but Mann was always prepared to offer practical solutions for getting both back on track.

In 1977, I wrote an article for *Cycle Guide* magazine, titled "The Mann Plan," in which Mann outlined the philosophical and tactical changes he believed motorcycle racing needed to undergo for it to grow and prosper. The sport had stalled in its drive to become a major league entertainment vehicle, and the captains of the business at that time didn't seem to know how that breakdown had occurred or what they should do to repair it. Mann felt that he fully understood the problem, however, and offered his thoughts about how the system could be fixed.

I don't know how many people read that article, but no one apparently paid it much heed. Yet today, even as this Foreword is being written, a small group of dedicated, knowledgeable individuals has been working diligently—and rather successfully—over the past few years to elevate motorcycle racing to higher levels. They are not using "The Mann Plan" as their operating guide and, as far as I know, aren't even aware of its existence; nevertheless, their strategies bear remarkable resemblance to those proposed in that 1977 article. Dick Mann had the answers; it took 25 years for the rest of the sport to understand the questions.

Although I can't say that I am one of Mann's closest friends, I have spent some time with him over the years. I worked with him briefly at Yankee Motor Company and later interviewed him on a couple of occasions for magazine articles. We've also shared several fun trail rides, done a bit of vintage racing, traveled together once or twice, and enjoyed a few high-quality lie-swapping sessions. Some of those encounters were fairly long, others were just a few fleeting moments. But not once in any conversation with Mann, regardless of how long or short it might have been, did I ever come away without having learned something valuable, something educational, something inspirational. Within his simple, straightforward observations about one thing or the other, there always was a message, a moral of the story, if you will. In his own simplistic way, this homegrown philosopher didn't tell me what to think about something; he told me *how* to think about it. I have never forgotten those conversations, and many of their messages have served as beacons that have helped me find direction for certain aspects of my life.

You are, therefore, going to read about a truly remarkable individual in this book, a man who has touched people's lives without even knowing he was doing so. In a society that sometimes seems populated only by takers, Dick Mann is a giver of the highest magnitude.

Indeed, perhaps Mann's greatest contribution to the sport of motorcycling is that, through his extraordinary wisdom and insight, this humble, unassuming gentleman has made those around him better, smarter people.

I know this to be true. I am one of them.

– *Paul Dean*

Introduction

At the beginning of his career, Dick Mann competed against legendary Indian racers Bobby Hill and Bill Tuman, and at the end of his career against three-time World Road-Racing Champion Kenny Roberts and America's first and only 500cc Motocross World Champion Brad Lackey. He was twice AMA Grand National Champion, and one of only four men to have won every type of competition included in the AMA Grand National Championship Series. None of the great host of riders of the Grand National Era came close to his achievement of holding a place among the top ten sixteen times during his nineteen-year career as an Expert ranked rider. He was—and probably always will be—the most versatile rider America has ever produced. He could flat track, scramble, and road race with the best of them, and he even qualified for the International Six Days Trial while he was actively campaigning the Grand National Championship series. To these competitive disciplines he added motocross, where he excelled in defiance of his years. His career bridged a period of extraordinary change, and he arguably influenced those changes more than any other professional racer. Not only was he a man of his time, but he helped, and continues to help shape his era.

This is the second book about the career of Dick Mann. The first—*Dick Mann: Motorcycle Ace*—was a memoir written by Dick in collaboration with Joe Scalzo. This book is indebted to that earlier work and is not intended to suggest in any way that it was unworthy or incorrect. To the contrary, it is an entertaining, informative, and valuable contribution to the history of our sport. However, *Dick Mann: Motorcycle Ace* was published more than 30 years ago, just after Dick had won his second Grand National Championship. I suspect it could have been motived by Dick's belief that his career was coming to an end, and hence his story was ready to be told. But that would have been a premature conclusion. Dick's greatest contributions to motorcycling were yet to come. Even after hanging up the steel shoe that symbolized his extraordinary professional racing career, Mann has continued to vigorously participate in racing and shape the future of our sport.

Dick Mann's accomplishments have been driven by two motives. The first was his childhood desire to become a professional athlete, which he could not achieve through stick-and-ball sports due to his small stature. The second was his love of motorcycling. Motorcycling brought him both joy and satisfaction, as well as the means to become a professional athlete. In Dick Mann's mind, motorcycling was compartmentalized into two distinct practices, fulfilling two distinct needs. Cow trailing and trials riding with his friends was, and still is, one of the great joys of his life. On the other hand, riding to earn a living was serious business, and he pursued it with as much grit, determination, and self-reliance as any racer in the history of American motorcycle racing. The latter fed him. The former feeds his soul.

His racing exploits alone could justify a book, but racing was only the prerequisite for Dick Mann's ongoing contributions to the motorcycle sport. He became an active force for improving the safety of racing and the treatment of professional motorcycle racers, he was a key player in revolutionary changes in the structure and operation of the American Motorcyclist Association that took place during the late 1960s, and he is currently a leader in the vintage motorcycle racing movement, which is still growing and evolving on a worldwide scale.

Dick Mann is a complex personality and a keen intellect who ponders, plans, and understands his actions. He believes in the future and understands how it is inexorably connected with the past. He is a man of conscience who has consistently and faithfully contributed his time and energy to the improvement of the American motorcycle sport. And in this arena—the politics of racing—he may have made his greatest contributions, though he would probably argue against such a notion.

I once wrote a book about another American motorcycling icon named John Penton. In the introduction of that book, I expressed regret that I had been unable to interview three of his great contemporaries because they were deceased. It is the same for this book, and in this case they are Al Gunter, Dick Dorresteyn, and Cal Rayborn. All three are men Dick Mann greatly admired, and there is little doubt they would have had a lot to say about him. But to the many, many living contemporaries of Dick Mann who have tolerated my questions and generously contributed their memories and observations to this book, I am genuinely grateful. They are far too numerous to mention here, and are acknowledged in Appendix E.

I want to thank the American Motorcyclist Association and the Motorcycle Hall of Fame Museum for giving me the run of their archives. I owe a great debt to John Penton, who motivated me to undertake this project, and to Dave Mungenast and John Sawazhki, who, along with Penton, helped make the project possible. Most of all, I want to thank Dick and Kay Mann for patiently answering my questions during two long interview weekends at their home followed by dozens of phone calls, and for reading and commenting on the manuscript. The project would not have been possible without their cooperation, support, and hospitality. I only hope this book succeeds in fairly capturing the truth and essence of a legendary motorcyclist who so profoundly influenced our sport, and so many of our lives and careers.

1

Little Bugs Discovers Motorcycles

Instead of going to his high school graduation ceremony, Bugs went cow trailing.
– Johnny Hall, friend

Richard Scott Mann, known to his friends as "Bugs," was born to Walter Scott and Rayola Mann in Salt Lake City, Utah, on June 13, 1934. He was a second son, having an older brother, Gary, born on exactly the same date in 1931. The Manns were not churchgoers, but they were Mormons who were aware of their history and their culture. Dick took a keen interest in American history—especially the Civil War and the era of western expansion—and he revered the early Mormons for their dedication, toughness, and resolve in the face of misunderstanding and adversity. These are qualities that he has exhibited throughout his life and his extraordinary career as one of the greatest, most versatile, and enduring professional motorcycle racers that America has ever produced.

Dick's father was a diamond drill expert, earning a living by moving from one desolate, Depression-era Nevada mining town to another, overhauling drilling equipment deep beneath the surface. The family lived in small places like Lebec and Valmy, never staying in one location for long. Although Dick was just a small child at the time, he still remembers the main features of that life: straight dirt roads disappearing into the distant Nevada mountains, huge mining machinery, burros,

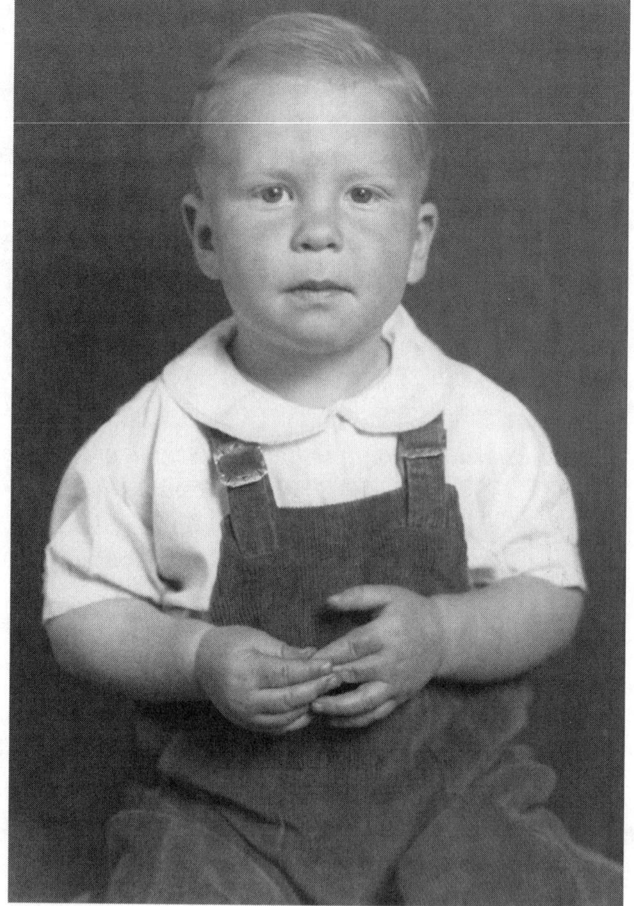

Dick Mann at the age of two. Dick says there was no way a small boy could stay clean in the dirty Nevada mining towns, but this photo stands as proof that mother Rayola buffed him to a fine sheen on at least one occasion. *Photo courtesy of the Dick Mann collection.*

summer dust, and winter mud. He recalls, "During the winter months there was nothing but mud. I was constantly dirty. There was no way for a little kid to play and be otherwise in those mining camps." He also remembers the family living in houses that ranged from earthen huts to tarpaper shacks, and sometimes even in dormitories with other mine workers and their families.

It was not an easy life. The Manns were able to stay in one place only so long as work remained available to Walter, then they would move on, seeking another mine that needed his services. For a time Rayola Mann helped make ends meet by managing a boarding house and cooking three meals a day for eight to a dozen miners. Then, when Dick was only four, his parents split up and his father disappeared. Rayola moved her family back to Salt Lake City where they lived with relatives for a couple of years, then to Reno, Nevada, where she clerked for a National Dollar store for two dollars a day.

These were the years of the Great Depression, and life was easy for relatively few Americans. But Dick recalls that he and his brother were well provided for. In fact, the Manns had it better than many, since the latter years of the decade saw entire populations throughout Arkansas, Oklahoma, and Missouri displaced by drought and a failing agricultural industry. Literally, they were refugees of economic defeat. Tens of thousands of these ragtag Americans gathered what possessions they could carry on their backs and in dilapidated Model Ts, and headed west toward a rumored paradise called California. Many found nothing to ease their plight on the west coast, but others were finally rescued financially by the outbreak of the Second World War. Rayola Mann and her two sons were among them.

Learning that jobs were available in the shipbuilding industry, Rayola Mann packed up the boys and headed for Richmond, California, a deepwater port on the San Francisco Bay. Richmond was founded in 1905 when the Santa Fe Railroad and Standard Oil arrived and sparked a turn-of-the-century industrial boom. Later a Ford Motor Company plant was constructed on the waterfront, employing more than 1,000 workers assembling 50,000 vehicles a year. The biggest change, however, came with World War II, when Richmond grew from 20,000 to over 120,000 in less than two years because Kaiser Steel had a government contract to build more than 750 Liberty Ships as rapidly as possible. So intense was the program, many ships went from keel to commissioning in fewer than 30 days, and on one occasion the Richmond workers built a complete ship in less than five days!

Kaiser, like other companies in the California-based defense and weapons industries, turned to the vast supply of manpower displaced by the collapse of the agricultural economy in the south-central United States. The tens of thousands of workers who migrated from Arkansas, Louisiana, Oklahoma, Missouri, and Texas to build ships made Richmond a bustling and multicultural city. They also made it a rough place to live. Some residents were not even literate enough to qualify for military service, as were characterized by the poor white trash in John Steinbeck's *The Grapes of Wrath,* or depicted by Dorothea Lange in her profound and haunting black-and-white photos from the era. Due to housing shortages, people not only worked in shifts, but slept in shifts as well, and many businesses were open 24 hours a day to cater to the defense workers. This bizarre, hardscrabble, non-stop city of wartime Richmond became the subject of some of Lange's most memorable photographs.

Individually, one might regard many of these displaced workers as the dregs of society, but collectively they created a proud and heroic persona of which America will always be proud. Traditional society was turned on its head as young women streamed into the shipyards and aircraft factories to fill the jobs vacated by the young men who went off to Europe and the South Pacific to fight for their country. Rosie the Riveter was born, characterizing America's will and ability to prevail against the dreadful threat of fascism. Rayola Mann was among the thousands of Rosies who took up traditionally male jobs to save their nation and feed their families. She found work as a burner in the Richmond shipyards, rising early to feed her children in the morning, spending her days cutting thick steel plate with a torch, then returning home in the evening to cook dinner for the family. Dick says, "It was heavy work. She spent long hours in noise and dirt, cutting steel, and dragging 60 or 70 feet of acetylene hose behind her." But hard work and self-reliance were not new for Rayola Mann. Being the second eldest in a family of twelve children, she raised ten kids before she was married and had two of her own.

Rayola Mann's contribution, and that of the thousands of women just like her, was recognized on October 14, 2000, with the dedication of Rosie the Riveter Memorial Park at the former location of the Kaiser shipyard. Designed by artist Susan

Schwarzenberg and landscape architect Cheryl Barton, the monument includes a 441-foot walkway reflecting the length of a Liberty Ship, a time line with quotations from the women who worked in the shipyard, and porcelain panels with photographs depicting the range of labor performed by the women.

No doubt, Dick Mann inherited or learned many of his strengths of character from his mother, including innovativeness, persistence, and determination. Rayola Mann also possessed a quick wit and a dry sense of humor that Dick's friends recognize in him as well. Lifelong friend and motorcycling buddy Johnny Hall tells of the time he dropped by Dick's place to find Rayola up on a ladder, cleaning the gutters.

Dick Mann's mother, Rayola, circa 1930. As a single parent, Rayola Mann raised Dick and his brother while maintaining a strenuous job of cutting heavy metal plate at the Kaiser ship building yards in Richmond. *Photo courtesy of the Dick Mann collection.*

Dick Mann, his older brother Gary, and relatives at the mining town of Mina, Nevada, circa 1937. Born in Salt Lake City in 1934, Mann moved with his family from one Nevada mining town to the next, eventually returning to Utah with his mother following the breakup of her marriage, then finally to Richmond, California where he lived most of his life. *Photo courtesy of the Dick Mann collection.*

When asked why she didn't make Dick clean the gutters, she laughed and said, "Dick can't deal with something like this. It doesn't have two wheels!"

Dick recalls the war years as a happy period in his life. The family had known greater adversity in the drab and desolate mining towns of Nevada and, by contrast, Richmond provided freedom and adventure for an inquisitive, growing boy. Dick says, "With mother working in the shipyard, we were pretty much on our own during the day, especially in the summer when we were out of school and had no adult supervision all day long. We could ride the bus to neighboring towns and hang out in the movie houses. Richmond was a rough place, but it was very different from the bad neighborhoods of today. There was no drug culture and no predators to bother young children. If we stayed away from the bars where people were getting drunk and fighting, we were unlikely to run into any kind of trouble."

Entertainment opportunities in wartime America were very different from today. Television had not yet arrived, and even the radio offered only three or four stations in even the largest cities. Dick says, "There wasn't much of anything to spend money on, including candy, since we had sugar rationing. We would buy and eat Smith Brothers cherry cough drops. I guess they could still get sugar to make them because they were supposed to be medicinal," he laughs. Remembering the cough drops, of which Dick preferred licorice, Mann tells about the exciting post-war return of Fleers bubble gum. He says, "At the end of the war when sugar and rubber rationing ended, we could get Fleers bubble gum again. People lined up down the block, and I stood in line and bought a piece. It was heaven. I chewed it and chewed it, and saved it overnight, then chewed it some more the next day. By about the third day it became real hard, and when I tried to blow a bubble, I accidentally spit it out on the ground. I picked it up and tried to clean the grass and dirt off of it, but it was too far gone. I was just devastated."

In the wartime economy a town the size of Richmond boasted more than a dozen movie theaters. Movies were the entertainment of choice of the era, and Dick loved them. As a young boy he would go to town, set up an orange crate, and shine shoes until he had earned enough money for the price of a ticket. Then he would while away the afternoon, enjoying the adventure and excitement of the latest cowboy movie. He recalls it as an age of innocence, stating, "Even the bad guys were dressed in clean and fancy shirts, and when people got shot, they just fell down. There was no blood or exploding body parts like the realistic violence we see in television and movies today." Because there were usually long lines for rationed goods, Little Bugs would also earn money by standing in lines as a proxy for others. He says, "I could get an easy quarter for holding a place in line." Wistfully, Dick recalls, "It was a good time to be a kid."

This was also the time when the nickname "Bugs" emerged, but no one knows its origin, not even Dick himself. He says, "My brother's friends called him Bugs for as long as I can remember. Then people started calling me "Little Bugs" and modified his name to "Big Bugs." Johnny Hall confirms, "I've known Dick as long as anyone. He delivered our newspaper when we were both kids. But I have no idea where the name came from. Dick's brother Gary especially liked to talk about Little Bugs. It was Little Bugs this and Little Bugs that. Gary was really proud of his little brother." (Neil Keen, the king of nicknamers on the AMA dirt-track circuit, started calling Dick the Bug Man. Then "Bugsy" emerged in the motorcycle press much later. Dick does not especially like that version.)

As Dick approached junior high school, football became a favorite pastime among the boys his age. He recalls that they became fanatical about it, forming neighborhood teams, playing constantly, and spinning out fantasies about their exploits as great professional players. Within this competitive sporting environment, Dick created a dream. Football is what he wanted to do with his life. He says, "I really wanted to become a professional linebacker, which is a pretty ridiculous aspiration for a kid who was 5-foot six and weighed about 130 pounds. But I was tough and determined, and that is what I really wanted to do."

Mann embarked on his dream by going out for football in high school. But he didn't even get to audition his skills. Rather, the coach lined all the boys up along a fence and announced that any below a certain height would not receive a uniform. Little Bugs was among a group of boys who didn't make the cut. The plan for his life's work was suddenly a shattered dream. Dick was angry. He mounted his small motorcycle and cut some broad-sliding laps around the field, letting the dust settle on those bigger boys who got the uniforms. He says, "I never looked back on football again."

But another great dream had been forming in Dick Mann's mind, and perhaps because of his intense focus on football, he had not yet even realized it. He had acquired a *San Francisco*

Examiner morning paper route and an old Cushman scooter with which to deliver his papers. The late Mike Indelicato, a local motorcyclist about eight years Mann's senior, said, "Dick used to constantly follow us around on that scooter, and he couldn't quite keep up with us older guys on our BSAs and Triumphs, but he sure as hell tried!" Finding the Cushman inadequate for his sporting needs, in 1949 Dick traded it in for a brand new a 125cc BSA Bantam that cost $280. He also obtained a beautiful pair of second-hand gentleman's riding boots, passed down by a motorcycle policeman. He says, "They were really beautiful. With my jeans over them, they looked just like shoes, but I could tuck my pants in the tops, and they were great for riding."

Still, real motorcyclists did not take something like the Bantam seriously. It was certainly not a scooter, but it was not considered a real motorcycle, either. But Dick loved to ride it and began to discover a joy that would eventually become the driving force for his life. His obsession with riding is described by Carthel Scoggens, a classmate of Dick's at Richmond High who later married Mike Indelicato. She says Dick was very intelligent, but was quiet and kept to himself, and did not care so much for school as he did about his motorcycle. She recalls, "I sat behind him during last period, and I could see him fidgeting, wanting to get out of there to ride. He sat there in his leather jacket and riding boots, and just watched the clock. He dearly loved to ride that motorcycle."

June Lawwill—formerly June Spenger—confirms this description of Dick's personality. Raised in neighboring El Cerritos, Spenger, who was about three years Dick's junior, first met him in 1955 when Dick ran with local motorcycling pals Rich and Bill Dorresteyn. Lawwill says, "Dick is quiet, but he is not antisocial. He came to parties and get-togethers, but he never got loud or rowdy. He would usually sit quietly and talk to one person, or sometimes just watch and listen to others."

Mann began to hang out at Walt Kreft's and Carl Huth's BSA dealership where he could read monthly magazines about what was happening in the motorcycle scene in England and

Europe. He says, "Right from the very beginning my heroes included Jeff Smith, Arthur Lampkin, and John Draper. I read about the American champions also, like Dick Klamfoth, but I dreamed of being Draper rather than Klamfoth, because Draper was small. He was like me." Reading about the great trials and scrambles champions overseas gave Dick ideas about the possibilities of living his life and earning his living as a professional motorcyclist. It also instilled in him a broad and global view of motorcycling that would eventually result in some of his greatest achievements and contribute to his remarkable versatility.

No one could have known it at the time, but Dick Mann and his motorcycling buddies were among the first generation of a new and exciting modern era of motorcycling in America. Prior to 1920, America had spawned a large and exuberant motorcycle industry. But the advent of the mass-produced Model T and a general economic decline brought the industry to its knees. Whereas there had been more than a hundred American brands in the early years of the century, by 1932 only Indian and Harley-Davidson remained, and Indian was already sliding toward eventual bankruptcy. With the arrival of the Great Depression in 1929, the American government took steps to protect domestic industry and the domestic economy, passing in 1930 the Smoot-Hawley Tariff Act which increased tariffs on imported goods. Higher tariffs made it economically unviable to import many European products, including motorcycles. Consequently, by 1940 the American motorcycle scene had become a rather monotone canvas, depicting little other than the big V-twin technology of Harley and Indian.

British motorcycles were few and far between prior to the second world war, but this changed rapidly with the passage of the Economic Cooperation Act of 1948, empowering the Marshall Plan for European economic reconstruction. Turning Smoot-Hawley isolationism on its head, the Marshall Plan encouraged international trade and the exchange of technology. As a result, a great number of British motorcycles were imported and sold in America during the 1950s, largely because they were inexpensive, exciting, maneuverable, available, and

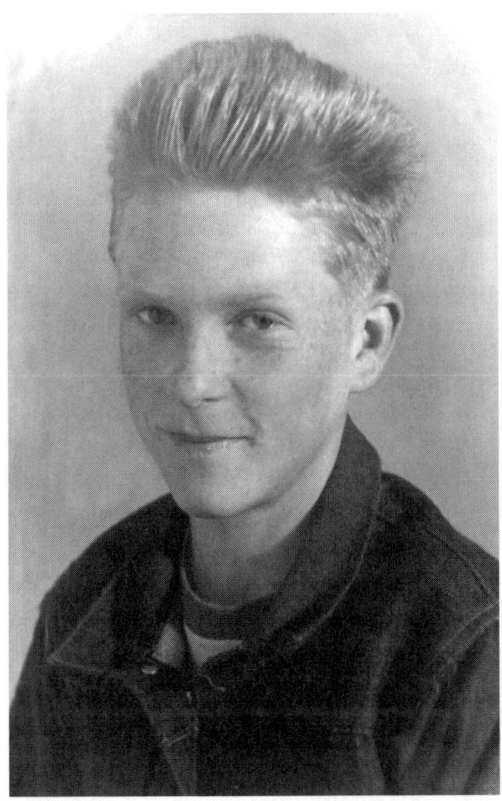

Dick Mann in his early teens. At this time Mann gave up his football dreams to pursue his life as an avid motorcyclist. *Photo courtesy of the Dick Mann collection.*

different from traditional American products. This, plus the influx of Japanese brands in the 1960s, turned American motorcycling into a more profitable, vibrant, popular business than it had been since 1920. While Oakland had long been a Harley town, Richmond became a hotbed of BSA loyalists, and El Cerritos spawned mainly Triumph enthusiasts. These, and other British brands, appealed to young men like Mann and his peers. This was the era of exciting growth and change during which Little Bugs and his buddies began to experience the joys of motorcycling.

Richmond was a great place for a young man to enjoy a motorcycle. When they could get away with it, Dick and his paper route buddies would street race or do hot laps around the high school running track, dispersing before the police arrived. On one occasion Little Bugs was racing around one of the athletic field tracks in the community when the janitor casually walked out, locked the gate, and called the police. Dick says, "I thought I was going to get arrested, but they just hassled me a while, then sent me home." In his memoir of 1972, Dick says, "Some of the greatest, wackiest bike races in the history of the world took place while we worked our paper routes . . . We were young, didn't know the meaning of fear, and always refused to back down." When the streets were too crowded for racing, or the running tracks off limits, Dick and his friends would take to the steep hills surrounding the San Francisco Bay. The little BSA Bantam was not very suitable for off-road riding, but Little Bugs was having too much fun to notice.

Prior to the 1960s and the advent of purpose-built dirtbikes, people who wanted to ride off the road used standard or slightly modified street motorcycles, which were never intended for use over rough and difficult terrain. For off-road pleasure riding, they often looked for reasonably passable terrain, and that—Dick Mann might tell you—is why God invented cows. When cows make their way from the barn to the pasture, and from one grazing place to another, they follow each other in single file. Like some kind of agrarian highway engineers, they seem to understand and adhere to minimum standards for turns and grades. They don't make sharp turns, nor do they take the shortest path over a steep hill. Rather, they seek a course along a gradual grade, dutifully following along, one after the other in single file, until they have terraced the hills with dozens of well-defined, hard-packed paths not more than a foot or two wide. These cow trails might well have been designed for motorcyclists who want to spend an enjoyable or exciting afternoon in the countryside riding over open terrain. Dick admits that he and his buddies did not invent "cow trailing," but through endless hours of practice, he says they raised it to an art form, becoming some of the best cow trailers in the West. In fact, cow trailing has become a term used by motorcyclists throughout the United States, even among eastern woods riders who use forested land where cows have never set foot.

After meeting Gary Nixon on the professional racing circuit in 1959, Mann invited him home to Richmond to visit and do some cow trailing. As an Oklahoma flatlander, Nixon had never seen hills like those around Richmond, and he was astonished that anyone could ride them with the casual ease displayed by Mann. Nixon says, "Later he came to stay with me in Maryland, and we went trail riding. These were *my* trails, that I rode almost every day, but Bugs was so fast he had to stop every five or ten minutes to wait for me to catch up."

As for Richmond and its environs, not only did it provide Dick Mann diverse opportunities for the development of a wide range of motorcycling skills, it gave him lifelong friendships with equally fanatical riders like Johnny Hall, Donnie Smith, and the legendary Rich Dorresteyn. In the hotbed of Brit bikes that the Bay Area had become, Bugs Mann became the king of the BSA crowd, and Dorresteyn the leader of the Triumph contingent, but their rival brands of choice never got in the way of their friendship as fellow motorcyclists.

His little BSA Bantam brought out the highly competitive aspects of Dick Mann's personality. Whereas he had previously envisioned himself as a competitor in team sports, as a motorcyclist he began to understand the thrill and excitement of competing one-on-one against other riders, and against his own self-imposed standards of excellence. One of Mann's first victories involved an autumn Turkey Run hosted by a local club. The winner of a Turkey Run—commonly held around Thanksgiving time—typically receives a turkey rather than a trophy. The contest is usually an off-road enduro or a road rally wherein competitors ride against the clock, seeking to complete a challenging course within a prescribed period of time. In his first Turkey Run, the youthful Dick Mann finished third, and for his reward he received a live goose. He recalls, "When the goose was handed to me at the award ceremony, the crowd of onlookers became hysterical. The goose was nearly bigger than I was."

Getting the live goose home was a bit of a problem. With no way to hook an unhappy goose to a speeding motorcycle, Dick simply squeezed it to his chest and zipped up his leather jacket around it, riding home with the head and neck of the goose sticking out in front of his face. Upon arriving home, Mann discovered that the poor animal had expressed its displeasure by shitting all over his shirt. Rayola Mann was not favorably impressed. What was a mother to do with a kid like this? Appropriately, she cooked Dick's goose!

2

Learning the Trade

He was this bright-eyed little carrot top. His bike didn't have much steam, but he was making the main on a regular basis. I knew he was going to be good!

– Joe Leonard, Three-time
Grand National Champion

In 1951 Dick Mann traded in the little Bantam for a 350cc BSA and got more seriously involved in scrambles, enduros, and other kinds of sportsman competition in the Bay Area. Don Brown, who would later collaborate with Dick to set speed and endurance records for BSA, reports that as early as 1952 Dick Mann was making a name as the rider to beat on the home front. Brown says, "I had just mustered out of the Army in the Bay Area and bought a new Triumph. I was looking for something to do and went to an event one weekend hosted by the Richmond Ramblers. It was kind of like an English endurance trial where riders were timed while they negotiated a course that wound around in the hills. Everyone was talking about Dicky Mann. They were going to get to see Dicky Mann ride that day, and were all excited about it. I realized he was a local star, and after I saw him ride I knew why. After the event he just happened to see my Triumph and came over to talk about it. He was really down-to-earth and friendly, and it made me feel good that he noticed my bike and talked to me."

Dick Mann with Peggy Spencer and hometown mentor Boots Curtis, 1957. *Photo courtesy of the AMA archives.*

Twenty years later Brown was an executive at BSA, and Mann was riding for him, in part because of the positive impression he left with Brown that day. Brown says, "Of course, I hired Dick for his skill and experience, but I had lots of good riders to choose from. I have no doubt my decision was affected by the good feelings I always had for him from our first meeting so many years before." Brown adds, "In fact, after my first encounter with Dick, I later traded my Triumph for a BSA, in part because that's what Dick Mann liked to ride. He was kind of a natural ambassador for motorcycling and any brand he was affiliated with. Over the years, I often wondered how many people Dick Mann influenced in that way."

In 1951 Mann began attending the weekly races at Belmont, a local quarter mile that attracted top California professional riders such as Charlie West, Kenny Eggers, George

Sepulveda, and Joe Leonard. He hung around the pits and helped a rider named Bill Verbiscio, better known as "Biscuits." When he graduated from high school in 1952, Mann purchased his American Motorcycle Association professional racing license and gave up his paper route. After a brief stint as a parts washer and general flunky at Walt and Carl's, he landed a good-paying job—$1.80 an hour—on a maintenance gang at the local Standard Oil refinery. Initially, he liked the job because he was active and always repairing something, but he soon got reassigned to the assembly line to affix labels to cans of oil, a mindless, soul-destroying job that was not to his liking. Within two weeks he quit and took a dollar-an-hour job at Hap Alzina's BSA dealership in Oakland. Mann reported to Bud Hines, an old-timer who provided knowledge and training that were worth a great deal more than money. Mann says, "Bud taught me a million things I never could have learned in school. I learned how to weld, how to paint, how to pinstripe a gas tank, how to tune engines and make them perform. In those days we did not just repair motorcycles by pulling new parts off the shelf. We actually fixed things. If you had a dented tank you fixed it, repainted it, and pinstriped it so it looked like new. We welded up things that were broken, and even straightened and rebuilt damaged frames, which would not be allowed today." Over time, all of these skills would be used by Dick Mann as he carved out a career as the most independent and self-reliant motorcycle racer on the AMA national circuit.

As soon as he had his AMA pro license, Mann disconnected the lights and front brake from his BSA, made a skid shoe from the bumper of a 1937 Hudson, and entered the fray at Belmont.

Belmont ran a progressive program, which meant it was possible for a Novice or Amateur (AMA terminology for first- and second-level professional riders, respectively) to qualify to race in the final feature against the Experts. The odds of that happening were slim to none, and all Dick wanted was track time. He was just getting in practice and trying not to get run over, with no aspirations to race any of the big guys. But he was better than he thought he was. Joe Leonard recalls, "I remember this little bright-eyed kid named Bugs Mann who would show up and try to race a little 350cc BSA. He only had about half the motor of everyone else, but he tried hard and he was really good, and sometimes he would make the main." Mann remembers, "The first time I pushed my bike out to the line for a heat race with Sepulveda, Eggers, and Leonard, I was so scared my knees were shaking. I wanted nothing but to get out of those guys' way, and I psyched myself into the perfect start, jumping off the line and leading them all into the first turn." Laughing about the terrifying experience, he continues, "I was first into the first turn, second into the second turn, third into the third turn, fourth in the fourth turn, and nearly last by the time we completed the first lap!"

His first race against the big guys may have been inauspicious, but Dick Mann was hooked. He went into hock to trade his little 350cc BSA for an old, track-worn 500cc single, bought a $17 Cromwell helmet, and rescued a set of tattered hand-me-down leathers from the dumpster at the local Triumph shop. Dick says, "I wouldn't take the leathers out of the garbage until late at night when no one was there to see me. The seat was ripped out and the crotch was hanging by a thread, but mom sewed them up and made me look pretty decent." Of course, no one looked too snazzy at Belmont. This was before the era of custom-made, form-fitting, colored leathers, and Mann's recycled suit fit in pretty well. But racing at Belmont was making life more complicated by the week. The old 500 added little to his performance, and he began to pour money into it to make it faster. And now that he had a full-fledged racing motorcycle not suitable for the street, he had to buy a used Chrysler to tow his racing bike to Belmont on the weekends. Not only was racing becoming expensive, but Mann was being actively discouraged at Alzina's. Bill Bulger, a fellow employee who had been with Alzina from day one and who rode an Indian Four, having never owned an automobile, told him he would never make it as a racer. Alzina threatened to fire him the first time his racing or an injury caused him to miss work.

Looking back, Dick figures the old BSA was good for him in that it was not fast enough to get him into trouble, and it forced him to try harder to improve his skills. From the more experienced racers he learned the tricks of the trade. For example, on a short track like Belmont, there was not enough room to pass people, but Leonard explained, "You just run the front wheel up to the other guy's leg, put it against the crankcase, and push him out of the way." In spite of these lessons and his best efforts, Mann still couldn't win at Belmont. After a season of racing, his best finish was fifth, so he decided to try his luck at Tulare, a half-mile track one hundred miles south.

At Tulare Mann had problems with his old single, and Ed Sumner, a Fresno BSA dealer, loaned him a new BSA Star Twin. Albert Gunter had already won an AMA National on just such a motorcycle, and it was the first really fast motorcycle that Mann had an opportunity to ride. Unfortunately, his front tire went flat diving into turn three off of the back stretch, and Mann hit the fence, smashing his $17 Cromwell into several pieces. The next day he rebuilt the helmet with fiberglass and joked that he felt better about having a helmet that was properly broken in. Restoring a damaged helmet would be

A youthful Dick Mann proudly displays his trophies and his Greeves racer. Though the photo is undated, the championship jacket would indicate that it was taken some time after 1957, the first year that Dick broke into the prestigious top ten AMA riders in the nation. *Photo courtesy of the Dick Mann collection.*

Dick Mann in the winner's circle after winning the Amateur final at the AMA national championship at the Bay Meadows mile in 1954. The Bay Meadows victory earned Dick his first recognition in the national motorcycle press, as well as the right to go on the road under the tutelage of Al Gunter. Note Mann's stocking foot. Having lost his steel skid shoe in the race, Mann continued to slide on the sole of his boot, nearly setting it on fire. He had to remove the hot boot before accepting his trophy. *Photo courtesy of the Dick Mann collection.*

unthinkable today, but in 1954 technology and safety standards were not what we have come to expect. In fact, the Cromwell patched up with fiberglass was probably better than new, because its shell was originally made of lacquered cardboard. Fiberglass was a brand new technology, styrofoam had not even been invented, and the inside of the Cromwell had straps and webbing like a football helmet of the same era. In retrospect Mann jokes, "The only thing the shell was ever good for was holding the webbing on your head!"

Despite his misfortune at Tulare, Mann decided he liked traveling and visiting different tracks. His next was Hollister, a big, wide bowl with a loose surface and six inches of dirt piled to the outside. Such a track—more common in the Midwest—is called a "cushion" track. It was a totally different experience from the hard, tacky surface of Belmont. Mann loved it. He says, "If you were nervy enough you could just plow into the corners wide open without backing off on the throttle. You just cocked your handlebars until the rear end started sliding out, then you just stayed on it and pretty soon your back wheel was spraying a big rooster tail of dirt all the way around the turns."

In 1954 he won his heat and qualified for the Amateur final at Vallejo. In the main event he was on his way to a sure victory but ran out of gas on the last lap. Mann says his BSA was a gas-guzzler, but Johnny Hall adds a little color to the story. Laughing, Hall says, "You gotta understand that Dick Mann always kept a pretty tight grip on a dime. If he had put 35 cents instead of 30 cents of gas into his tank, he would have won that race!" Yet, in a greater sense, Mann *was* a winner because Vito Durante, a motorcycle dealer and racing bike sponsor from Cheyenne, Wyoming, had watched Dick race that night and was impressed with what he saw. He approached Mann and said, "I'm looking for a good Amateur to race the Kansas county fair circuit this summer. I like the way you looked out there. How would you like a full sponsorship to race for me?" Mann said, "Where's Kansas and when do I leave?"

Filled with confidence and dreams of glory, Mann marched into Hap Alzina's office on Monday morning and asked him for a month's leave to go racing in Kansas. The reaction he got brought him quickly back to earth. Alzina said, "No way! If you take a month off, just don't come back. Why do you want to go all the way to Kansas to go racing? You can't even win races around here!"

Mann says, "I was just devastated, but Hap had a point. I couldn't figure out whether to call Mr. Durante and call it off, or whether to just quit and go racing in Kansas." When Dick started working on his BSA to try to sort things out in his mind, the picture became even bleaker. The BSA had a cracked piston. There was a big national championship coming up at Bay Meadows the following Sunday, and Mann couldn't see any way to fix his bike in time. Knowing there would be no sympathy from Alzina, Mann bemoaned his fate to his longtime friend and mentor Boots Curtis. Boots listened patiently to his troubles then said, "I'll call Ang Rossi, the BSA dealer up in Santa Rosa. Maybe he has something for you to ride at Bay Meadows."

Rossi did not have a racing bike, but his son Don, who was an excellent tuner, had just completed a fast street bike for a good customer, and Ang called him to see if he would let Dick Mann race the motorcycle. The bike owner agreed, and to his surprise, Mann discovered that the bike was faster than any racing machine he had ever ridden. Bay Meadows was a big mile oval, and he could get terrific speed out of the motorcycle on the long straightaways. Joe Leonard won the National Championship and Mann won the Amateur main event and set a new Amateur track record. More remarkable still, his old 1937 Hudson bumper skid shoe disintegrated during the race, but Mann finished by sliding on the sole of his boot, nearly setting it afire. The winner's circle had to wait until he could remove the smouldering boot. Mann says, "I thought I had done some serious damage to my foot, but when I got the boot off it wasn't so bad."

The big Bay Meadows victory brought Dick Mann into national prominence. He is pictured in the August 1954 issue of *American Motorcycling,* the official magazine of the *AMA,* grinning in the Bay Meadows winner's circle, complete with his patched-up Cromwell, baggy hand-me-down leathers, only one shoe, a trophy in one hand, and a trophy girl in the other. But Dick's debut story did not quite get it right. Although his name was listed correctly in the results of the race, the text of the story referred three times to the upcoming Bay Area star as "Duke Mann."

With the Bay Meadows victory under his belt, Mann decided that he was right and Alzina was wrong; it was time to take on the Kansas circuit, and Hap could just fire him if he didn't like it. Mann approached Alzina and declared his intentions, fully expecting to get fired. Rather, Alzina ignored Mann's ultimatum and said matter-of-factly, "Have you heard of Louie Thomas?" Louie Thomas was a Los Angeles-based tuner, widely known as one of the best, and Mann said certainly he had heard of him. Alzina continued, "Well, I just finished talking to him. He heard about your Bay Meadows win and he has a BSA for you. You can take it back East to race, and you'll be traveling with Al Gunter." Then he added, "And your job will be here waiting for you when you get back."

That proud grin is well justified, as Dick displays the trophy from his big Amateur class win at Bay Meadows in 1954. Mann won the race aboard a borrowed BSA street machine, and the victory earned him support from Los Angeles tuner Louie Thomas. *Photo courtesy of the Dick Mann collection.*

Mann was speechless. Not only would he be sponsored on a racing bike built by one of the best in the business, but he would be traveling under the tutelage of one of the most famous Experts on the circuit. What's more, Mann says, "I don't believe Alzina heard from Thomas that morning. I think it was the other way around. I think Alzina called Thomas and set it up for me. I never figured Hap out. One minute he would bring me down to earth hard, then the next he would secretly do something nice for me. You just never knew what he was going to do."

Dick Mann at Ascot in 1964. *Mahony Photo Archive.*

Mann called Durante to tell him about the opportunity, and Durante agreed that it was a far better program than he could offer. Mann recommended his friend Chuck Eastman for the Durante ride, and Durante agreed. Everyone was happy, and Dick Mann climbed into his old Chrysler and headed for Los Angeles to meet Albert Gunter, one of the most ingenious, inscrutable, and unpredictable characters he would ever know.

Those who have known both men find them one of the oddest couples that could ever travel the circuit together. Dick Mann is quiet and never speaks before he thinks. Albert Gunter rarely thought before he spoke. Dick Mann is one of the most unselfish men you will ever know. Al Gunter was self-absorbed. Impetuous, abrupt, fastidious, opinionated, and hot-headed, Al Gunter got away with abrasive behavior through the sheer heat of his genius. Lacking even a high school education, he was a self-taught and brilliant man who was always dreaming up novel solutions to problems. Most people who met him immediately recognized that he was "out there," and very bright. He was an accomplished engine builder and constantly thought of ways to make bikes run faster and equipment work better. He can be called the father of the modern full-coverage helmet, having designed the revolutionary Bell Star while working for Bell. He pursued theories and ideas that were totally alien to his milieu. For example, he became a vegetarian and set up a rigorous program for personal nutrition when other riders were satisfied with any greasy spoon that was cheap and quick.

In Dick Mann's own words from his 1972 memoir: "I can still see Gunter now, walking out to the starting line at the last minute, pulling on his gloves and adjusting his goggles just so. Did he care that he'd kept all those other riders sitting on their bikes in the hot sun waiting for him? Not Albert. Albert Gunter was an individual unto himself, a freethinker, and the smartest, shrewdest motorcycle racer I have ever known." Mann also has said, "Among the many things I learned from Albert Gunter, one was restraint, because he didn't have any!"

Mann's old Chrysler crapped out on him on the way to Los Angeles, and he had to abandon it and catch a bus. He was a day late and thought he had gotten off on the wrong foot, but Gunter seemed not to care. Right away he announced they were not going to Kansas. Rather, they were going to go to Sturgis, then on to race the rest of the Nationals. Racing at the national championship level was an even greater opportunity than Dick Mann expected. Gunter won Sturgis, and Mann finished second to Al Laur in the Amateur final. He finished third at the Northwest Championship and was running second to Brad Andres at the Springfield Mile when he bumped Andres and fell, only to remount and finish sixth. At the Pacific Coast Championship Mann took the fastest time, won his heat, and won the final. At Milwaukee he won the Amateur final. Andres, the hottest Amateur on the circuit, won practically everything else. In summary, Dick Mann was overshadowed that year by Brad Andres, who was nearly unbeatable aboard a hot Harley-Davidson built by his father, Leonard Andres. But Dick Mann's performance was nothing to be ashamed of, and it brought him recognition as a new and worthy competitor who was quickly learning his trade.

Gunter and Mann made a good team. Gunter had a protege who was quick to learn, and Mann had a mentor who taught him the skills and tricks of the trade it might have taken him years to discover on his own. The two men developed a mutual admiration that lasted for the rest of Gunter's life. Al Burke, a professional racer from Minnesota, recalls the summer of '54. Burke says, "I was standing in the pits at Sturgis, talking to Al Gunter. Suddenly I heard someone making a screaming qualifying lap, circling the track without ever shutting off the throttle. It was a BSA Star Twin with megaphones. I looked up and said, 'Who the hell is that?' Al Gunter said, 'That's a young guy named Dick Mann. You're going to want to remember that name.' "

3

Life on the Road

Dick Mann is the original stick shift guy. He did it all and slept in his truck, even when he didn't have to, because he was just that kind of guy.
– Neil Keen, motorcycle racer

The greatest public works project in American history began in 1956 with the passage of the Interstate Highway Act. For a nation that had just fought a world war simultaneously in two theaters on opposite sides of the planet, a vast interstate highway system was conceived for national defense to enable the military to rapidly deploy troops and materiel from coast to coast. But like today's Internet—the so-called information super highway—which also was developed for use by the Pentagon, the real benefit of the interstate highway system accrued to the public at large, and it forever changed commerce, culture, and the life of the average American.

Over the next four decades more than 41,000 miles of high-speed, limited-access highways would lace across America, giving citizens access to those wonderful places they had previously seen only at movie houses and through Viewmasters. Travel became a national pastime, Detroit geared up to provide two cars for every family, chains of convenient and clean eateries sprang up at every offramp, and Holiday Inn launched the revolutionary concept of good hotel rooms that were affordable to anyone. The interstate highway system became a magic

Following his first season on the AMA national circuit as a factory-supported rider, Dick poses for a BSA publicity shot with his friend and mentor Al Gunter, left. In the center is BSA racing chief Ted Hodgdon. *Photo courtesy of the Dick Mann collection.*

carpet that propelled Americans to greater prosperity, giving them a lot of adventure and excitement along the way.

But the network of highways we take for granted today was not yet approved by the U.S. Congress when Dick Mann left Richmond in 1954 to hit the road to pursue his passion and profession as an itinerant motorcycle racer. When Dick Mann began to cross America, there were no limited-access highways, there were no reliable fast food chains, there were no franchised hotels. It was still an America of dusty roads, two-lane blacktop interrupted by small towns, greasy spoon eateries, flop houses, and tourist cabins. It was populated by people who knew their neighbors, recognized outsiders, and frequently distrusted "drifters" passing through. Many people on the road during the decade following the war were displaced workers, troubled vets, hobos, or misfits. And the distrust accorded to such outsiders just might go double for guys hauling a trailer full of racing motorcycles, tires, and other paraphernalia. America's first civil rights legislation would not appear for another three years and the Supreme Court's creation of Miranda warnings was more than a decade away. Outsiders just passing through in 1954 America did well to keep in mind that cops were kings, except in the deep South where they were gods! Mann recalls: "The South was a foreign country. People spoke a different dialect, behaved differently, and the food was different. The only thing that was the same was the money."

When Dick Mann started traveling the AMA national circuit, there were only eight to ten Nationals per year, but the annual trek was no less daunting than it is today. A northern Californian had to make four trips per year across the country. The first was Daytona in March, followed by a Spring swing that included Laconia, New Hampshire; Heidelberg, Pennsylvania; and Columbus, Ohio. Next came Sturgis and a side trip to the Kansas circuit, followed by Peoria and Springfield in Illinois. Then came another trip all the way back to Pennsylvania for Langhorne, before returning to Southern California for Ascot. This roughly 20,000 miles had to be travelled over two-lane blacktop at best, and dirt roads otherwise. Most of the racers used dilapidated sedans that towed homemade trailers. Some used pickups. About life on the road, Neil Keen says, "It is exciting. You are in charge of things. It is like the mountain men of a hundred years ago. You lived where dark overtook you." Of course, Keen is speaking figuratively, because the racers usually continued on until they were overtaken by exhaustion or some catastrophic failure with their tow vehicle or trailer.

Life on the road was enough to wash out many who aspired to racing glory. It was dirty and demanding. Decent food was nonexistent, and no one had any money. Many traveled in pairs, and drove around the clock until they could drive no farther. Then they slept in or under their vehicles, and found a creek somewhere the next day to take a bath. Joe Leonard recalls, "We would wash our clothes in the creek, then drape them over the handlebars of our race bikes and take off down the road." Tom Cates, an Ohio-based racer, recalls, "After the race at Sturgis we would head out to Bear Butte Lake. Sometimes it looked like a National final. In the water would be Brashear over here, Resweber over there, and all the other top riders, all naked and taking a bath." He chuckles, "There was so much soap film on the surface, if we tried it today the EPA would probably shut us down!"

John Hateley reports an alternative and more creative method for personal hygiene: "We would park on the back side of a motel early in the morning and watch the people leaving their rooms. Sometimes a guest would leave and not pull the door shut behind him. When that happened we could rush in and get a nice, hot shower and be gone before the maid made her rounds." When someone had enough scratch for a motel, he usually invited three to five of his buddies also. The idea was to get a motel room large enough to pull the mattress off the double bed and toss it on the floor. That way two guys could sleep on the box springs and two on the mattress.

But there were other ways to get a good night's sleep. For example, Joe Leonard is a big man who didn't find it easy to sleep in his car. He recalls, "Somehow I figured out that camping trailer dealerships usually didn't lock up the campers. I would come into town late and find one of these dealerships and sneak inside a camper to get me a good night's sleep. I had a little windup alarm clock so I could be out of there early and on my way." However, on one occasion Leonard's alarm clock did not go off. He explains, "I was awakened by the camper jostling around, and here was the salesman coming in with a young couple. He was busy preaching about all the great features of this camper and still hadn't seen me. Finally the woman stopped him, pointed at me, and said, 'Does that come with it?' " Leonard grabbed his pants and ran for it while the salesman stood there with his mouth hanging open.

Some journalists have painted an exaggerated and dramatic picture of the AMA national circuit as warring camps: Harley guys versus BSA guys versus Triumph guys, all mindless brand loyalists who fairly hated each other. It simply is not the truth. Life on the road was their common ground, no matter what they rode, and it was not unusual for riders of different brands to travel together. Through shared adversity, they became more like an itinerant carnival community, trekking together from race to race and helping each other whenever they could. Relying on their different talents, they developed community support systems that often went beyond brand loyalty. On one occasion Indian star Bill Tuman, who was a superb mechanic, helped Leo Anthony install new racing cams in his Harley, then was rewarded by getting beaten by him.

Different members of the community took on important roles. For example, Neil Keen was one of the most widely-read riders on the circuit. He knew physiology and the proper names for injuries and broken bones. Keen learned how to temporarily but effectively treat sprains and minor breaks with makeshift casts made of duct tape. Because he was from the South, his monikers included "Peaches," "Peachy Keen," and

Having earned AMA National Number 64, Dick Mann sits aboard his factory Gold Star on the famous beach course at Daytona in 1956. Mann led the race until his clutch failed on the 36th lap. *Photo courtesy of the Dick Mann collection.*

"Dr. Peach," in reference to his medical skills. Getting patched up on site could be important. If you took a ride in the ambulance, the AMA would retain your license until you received a medical release, and that might put a rider out of work for several weeks.

Keen and Dick Mann also gave the other riders haircuts for a couple of bucks. Mann says, "I knew how that was done. My mother cut my brother's and my hair until we were about 20." Mann also earned pocket money by changing tires, a frequent task that some of the riders despised. He recalls, "I could make five bucks changing a tire. But sometimes I would gamble on whether the guy was going to win that day, and if he did, my share of the purse could be as much as $25. But if it went the other way, I might get nothing. Then there were races when the best money I made was from changing tires." Riders would share machinery for their mutual financial benefit. On one occasion Dick Mann had a broken ankle and Dave Aldana had a destroyed engine. Neither man was going to earn a penny that day, so Mann loaned Aldana his BSA in return for half his earnings, and Aldana used the bike to win a National.

When Gary Nixon arrived on the scene, he was an unsophisticated little redhead from Oklahoma who had a craving to race, but meager means. He was always broke, and would sometimes go down the line at racetrack registration, panhandling for his entry fee. Fellow Okie Ted Davis recalls with amusement a time when Darrel Dovel threatened to beat the hell out of Nixon, just trying to get back the four dollars that Gary had owed him for weeks. At one point Nixon didn't even have a tow vehicle. He had nothing but a trailer with a motorcycle on it, which he talked other riders into towing from one race to the next. He would hitch his trailer to the back of some sympathetic comrade's pickup, then ride in the bed to the next event. Finally, he arrived one day resplendent with his trailer behind a big, clapped-out old Lincoln that he had purchased from Everett Brashear. At the end of the day when the Lincoln wouldn't start, Nixon talked Dick Mann into towing his whole mess—the Lincoln plus his trailer—to the next event. Of course, at the end of that event the Lincoln still wouldn't start, so Gary asked Dick to tow him to the *next* race. Facing the horrifying vision of dragging Nixon and his Lincoln junker all over America for the rest of his life, Mann put his foot down and said, "No, Gary, we can't keep doing this! You gotta get yourself some transportation." Mann continues, "We just left the Lincoln sitting, and I towed Gary to the next couple of races until he could earn enough for another car." With a laugh, Mann adds, "I think Nixon never forgave Brashear for selling him that Lincoln."

When the circuit was in the Midwest and the corn crop was coming along, the riders would stop, pick some corn, boil it in water in a hubcap, and have a feast. Mann says, "I never figured it out. The farmers didn't seem to mind us taking corn, but they were apt to shoot you if you tried to steal a watermelon." John Hateley recalls, "One time I was with someone and we had to fix a flat. We pulled off the hubcap, and it was filled with encrusted, burnt beans. We became hysterical, laughing about how it must have been previously owned by some old racer."

Riders with status, such as those with National Numbers, had little trouble bunking at key motorcycle dealerships around the country. Often the accommodations were primitive, but they beat sleeping under a car. Ted Davis says, "The first time I went back east with Dick Mann, he got us in at Joe DiSimone's just outside Philadelphia. We had to climb a ladder up to a second story window of an old building behind Joe's shop, but we thought nothing of it. Those were pretty good accommodations."

The Midwestern swing of the AMA circuit spawned the great legend of Lund's. John Lund was a young BSA dealer in Decatur, Illinois, whose shop served as headquarters for many of the racers. So popular was the hangout, that Lund's earned an official designation as BSA's Midwestern Racing Headquarters, and was supplied with parts that Lund was authorized to distribute to the sponsored riders. Lund's mechanic Claude McElvain says, "At peak season it was like a hobo jungle. There were racers sleeping on John's front porch, back porch, in the yard, and at the shop. They would come to the shop every day and hang out and work on their motorcycles, then go home

Fellow warriors of the road: Dave Bostrom, Joe Leonard, Dick Mann, and Dick Dorresteyn. Mann considers his hometown buddy Dorresteyn one of the greatest natural racing talents ever. *Mahony Photo Archive.*

with John for dinner in the evening." Lund adds, "All of us had little pit bikes, and when we closed the shop at the end of the day, we would grab our bikes and road race right through the middle of Decatur. There went Nixon, Keen, Mann, me, and a bunch of other guys, kicking and shoving each other, and speeding through traffic." For some reason, Dick Mann seemed to have trouble with his laundry at Lund's. For example, there was the time when Rebel and Charlie, Lund's mean-spirited Doberman guard dogs, decided to make sport with Mann's duffle bag. Lund says, "It was unbelievable. I walked into the shop one morning and there were rags everywhere. Then I realized they were Dick Mann's clothes. The dogs had emptied his duffle bag and absolutely shredded everything." Then there was the time when Mann's unattended dryer got raided. Mann says, "I saw a bunch of kids running around the neighborhood wearing clean BSA shirts!"

Today Dick Mann recalls life on the road and wonders how he and most of his peers survived. He claims, "For risk and danger, racing was no comparison to getting from one place to the other. We traveled for thousands of miles over bad roads with bad vehicles, driving without enough sleep, and doing crazy things out of sheer boredom." He elaborates, "We would all be going from one town to the next on the Kansas circuit, so we would just make a caravan, running bumper to bumper at about 60 miles per hour across the Kansas countryside. Usually we would hook up in strings of three vehicles with trailers, but sometimes we would put together a train as long as five guys." He continues, "At night we would run just as fast, but everyone except the lead driver would turn off his lights so we wouldn't blind each other. I always wondered what it was like to be one of those Kansas farmers, poking along home late at night. Here he would see a set of lights in his mirror, approaching fast. Then ZOOM, ZOOM, ZOOM, ZOOM, a whole string of vehicles with motorcycle trailers would thunder past and disappear into the night. It must have scared him to death!"

Once Dick Mann and Joe Leonard were caravanning across Nevada. Digger Helm and Jimmy Plain were running ahead in Leonard's pickup and Mann and Leonard were following in Mann's car with his homemade trailer. Mann says, "I was flying along and looked out the window to see a trailer full of motorcycles heading off across the desert. Then I realized it was mine." The trailer hitch had broken off, and Mann watched helplessly as it sped away, then finally looped and crashed, end over end, utterly destroying the trailer and everything on it. When Helm and Plain noticed that Mann and Leonard were no longer following, they turned around to see what had happened. Mann says, "The devastation was so complete we put everything worth keeping in Leonard's pickup, and he was already carrying a full load. I just left the trailer in the desert. There wasn't enough left to try to fix." Leonard recalls, "Poor Bugs was crying. He said, 'Digger, I'm out of business! I'll sell you everything here for a hundred bucks.' Digger patted him on the back and said, 'That's the best offer I've ever had, but I think next week you might regret it. Don't worry, Bugs; we'll make something out of this mess.' " Helm adds, "It was terrible. It is the only time I've ever seen a three-foot-long Gold Star."

On another occasion Mann and Donnie Smith were driving across Kansas at night, running along a road that was straight as an arrow. Then suddenly the road made a 90 degree turn at the edge of an embankment that dropped some 35 feet. Mann managed to throw the car sideways and slide to a stop at the edge of the embankment, but the trailer went over. When they dragged it out, they discovered that the axle was bent, one of the tires was rubbing on the side of the trailer, and they had no way to fix it. Mann drove to the next town while Smith squatted on the trailer, hanging on to one of the motorcycles, and dribbling oil from a can onto the side of the spinning tire so it wouldn't burn through and explode.

Another time Mann and Al Gunter were traveling together, pulling a trailer full of bikes through Troy, New York, on their way to Laconia. Gunter turned a corner just as an old lady on the sidewalk keeled over with a fatal heart attack. Somebody told the police the trailer had hit her, but by then Mann and Gunter had changed drivers and were out of town and heading down the highway. Mann says, "I was rolling merrily along, carefully obeying the speed limits, when suddenly in my mirrors I saw two police cars bearing down on me. I wasn't speeding, and I figured they were going to an accident or something. I moved off onto the shoulder to let them by." When Mann started to pull over, the lead squad car wheeled in front of him and forced him off the road. It squealed to a stop in front of him, the second car roared up and boxed him in from behind, and the cops piled out with guns drawn. He continues, "Gunter and I were taken back to town and roughed up pretty good while in custody. Later that day we were taken to court, and the whole matter was sorted out." By then it was known that the old lady on the corner had suffered a stroke, the trailer had not hit her, and Mann and Gunter turned out not to be maniac motorcyclists bent on terrorizing the small towns of New York. Mann says, "If there was any place that had meaner cops than in the South, it was New York. I hated driving through New York."

Some of the antics on the road were quite insane. Mert Lawwill tells about the time he and his crew loaded up to go to

Daytona. They could not carry all their gear in the pickup, so they rented an enclosed U-Haul trailer. Mert says, "There was only enough room in the cab for two people, so Bob Walls crawled into the U-haul and we would shut him in to ride with the rest of the gear." Mert describes how he was driving at night and came upon a poorly-marked construction zone. He says, "I nearly ran off the road, then swerved and got on the brakes. I could feel the trailer yanking the truck from one side to the other, and when I looked in the rear view mirrors, I could see the trailer on both sides, swinging so violently that it would appear in one mirror, then in the other." He adds, "You can imagine how Bob was shaking when we finally got the truck stopped and went back to let him out!"

When stylish Chevy El Caminos and Ford Rancheros became available, they were ideal for race bike transportation. Although it was a snug fit, a racer could put two motorcycles, spare wheels, a tool box, gas cans, and a little luggage in the back. They were available with big V-eight engines, which made them great high-speed haulers for running from coast to coast. Dick Mann and Al Gunter bought identical 352-cubic-inch, 300-horsepower Rancheros, except Mann's was an automatic and Gunter's had a standard shift. One time Mann was heading east when he looked up in the middle of New Mexico and recognized Gunter coming the other way. They screeched to a halt and Mann said, "Aren't you going to the races?" Gunter replied, "Naw, I've had a great idea about how to make my engines run better, and I'm heading back to the shop to work on it." This was typical Gunter, foregoing a race to pursue his brainstorm du jour. The two friends talked a while and ultimately decided it was time to figure out whose Ranchero was faster. Mann says, "We lined them up and took off, winding them out. We roared down the highway side by side, flat out for about ten miles, in a dead heat. No one could pull an inch ahead on the other. So we finally gave up, said goodbye, and I went east and he went west."

When enclosed vans arrived, they became the vehicle of choice for racers. Not only would they carry a lot of gear, but owners installed bunks just above and behind the passenger

Undoubtedly, Al Gunter is lecturing Dick on the art of riding with broken bones, a practice that Mann would take to the level of a fine art during his career. *Mahony Photo Archive.*

cabin where one rider could stretch out across the van while the other drove. In 1969 Cal Rayborn, Sid Carlson, Jim McMurren, and Joe Connolly were in Carlson's new van, heading west from Houston after dark. Connolly was driving, Carlson was riding passenger, McMurren was asleep on the floor behind the seats, and Rayborn was in the bunk. Suddenly, just west of Abeline, they came upon a drunk who had parked in the middle of the freeway, turned off his lights, and gone to sleep. They hit him, destroying both vehicles. Rayborn flew out of the bunk and through the front windshield, nearly taking Carlson's head off in the process. Everyone was beat up and badly shaken. Connolly had some broken ribs, and McMurren broke two vertebrae. Carlson says, "Rayborn came wandering out of the night, shaken and barely conscious, asking, 'What did I do that was bad enough to make you guys throw me out of the van?' " He had a broken collarbone and some broken ribs. Less than a month later he rode and won Daytona.

Incredibly, the drunk who caused all the chaos sued Carlson, but the insurance company settled without going to trial. Carlson says, "We had our dress clothes on and were ready to go to the airport to fly to Texas for the trial when the insurance company called to tell us it was settled. We were really relieved. That drunk had no case, and we were really afraid of how some Texas jury was going to take to a bunch of motorcycle racers from California." Following this incident, many riders installed netting in front of their bunks.

As luck would have it, Neil Keen also rolled his van right after Houston. Although the front windshield was gone, Keen's van still ran, so they loaded everything into it and McMurren drove it to El Paso. McMurren recalls, "We were going 70 miles per hour with no windshield, and it was not very warm. I put on my Bell Star helmet and my racing leathers to drive the van down the highway." At El Paso they hooked up with Gene Hartline, mounted a tow bar on Keen's van, and towed the whole mess back to California behind Hartline's truck.

Aerodynamically, vans were even better for bumper-tagging than cars and trailers. Racers would organize a caravan and roar across the country like a freight train, one van literally inches behind another. John Lund says, "It seemed really cool at the time, but I look back on it with horror. I remember sitting in the passenger seat of some guy's van, roaring along at seventy miles per hour, and all I can see in front of me is the back windows of the van ahead of us." Mert Lawwill recalls, "Cal and I left San Diego for the mile race in Atlanta, which was on Friday evening. When we got there on Friday, it was rained out. We had a contest to see who could drive the longest without going under 80, and by noon on Sunday we were watching *Bonanza* in Cal's living room in San Diego." Mann says, "The record from the Bay Area to Daytona in the old days before Interstates was 58 hours. After the Interstate highways were built it was 52. We really didn't gain that much more time, and the Interstates removed a lot of the adventure."

Some of the stories about life on the road have taken on the dimensions of urban legends. For example, there is the story about the racer who drives four hours into the night with his buddy asleep beside him. Finally he pulls in for fuel, circles the pumps, shakes his buddy awake and says, "It's your turn to drive. Gas us up and take over." The exhausted driver then collapses into slumber and his sleepy buddy fills the tank, climbs behind the wheel, and takes off in the direction from whence they came. Four hours later, day breaks and the hapless racers find themselves exactly where they started the previous evening. This story has been told about at least three different people, places, and times. Depending upon the teller, it happened to Dick Mann, or Neil Keen, or Charlie West. But there is little doubt that the legend arose from a real event somewhere on the AMA national circuit.

Some of the stories are a little less innocent. There's the one about the racer who installed two 20 gallon tanks on his van with fillers exiting on either side. These were the days before service stations had recording equipment at the cash register, and the racer would pull into the station midway between two islands of pumps. He would conspicuously pump and pay for 20 gallons on one side of the van while his passenger—out of sight of the station attendant—would pump and steal 20 gallons on the other.

As the 1950s evolved into the '60s, then into the '70s, the AMA Grand National Series became more prosperous, fueled by tobacco sponsorship money and the racing budgets of several leading motorcycle manufacturers. Two-lane blacktop gave way to interstate highways as the days of rag-tag caravans, careening wildly across the dusty landscape of Kansas like mad, mechanical centipedes, came to an end. Riders began to travel and take their hot showers in big, luxurious motor homes, and some even began to fly to the races to mount bikes owned and maintained by factory-sponsored teams. As interstate highways became more common, and motorcycles became more popular, life on the road for the true vagabonds of American racing came to an end.

4

Finding the Combination

Now I know why it was so hard to beat that guy!
– George Roeder, after riding Dick Mann's G50 Matchless at a vintage exhibition in 1999

When Dick Mann earned his Expert license for the 1955 season, he and Gunter were no longer mentor and pupil. Rather, they were peers and competitors on the white plate battlefield, so the two men remained friends, but went their separate ways. Gunter continued to campaign the national series, but for the most part Dick Mann chose a less ambitious path. Although he raced selected nationals, a first year Expert still has much to learn, so Mann teamed up with hometown buddy Donnie Smith, kept his day job with Alzina's, and concentrated on local races and the Kansas circuit. He explains, "The racing situation was like this: Joe Leonard, Everett Brashear, and Brad Andres were the big guns with their factory Harleys. Bill Tuman challenged them on his big Indian, as did Gunter on his BSA. Beneath these were another twenty guys with a lot more experience than me. Why should a beginner like me rush out and butt heads with so much good talent, knowing I was unlikely to make the main? I figured I would spend 1955 picking up a few bucks and learning as I went along." This attitude typifies Mann's calculated approach to his racing career. Though he had a burning passion to race, he never let it drive him toward unreasoned decisions.

Mann shakes hands with Joe Leonard in the winner's circle at Daytona in 1958. Mann finished second aboard a factory Harley-Davidson arranged by San Francisco Harley dealer Dudley Perkins. Mann rode a Harley twice at Daytona—in 1958 and 1959—finishing second on both occasions. *Photo courtesy of the Dick Mann collection.*

Mann rode his first Daytona in March of 1955, where Joe Leonard won. But Mann ran as high as fourth on the challenging beach course, fell off, remounted, and finished seventh. Bay Meadows was the only other national he entered that season, finishing eighth in a field topped by Everett Brashear. Venturing south, Mann entered the famous Catalina Grand Prix, stomping grounds of the mighty Bud Ekins and other District 37 (the AMA's Los Angeles area district) champions. Mann was sponsored by Joe Koons, a famous Indian tuner and BSA dealer. Koons had a yacht called "101," named after the famous Indian 101 Scout, on which Mann, Koons, and his entourage sailed to the island. The official results say Mann finished an impressive fourth, but Joe Koons said otherwise. Mann, who finished second, was given a two minute penalty by the officials, who claimed he did not shut off his engine while refueling. Koons said that was not the case, and believed that the organizing club simply did not want to see a Northern Californian finish hot on the heels of local hero Ekins. Mann was not too concerned, having found Catalina somewhat disappointing. He says, "There was a lot of mystique surrounding the event. The trip over to the island was fun, and I liked the pavement part of the race through the town, but I was disappointed with the dirt sections."

When Mann and Donnie Smith embarked on the Kansas circuit in 1955, they both had Ang Rossi BSAs and about $45 between them. As they headed out in Dick's '49 Olds, they stopped at a local diner where they found their buddy, Bunky Murphy. "Hey, Bunky, you wanna go to the races?" Bunky piled in to go along. Three hours later, as they were crossing the Nevada state line, Bunky asked, "Where the hell are we? Where are these races?" "Kansas!" both Mann and Smith roared in unison. Poor Bunky had been shanghaied, but it was not so he could bankroll the adventure. He had nothing but the clothes on his back and fifteen cents in his pocket.

Riding a factory BSA, Dick Mann stormed to victory at Laconia in 1960, setting a track record and lapping every rider in the field except Carroll Resweber. *Photo courtesy of the Tom Clark collection.*

The racetrack at Norton, Kansas was a dilapidated facility with huge potholes. Mann and Smith went out and painted the potholes with white wash so they could see and avoid them while racing. Nevertheless, Smith hit one, bailed off, and injured his foot. Seeing the crash, Bunky raced off across the infield to help his buddy, promptly suffered a sunstroke in the 105 degree Kansas heat, and fell face first into a mud puddle. Mann says, "Smith was hopping around on one foot, yelling to the ambulance crew, 'Forget about me! Go help Bunky!' " Bunky recovered, and Mann won at Norton.

Dick Mann first met Bill Tuman at Norton, and learned the old lesson about how old age and treachery can beat youth and enthusiasm any day of the week. After Mann won the Saturday event, Tuman came around and congratulated him on his victory and flattered him about what a good rider he was. Tuman just couldn't understand how Mann could get so much traction, and he went on and on about what a great rider he must be. Mann, duly flattered by one of the great names in racing, explained to Tuman what kind of tires and pressure he was using. The next day Tuman equipped his bike similarly, and beat Mann's pants off. The two became great friends, and on more than one occasion Tuman helped Mann out of a jam.

For a while, the season was going very well. Mann and Smith raced in Kansas, Nebraska, Iowa, and Colorado. At a race in Colorado, Joe Leonard showed up and Mann beat him. Then disaster struck at a dusty and potholed track in Stockton, Kansas, where Mann hit a giant hole, cartwheeled off the motorcycle, went through the fence headfirst, and tumbled into a gully. He says he was feeling no pain, but realized he could look down and study the bottom of his skid shoe. He had torn his knee loose. Both the fibula and the tibia had slipped up by his femur and his lower leg was twisted around backwards. The ambulance ride turned out to be more traumatic than the crash. Noticing that they were creeping along at a steady 35 miles per hour with no lights or siren, Mann asked what was going on. The driver explained that they had installed a new engine in the ambulance only the day before, and they had to

Victory at Heidelberg, 1961. *Jerry West photo, courtesy of the AMA archives.*

break it in! Mann reflects, "It was a good thing I did not tear a major artery."

With Smith taking the bikes back to California, Mann found himself wearing a cast, stuck in a hospital room in Hays, Kansas, and wondering when and how he was going to get out of there. Finally, five days later, after winning the National at Minneapolis, Al Gunter arrived to spring him. Telling the nurses he was taking Dick out to get a haircut, Gunter put him into a wheelchair, rolled him out to his truck, and the two set off for California. Upon returning home, Mann underwent additional surgery on the knee. Worse yet, Alzina stood by his threat of the previous year, and fired Mann for missing too much work for racing and the injury. After losing his job at Alzina's, Mann went to work as a mechanic at Carl and Walt's, starting a friendship that lasted for the next fifteen years. Mann says, "They were really good to me. I could take off and go racing for as long as necessary, and when I returned there was always work for me." Working at Carl and Walt's also taught Mann a lot about quality work and how to treat other

Borrowing Mert Lawwill's Harley Sprint for an indoor short track. *Photo courtesy of the Dick Mann collection.*

people. He says, "No matter what a bike was in for, they insisted that with every job we adjust the carb, set the timing, and adjust the clutch before we returned the bike to the customer. That way the customer left the shop feeling really good about his motorcycle. He might not even realize it, but we knew he would have a good feeling about coming to our shop." Mann's first year as an Expert had proven to be a big learning experience, and having raced only a couple of Nationals during the season, he finished 29th in the nation.

The injured knee bothered Dick for the remainder of his racing career. At times he had to wear a metal brace which, on one occasion, he used to good advantage. During the Korean conflict Mann feared he was going to be drafted and did not want to go into the Army. At first he tried to sign up for the Coast Guard and the Marines, and though he did not wear his brace to the physicals, the doctors spotted the injury and disqualified him. Finally, he was called up for an Army physical.

Dick says, "I took the brace apart and cleaned off all the lubrication in the joint with carbon tetrachloride so it would squeak really loudly when I walked." Eyes twinkling, he continues, "I walked into the Army physical squeaking really good, and I did not have to go to the service."

After recuperating from his knee injury over the winter, Dick Mann was ready to race, and in March 1956 headed for Daytona. The results show he finished 26th, but this does not accurately characterize his remarkable performance. With Andres and Gunter dropping out early, Dick Mann and his BSA did battle with Paul Goldsmith and his Harley. The two swapped the lead and were never more than two seconds apart until the 26th lap when Goldsmith made a 14.6 second pit stop. Mann made an equally quick stop on lap 27, and maintained his narrow lead until the 36th lap when his clutch began to fail, forcing him out of contention. Andres, Brashear, and Leonard continued to dominate the remainder of the season, but Mann finished a respectable 15th in the nation.

The following year Mann's BSA threw a chain early at Daytona, and he failed to finish at both Milwaukee and Laconia. His best finishes for the season were a second at Vallejo, a fourth at Minneapolis, and a second at Peoria, but consistent work landed him sixth in the Grand National Championship standings for the year. Off the track in 1957, Daytona produced one of the great and much-retold tales in the history of American motorcycle racing. In the old beach course days, there was no official practicing for Daytona. Riders just came, entered, and rode the event. To prepare their bikes, many went out to a bumpy, narrow, paved road through the jungle, known simply as the jungle road. When the noise and commotion became too great to ignore, the Volusia County sheriff would chase everyone away. On Saturday morning before the race, Mann and Gunter were on the jungle road making their final tests and speed runs. Both had just completed 125-mile-per-hour runs. Mann had just removed his spark plug for a plug check. Gunter was getting ready to make another run when a squad car arrived, containing a big county sheriff who smiled and said, "I'll take you boys off to jail now." "What for?" demanded Gunter. "For speeding," said the sheriff. Following a brief debate instigated by Gunter about whether the sheriff had actually witnessed any law breaking, Albert suddenly fired up his bike and sped away.

Enraged, the sheriff put Mann in the back of his cruiser and started shouting into the radio about throwing up a road block to catch Gunter. He had seen the number 54 on Gunter's bike, and he instructed deputies to go to the racetrack and arrest number 54. Deputies mistakenly grabbed Amateur rider number 54 and hauled him off to jail, just as the Amateur race was about to begin. Because Mann was not responsive to the sheriff's questions about Gunter's identity, the sheriff put Mann in handcuffs and roared off after Gunter, continuing to scream hysterically into the radio. Mann found the whole scene so absurd he started laughing, and that made the sheriff even angrier. Finally, Gunter was identified through his riding number, apprehended at his motel, and thrown in jail with Mann. BSA operations manager Ted Hodgdon had to post a $350 bond to get them out in time to race the next morning. Gunter was fined $500, but Mann got off without a fine. According to BSA racer Glenn Jordan, when the sheriff came to release the riders, Gunter asked, "Where are you taking me now?" The sheriff said, "I will release you into the custody of E.C. Smith," who was the AMA's authoritarian executive secretary. Gunter replied facetiously, "Oh, no! Just put me back in jail."

Although Dick Mann had pulled together a successful program by building and maintaining his own equipment with a little factory financial support, a cutback in the BSA racing budget in 1958 caused him to accept a ride at Daytona on a factory Harley-Davidson, arranged by San Francisco dealer Dud Perkins. Joe Leonard, riding a Charlie West Harley, won the race, with Mann finishing second. Mann says, "Although it was a factory bike, Dud Perkins made me give him half my winnings." Mann went back to his BSA for Laconia, finished second to Andres, and found himself leading by a margin of 14 points in the Grand National standing. However, a series of failures to make the main event at mid-season netted him a final position of eighth in the standings. Mann explains his decision to return to a self-sponsored BSA in favor of a factory-sponsored Harley: "The Harley performed well at Daytona, but it was someone else's bike and I had to split my earnings. I realized I could continue to finish fifth or sixth in the pack on my BSA and still take home more money. Besides, there was really no magic to having a Harley. There were only a few who had the really hot engines—Andres, Leonard, Resweber—and the rest were no faster than my BSA. Besides, at that time there was no points fund, and all the Grand National Championship got you was a jacket with your name on it." With such a statement, Dick Mann reveals his professional racing philosophy. For Mann, racing was to make a living, not for glory or the prestige of the Grand National Championship.

This philosophy was reflected not only in Mann's strategy, but in his equipment. Mann, more than any other rider, conducted his own preparation, engine development, and

Though his name was commonly associated with BSA, Dick Mann rode a wider variety of brands than any other champion. This Bultaco advertisement celebrates Mann's victory in the lightweight race at Laconia in 1963. *Photo courtesy of John Taylor and the Yankee Motors archives.*

The BSA team at Laconia in 1961. BSA hoped for a clean sweep after Tom Clark, right, won the Amateur class. However, mechanical problems gave Mann a 20th place finish in the Expert national championship. *Photo courtesy of the Tom Clark collection.*

maintenance. He placed greater value on chassis performance than on horsepower and admits, "My bikes were more like work horses than race horses." Dave Aldana says, "Dick Mann taught me that you only have to go fast enough to win. We young lions were always trying to go flat out. It wasn't enough to beat a guy. We wanted to lap the guy too, but in the end you break more motorcycles and lose more races that way. Dick's equipment was always kind of homemade and cobby looking, but it handled better, especially on a rough track, than anyone else's motorcycle. Dick usually didn't have the fastest bike on the track, but he knew how to make it go fast enough to win."

In 1959 Mann was offered a Charlie West Harley for Daytona, and again he finished second, this time behind Andres. For the remainder of the season, he showed improved consistency, finishing fifth at Heidelberg, third at Laconia, fifth at Sacramento, third at Springfield, second at St. Paul, and won his first AMA National in the lightweight class at the Peoria TT. *American Motorcycling* reported, ". . . no rider has been more deserving of the big one. Mann has been knocking on the door for three years, but someone always managed to beat him across the finish line with a little more steam or more luck. Today the popular redhead, after taking second to Joe Leonard in his qualifying heat, came back in the national championship and got the jump on Leonard and the rest of the field and stayed in front all the way, after an early challenge from Andres." The story continued, "Mann has had a long wait for his first national championship, and he has always taken disappointment graciously. Mann's win was popular with the other Experts; this was evident by the fact that Leonard, Resweber, and Andres were the first to pat him on the back and congratulate him." Just like Mann's first big Amateur victory at Bay Meadows five years before, he won the event on a borrowed machine. Mann had only a dirt tracker during the 1959 midwestern swing, and had no intention of entering Peoria until Kansas City BSA dealer Ray Hendershot offered him his TT motorcycle. Thanks to season-long consistency and the Peoria win, Mann finished second to Carroll Resweber in the 1959 AMA Grand National Championship.

The 1960 season began poorly with a frightful spill and a last place finish at Daytona. Mann says, "It was my shortest Daytona. I went a mile and a quarter; a mile on my motorcycle and another quarter of a mile off of it." He continues, "The race began and the pack was roaring for the first turn. Suddenly Sammy Tanner sat straight up and put on his brakes right in front of me. I stuffed my front wheel right behind his muffler and rear wheel, and went flying off the motorcycle at 100 miles per hour. I grabbed my knees and rolled up in a ball and went tumbling down the beach. I remember it took all the strength I had to stay rolled up in a ball and not have my arms and legs start flying all over the place. Everywhere something was sticking out got the hide beat off it. My elbows, knees, ankles, hips, and shoulders ended up raw and bleeding." Immediately after the race, Mann and his companions, Dick Dorresteyn and Myron Hendrickson, loaded up and headed home, driving non-stop from Daytona to Richmond. Mann recalls, "When I got home I was healing up into my clothes. I couldn't take anything off because my clothes were stuck to all the scabs. I had to soak in the bath tub with my clothes on before my mother could peel them off me."

But Mann came back to win Laconia, clipping a full minute off the track record set by Andres the previous year. He rarely finished better than fourth for the remainder of the season, but consistent top ten finishes placed him fifth in the Grand National Championship, won again by Carroll Resweber. Mann was involved in a bizarre and crowd-pleasing event at Springfield in 1960. Describing the event, Jack Mercer wrote, "Tanner, working like mad all day to try to get by Brashear, went into a king-sized slide in corner four, slid right, overcontrolled to the left, and started to nose dive when Bugsy Mann slammed into his weaving rival, straightening him right up, and neither rider fell."

In 1961 Daytona moved from the old beach course to the newly-completed Daytona International Speedway. Mann qualified third fastest, but finished 39th due to clutch trouble. Roger Reiman won. After a 20th at Laconia, Mann won Heidelberg, got a fifth at the Charity Newsies in Columbus, then was awarded a tie for second at Springfield with Bart Markel while running on a flat front tire. *American Motorcycling* reported, "Dick Mann took over the lead from Al Gunter on the second lap and held it until the 22nd when he and Resweber began what might have ended in the best two-man fight in the history of the event. The pair exchanged the lead three times until the 43rd lap when Mann's front tire lost pressure and Resweber went in front to stay. But Mann stayed in it to the finish, managing to tie with Markel for second." Mann's pit man John Lund says, "Bugs's courage and determination were just unbelievable. When he came off the track, that tire was completely

Many think that Dick Mann's finest hour was the night he won the Ascot TT aboard his G50 Matchless while riding injured, earning his first AMA Grand National Championship. *Mahony Photo Archive.*

off one side of the rim." With a fifth at Schererville, Indiana, and a second at Peoria, Mann finished the season third in the standings, following Leonard and Resweber, who earned his fourth consecutive and final AMA Grand National Championship.

The 1962 season brought some big changes to Dick Mann's program, leading ultimately to a serious dispute with the AMA. Indian, which was the importer of several brands of British motorcycles, got AMA approval to run the G50 Matchless in AMA competition, and sponsored Mann a ride. Mann brought the Matchless home second at Daytona, just ten feet behind and gaining on the factory Triumph of Don Burnett. Next he got a fifth at the road race at Bossier City, Louisiana, losing a podium finish because the Matchless ran out of gas and he had to push it across the line. He got third at Heidelberg, third at Columbus, and won Laconia. But then Mann's trouble with the Matchless began. To campaign the Matchless on half mile and mile tracks, he installed the engine in a modified BSA Gold Star rigid frame, and the AMA told him this was not legal, and he had to stop using it immediately.

From there the season went steadily downhill. A horrendous seven-bike crash during practice at Lincoln, Illinois, killed Jack Gholson, broke Babe Robertson's leg, seriously injured Dick Klamfoth's neck with three compressed vertebrae, and ended Carroll Resweber's short but brilliant career with a savage compound fracture to his leg and nerve damage to his neck and left arm. Earlier in the season, Mann smashed his knuckles into the inside fence at Springfield, injuring his hand badly enough to potentially end his career. The race was not even stopped, so Mann had to crawl under the fence, and then

BSA teammates Dick Mann and Jody Nicholas at Daytona, 1962. *Photo courtesy of the Jody Nicholas collection.*

walk through the crowd of spectators to get around to a gate and cross the track after the heat to go to the ambulance. With a referral to a good physician named Dr. Jersuel in Rockford, Illinois, by his friend Bill Tuman, Mann ended up in a special cast shaped around a ball in the palm of his hand. Metal rings were inserted in the tip of each finger and pulled toward his wrist by rubber bands. The design was to insure that if Dick lost mobility in his hand, it still would be properly shaped to hold a handle bar. When Tuman saw the contraption around Mann's hand, he joked to Dr. Jersuel, "I hope this works. He has a race next week." Tuman says, "I was joking, but I've never known anyone who could heal up like Dick Mann. Six weeks later he removed the cast at Sacramento and went racing." Mann finished the season third, with Bart Markel taking his first Grand National Championship. Following the horrendous Lincoln crash, three-time Daytona winner Dick Klamfoth decided to retire at the age of 34 to open a Honda dealership.

Over the winter the AMA Competition Committee reconsidered the approval of the G50 Matchless and decided that Mann and others had been using an unapproved road-racing frame. The ruling resulted in Mann's sitting out Daytona in 1963, but not until he had stirred up a hornet's nest by threatening to get an injunction against the event. Mann was forced back to his aging BSA single for both road races and dirt track, but incredibly, the AMA allowed him to continue to use the Matchless frame for TT racing that had been ruled illegal for road racing.

Although Mann had not had an especially good season at the Nationals, 1963 was turning out a very profitable year at the local races, where he was consistently earning and frequently winning. Then, disaster struck on a rough track at a local race in Freeport, Illinois. Mann fell while leading the race, and was struck hard from behind while trying to get up. The impact ripped him open in his crotch alongside his rectum, with a gash large enough to insert a hand. Then he was hit again and again by subsequent riders as he tumbled toward the outside rail. In his 1972 memoir Dick explained, "Much of the pain seemed to be centered in my rump. I reached back and felt down there, and everything was pretty sticky. Then I got a handful of something . . . and that's when I knew that my insides were dripping out on the ground." Mann's friend, Thad Coleman, rode with him to the hospital, then quit motorcycle racing for good. While Mann lay in the emergency room at the local hospital awaiting treatment, an injured Novice was brought in and died ten feet away because there was no attending physician on hand on Sunday. Mann most feared infection in the huge injury because dirt tracks aren't just dirt. They consist of horse manure and calcium chloride and lord-knows-what kind of filth and corruption. He insisted that the staff bathe his wound again and again.

After getting sewn back together, Mann was soon able to get up and walk around, but he continued to experience pain in his back. After some X-rays, he was advised he had a broken back and would need to be placed in a full body cast for at least six weeks. This frightened him more than any of his injuries, so he called his friend, Bill Tuman. "Bill," he said, "You've got to get me out of here. I don't think these people know what they're doing." Tuman came to the rescue in the dark of night, told the night nurse he was taking Mann out to look at the moon, and spirited him away. Tuman gave Mann a cushion to sit on, and put him on an airplane to California. Mann's bikes had already been taken home by Neil Keen. Keen had broken his left ankle at Jerseyville, Illinois, the week after Mann was hurt, and he drove his pickup full of bikes all the way from Illinois to his home in Southern California by depressing the clutch pedal on his standard-shift truck with a cane!

Just three weeks later, Dick Mann entered the Ascott TT National Championship aboard his Matchless. No one thought Mann had much chance against the Ascot specialists aboard their hot Triumphs and Harleys, especially since he was riding with a wound in his crotch the size of a fist. But luck began to turn his way when championship contender George Roeder failed to qualify for the National. The second bit of good fortune came when one of the nation's best TT riders, Skip Van Leeuwen, dropped out of the race early. Mann rode one of the smoothest, best-executed races of his career, perhaps *because*

Dick Mann chases Mert Lawwill at Sacramento in 1963. Newcomer Lawwill had not yet earned his AMA National Number. *Photo courtesy of the Mert Lawwill collection.*

of his injury, rather than in spite of it. And he won—to everyone's astonishment. Ralph White recalls, "Mann and that Matchless just motored right by me. I couldn't believe he could make that little 500 single go so fast."

There was only one race remaining that season, and the Ascot victory ultimately gave Mann the 1963 Grand National Championship by a single point over George Roeder. Though he failed to make the main at Ascot, George Roeder qualified as first alternate. If Harley-Davidson racing boss Dick O'Brien had instructed Ralph White, another factory Harley rider, to stand down and let Roeder come to the starting line, it would have been a different story. With just two points—which Roeder could have earned by finishing last—he would have become Grand National Champion and Harley would have had brand bragging rights for yet another season. As it was, Dick Mann had gone through what were likely the two worst seasons of his career since becoming an Expert. He had been forced by the AMA ruling against his Matchless to race old and uncompetitive equipment, he had incurred an injury that would have ended the career of many men, and he won only one National all season. But he battled on to earn the highest title in American motorcycle racing, the AMA Grand National Championship. Better still, the title was his and his alone. No motorcycle brand could step up and claim the season, since Mann had pulled it off with a patchwork program using both his Matchless and his BSA. On December 15, 1963, AMA District 36 welcomed home their triumphant local hero by dedicating their annual Christmas Seals Benefit TT Scrambles to Mann.

Dick Mann talks about The Combination in his 1972 memoir. He said, "When you have The Combination, your bike is running perfectly, and you've really got your head on straight, and you *can't do anything wrong*. It's a little uncanny, and it's hard to explain unless you've experienced it yourself. Everything you do is right. Winning becomes easy. It all falls into place." The Combination is hard to define, but it involves skill, experience, equipment, luck, and even a state of mind. Often it involves actions and events beyond your control, like Skip Van Leeuwen breaking down, or George Roeder falling just a fraction of a second short of qualifying for a race, or Dick O'Brien not making a certain strategic decision. When you have The Combination, everything comes together and works right. A rider can't make The Combination happen, but part of having enough experience is when you're able to recognize that you've got The Combination, then you let it work for you just as long as you can. It rarely lasts long, and it comes and goes throughout a racing career. When The Combination happens, races seem easy to win. When you don't have it, you can't win, no matter how hard you try. The Combination can work against all odds, as it did for Dick Mann at Ascot in 1963.

Every rider deserves to find The Combination from time to time. But the real professionals are the guys who struggle on and try their hardest when it isn't there. Sometimes, when they keep trying, The Combination seems suddenly to return, as if it were a reward.

5

The Matchless Fiasco

They obviously were worried about that Matchless breaking up the iron triangle.

– Howard Utsey, rider

The American Motorcycle Association—later renamed American Motorcyclist Association—was founded in 1924 as a spin-off of the Motorcycle and Allied Trades Association. With the economy in recession and motorcycle sales continuing to decline under the weight of a burgeoning automobile market, the industry needed something to create excitement and get people involved with motorcycles. As a sport-governing organization, it was the mission of the AMA to promulgate and enforce racing rules in a fair and impartial manner. In addition, it was the job of the AMA to stimulate the formation of local motorcycle clubs and encourage tours, rallies, and other non-competitive social programs for motorcycle enthusiasts. This, it was hoped, would lead to more opportunities for people to use and enjoy their motorcycles.

The AMA was structured like a trade association because that was what its founders were familiar with. Its governing committees and boards were composed of individuals appointed by the various manufacturers and aftermarket companies who were members of the Motorcycle and Allied Trades Association. Although it was the intention of the AMA to sell general memberships and competition licenses, there was no provision in its governing structure for representation for rank-and-file members or professional competitors. Broader and more democratic representation eventually would arrive, but not for almost another half century.

Probably the most powerful and important body within the AMA was the Competition Committee, composed of 24 to 28 seats held by representatives of the leading companies involved in racing. The benefit of this structure was that it provided great engineering and marketing expertise. The disadvantage was that every member of the Committee had a built-in conflict of interest. Each, though perhaps sincerely dedicated to helping build a better motorcycle sport, ultimately answered to an employer who was in commercial competition with the employer of every other member of the Committee. Theoretically, their competitive conflicts of interest would cancel each other out and the Committee would pursue a higher vision beneficial to all concerned. It actually worked that way much of the time, but not always.

Another weakness of the structure was that it provided for no separation of powers. The Competition Committee legislated rules and adjudicated protests and appeals, and some of its individual members functioned as officials at the races. By so doing, a single individual could play an active role in legislative, executive, and judicial branches of government, thereby gaining extraordinary and potentially dangerous power and influence.

Because the AMA was conceived as a marketing arm for the motorcycle industry, there evolved a vision of the sport that was different from that in other industrialized nations. Prior to World War I, motorcycle racing in America had been an elite arena where the leading manufacturers could test designs and gain bragging rights over one another through advanced technology and large racing budgets. By the early teens both Indian and Harley-Davidson were producing prototype racers with four overhead valves per cylinder, a technical feature that did not become commonplace in series production motorcycles for another seven decades. To build and campaign such machines, the factories allocated significant funds for technical development and top racing talent. The result was a program similar to today's Formula One, where elite racing stars, backed by technical support teams, took their special motorcycles throughout America to stage races in major cities before large crowds. But such events were few and far between. Except for impromptu and poorly officiated races on local fairground tracks, motorcycle racing for the common man did not exist as it does today.

By the 1920s, most of America's motorcycle manufacturers had gone bankrupt, and those that remained could no longer afford to dump large sums of money into programs for special machines and highly paid riders. Survival depended upon a different approach that would take racing to the masses and get many people involved with motorcycles they could buy from their local dealers. By the early 1930s the AMA delivered just such a program. Referred to as "Formula C" in the minutes of the AMA Competition Committee, it became popularly known as "Class C," and it was based on the idea of racing mass-produced standard street motorcycles.

Rules were written that provided that AMA racing, including national championship titles, would be based on roadworthy motorcycles that one could buy through his local dealership. Access to a specially built hot rod or a factory prototype would no longer be required to win. In fact, by 1934 such bikes were no longer allowed at AMA championship events. Although controversial in the beginning, Class C proved to be a brilliant concept, and likely played a significant role in getting the American motorcycle industry through the Depression. From this egalitarian approach, a whole new generation of working class, grassroots heroes emerged, typified by Ed "Iron Man" Kretz.

Of course, when rules are strict and detailed, there are more opportunities to bend, stretch, or outright break the rules. Enforcing and protecting the integrity of the Class C program became one of the most important jobs of the AMA Competition Committee, and to eliminate the appearance of prototypes disguised as street machines, the Committee set up strict approval procedures that each manufacturer had to

Dick Mann aboard his Matchless G50 road racer in 1964. Mann won the 1963 AMA Grand National Championship despite having his fast Matchless banned for the season. *Jerry West photo, courtesy of the Dick Mann collection.*

follow in order for its products to appear at AMA sanctioned events. The requirements have changed from time to time, but basically, the manufacturer was required to submit the technical specifications for a new model to the Committee, make that model and its parts available through its dealers, include it in its catalog of standard models, and subsequently provide documentation proving that a specific number have been produced and delivered into the market. At some times that number has been as high as 200, sometimes as low as 25. By 1961 the rules read, "The motorcycle must be basically the counterpart of a standard production model, fitted with generator and lights, regularly sold for everyday use." Any legalistic mind would immediately recognize that there could be a dangerous amount of ambiguity in the words "basically a counterpart of a standard production model."

After the Indian Motorcycle Company ceased production in 1953 and went into bankruptcy shortly thereafter, the Indian Sales Company—a separate corporation—continued to provide a line of British-built motorcycles to the Indian dealer network. These included Matchless, Vincent, Norton, and others. In 1961 Indian undertook the process of getting its Matchless G50 approved for AMA Class C racing. The G50 had begun life as an AJS 7R, a 350cc motorcycle known as the "Boy Racer." It was a single-cylinder machine with a chain-driven overhead cam. Its engine cases and cam drive tower were cast in magnesium, and its narrow duplex frame provided excellent handling. It was, in its day, a Grand Prix quality machine. When enlarged to 500cc, it became the Matchless G50. But, as a purpose-built racer, it did not come with street-legal lighting, as required by the Class C rules. To create a model raceable in America, Indian and the Matchless factory came up with the Matchless G50CSR. The G50 engine was intact, but the bike featured a heavier and less race-worthy frame in addition to full lighting equipment. It was approved for the 1962 season, and 26 were immediately assigned to dealers throughout the nation. Indian also purchased four 7R frames, believing it had been approved, along with racing brakes and fuel tank, as accessories for the CSR.

Jimmy Hill, the head of Indian's racing department, negotiated a sponsorship with Dick Mann, sending him a new CSR, a spare G50 engine, and a 7R frame. Mann began to race the motorcycle, using the 7R frame for road racing and TT, and installing the engine in a modified BSA rigid Gold Star frame for dirt-track racing. He very nearly won Daytona in the bike's first outing, finishing ten feet behind Don Burnett's Triumph. Remarking on the debut performance of the Matchless, a story in *American Motorcyclist* related, "Only ten feet separated Burnett's Cliff Guild-tuned Triumph from the charging

Matchless of Dick Mann. If Mann had not had a spot of trouble in the pits that cost him precious seconds, the finish might have been a different story." The "spot of trouble" referred to was the fact that during a fuel stop, a crew member accidentally pulled a fuel line loose. Mann did not discover it until he was underway and well down pit road, and had to stop to replace the fuel line. That he nearly won after losing so much time indicates how dominant the Matchless was against other brands.

After his near win at Daytona, Mann turned the tables at Laconia, winning the race while lapping the field, with Burnett and his Triumph taking second. He finished fifth at the 130-mile road-race at Bossier City, Louisiana, third at Heidelberg, third at Columbus, fourth at Ascot, and by mid-season was tied for first place in the Grand National Championship with Bart Markel, who was having a tremendous season, having finished fourth at Bossier City and winning Heidleberg, Columbus, and Springfield.

But the Competition Committee balked at use of the BSA frame on dirt, and on June 14th Mann got a letter from the AMA stating, "Although the existing rules do permit the modification of frames, it was not the intent of these rules to permit the interchange of engines and frames from one make of motorcycle to another. This is your official notice that the frame in question cannot be used in AMA Formula C competition and any further use of the frame is in violation of AMA rules and will result in disciplinary action by this office." Mann soldiered on, using the 7R swingarm frame at dirt-track events; thus becoming the first rider to bring a bike with rear suspension onto half mile and mile tracks. Conventional wisdom said it would not work, but Dick earned enough points to finish the season third in the Grand National Championship.

But something happened at Watkins Glen in 1962 that would profoundly affect Dick Mann and other G50 owners in the coming season. Anthony Woodman won the Amateur final aboard a G50 and second place finisher, BSA rider Howard Utsey, protested it as an illegal machine, maintaining that its 7R racing frame had not been submitted for approval with the

G50 CSR. In fact, Utsey had very little to do with the protest. According to AMA rules, the only person who can file a protest is an entrant in the event, thus the protest was technically filed by Utsey. However, Utsey reveals that BSA chief Walt Brown—a member of the AMA Competition Committee—came around after the event and urged him to file the protest. According to Utsey, Brown said, "If you will file a protest, BSA will take care of it," meaning his company would pay the filing fee and handle the paperwork. Utsey says, "That G50 was really fast, and they obviously were worried about it breaking up the iron triangle." The "iron triangle" to which Utsey refers was Harley-Davidson, Triumph, and BSA, which were the dominant brands in AMA racing at the time. Presumably, the "they" he refers to were the individuals representing those brands who served on the AMA Competition Committee at the time, including Brown and Triumph representative Rod Coates.

Meeting the following November, the AMA Competition Committee upheld the protest and directed that the distributor—Indian—and the riders of G50s be advised that the motorcycle could be raced only as the G50 CSR submitted for approval. Unfortunately, during the fall of 1962 Indian consummated its slow slide into oblivion. Its name and import rights were sold to the Berliner Corporation, Jimmy Hill lost his job, and Berliner's Walter von Schonfeld inherited a growing and confusing controversy surrounding the approval of the G50 Matchless.

Jimmy Hill appealed to keep his seat on the AMA Competition Committee, but he received a letter from the AMA's executive secretary, Lin Kuchler, stating, ". . . the majority of the officers and directors felt that they should adhere to the established policy of appointing Competition Committee members on the basis of their current motorcycle manufacturer, distributor, or dealer affiliation. For this reason you were not reappointed to the Competition Committee for 1963." Ironically, this letter declared in so many words that personal expertise was not enough to hold a seat on the committee. Basically, as the letter suggests, you *had to have a commercial conflict of interest* in order to be eligible! Furthermore, the AMA's reason for dismissing Jimmy Hill from the committee was disingenuous, since Jim Davis remained a member in good standing, despite the fact that he was in no way involved in the motorcycle trade. With Hill officially out of the picture, Mann and other G50 owners no longer had an insider within the AMA hierarchy to champion their cause.

Mann was incredulous toward the news. The ruling of the Competition Committee defied logic. Did he not have a Laconia victory with the machine, and a string of top ten finishes? How could it now be illegal? Had he not been allowed to race the G50 in the 7R frame at dirt-track championships following the disapproval of the BSA frame? How could a road-racing frame be legal for dirt, but not legal for road racing? Dick Mann has never been a trouble maker. He typically rolls with the punches and works within the system, but he is also a man who will stand up and fight when he thinks an important principle is involved. Mann decided to enter Daytona on his G50 Matchless, and test the AMA's rulings in a court of law if necessary.

At Daytona the Matchless was predictably rejected during technical inspection, and Mann was advised he could race it only with a production CSR frame. He did not have a CSR frame, and there was no time to modify one even if he did. To race a CSR, the footpegs would have to be relocated, unnecessary lugs and brackets would have to be removed, mounts would have to be affixed for the road-racing seat and number plates, and the carburetor would have to be relocated with a different intake manifold. Mann set out to find a lawyer.

Today he relates, "I had never done that kind of thing before. I didn't know anything about the law, but I thought I would seek an injunction to stop the race if the AMA would not let me ride." He continues, "The first thing I discovered is that it was nearly impossible to find a lawyer in Daytona Beach who could take legal action against International Speedway Corporation. Although I was intending to sue the AMA, the owners of the Speedway would have been co-defendants, and most of the lawyers in town had a conflict of interest because they had worked for ISC at one time or another." However, Mann found a lawyer to review his case, and by that time word had gotten back to the AMA that he was serious in his intention to seek legal relief.

Dud Perkins, a San Francisco Harley-Davidson dealer who held a seat on the Competition Committee, and whom Mann had known for many years, approached Dick and urged him not to sue. Mann says, "The AMA was really worried that I could stop the race, anger the fans, and mess up their relationship with Bill France, the owner of the Speedway. Dud asked me to back off. He said there would be a meeting of the Competition Committee on Friday and they would get the matter straightened out for me. I figured I had gotten their attention, and that the Committee would let me ride, so I agreed to drop my legal action. I never wanted it to come to that anyway." Jimmy Hill, who was in Daytona at the time, offered to address the committee to verify that he had properly submitted documents and photos for the road-racing frame during the G50 CSR approval process, and that no action had been taken to reject it, thus explaining why the bike had been legally raced throughout 1962. According to the May 1963 issue of *Cycle Sport,* ". . . he was unable to even get a hearing from his former associates, [after] a quarter century of service to the sport."

Early Saturday Mann sought out Perkins and asked, "What happened at the committee meeting?" Perkins replied, "I'm sorry Dick, you can't ride." Dick responded, "But you said the committee was going to meet and straighten this thing out!" Perkins said, "I know. I lied." Dick was devastated. What had begun as an apparently honest dispute over an interpretation of the rules degenerated into a game of dirty pool. The AMA, through Perkins, had drawn him into its trust, earning enough time to make a last-minute injunction impossible. Then it had squashed him like a bug.

Dick Mann is and always has been one the AMA's most loyal supporters. For example, in January, 1962, the Association published an advertisement featuring Dick's photograph and testimony. In that ad, he said, "I take my helmet off to the AMA. Its Competition Committee has done wonders to standardize and equalize all phases of motorcycle competition. It's

Dick Mann on his way to a win aboard the Matchless at the 120-mile road race at Wentzville in 1965, after the motorcycle was reinstated by the AMA Competition Committee. *Photo courtesy of the Dave Mungenast collection.*

a pleasure to compete in AMA sanctioned races." It is sad that before the year was out, the organization's rule-making system—the Competition Committee that Dick praised—would militate against Mann and other G50 owners, and, in fact, ban him from competing in the AMA's most important race. One must wonder if he would have consented to such an advertisement a year later!

But Dick Mann is a person who refuses to dwell on adversity or wallow in self-pity. Rather, he seeks to find a useful lesson in events that seem unfair, unreasonable, or illogical. Looking back on the matter years later, he said, "I was really upset and angry about that for a short time, then I began to realize that it would have been wrong for me to punish the fans over my problem. Too often, we solve our problems by punishing people who are innocent bystanders. The fans are the people who admire us and pay our salaries. It would have been a big mistake for me to stop the race just because I felt I had been treated unfairly. The AMA was really wrong in what they did, but what I had in mind was wrong also, and it would have hurt the whole sport to punish the fans."

After the Daytona decision, the Matchless fiasco became even crazier. Mann was allowed to use the outlawed 7R frame for TT racing but not road racing. Even more incredibly, the AMA reversed itself and let him run the G50 engine in the Gold Star-based rigid frame on dirt. In regard to the G50, both the letter and the spirit of Class C racing became totally obscured in a bizarre morass of contradictory rulings and counter rulings by the Competition Committee. Finally, in 1964 the AMA allowed the G50 to appear at road races in full racing trim, 7R frame and all, although no record exists of the Competition Committee reversing its earlier decision to ban the bike.

Unfortunately for the AMA, such egregious missteps have always been better remembered than the countless times it made a correct and wise decision on behalf of the sport. There have always been journalists and conspiracy theorists who believe the AMA is in unholy alliance with Harley-Davidson, and when a controversy arises, they leap to the easy solution of identifying Harley's alleged hidden motives, rather than the more difficult job of searching for the facts. Such is the case with the Matchless fiasco, especially since a Harley-Davidson dealer figured prominently in the AMA's process of sandbagging Mann at Daytona in 1963.

But it is not quite as simple as that, and the evidence still available would suggest that Harley-Davidson—while certainly involved—was not the driving force behind eliminating the Matchless. The game of dirty pool likely began the minute Dick Mann very nearly overhauled Don Burnett's factory-sponsored Triumph at Daytona in 1962. Rod Coates, Triumph's man on the AMA Competition Committee, was one of the members most actively involved in the legislative, executive, and judicial processes of the organization. Not only did he help make the rules and judge the infractions, but he had executive powers as a technical inspector at the races. That the agenda of Rod Coates went beyond merely upholding the integrity of Class C racing may have been revealed at Watkins Glen as early as August, 1962. Bob Hansen was another owner of a G50 road racer with a 7R frame, just like Dick Mann's, and in a letter to Jimmy Hill dated August 29, 1962, Hansen wrote, "Rod Coates said to me at the Glen, 'Nice bike, Bob. Course you'll probably have to run it somewhere else next year.' Wonder what he has in mind?" Presumably, Hansen wrote this last sentence with tongue firmly planted in cheek!

Consider the implications of Triumph's Rod Coates making such a prediction on the very weekend that BSA's Walt Brown bankrolled a protest against the Matchless. Utsey's protest gave Triumph and BSA their Trojan Horse to carry the issue back before the Committee. Brown would not have urged a BSA rider in the 1962 Laconia National to protest Dick Mann's victory. Mann had brought a lot of glory to the BSA brand, and it would have been too crass and conspicuous to protest the winner of a points-paying National over an issue as contrived as this. But funding a protest by Utsey was different. Few would pay attention to a protest filed by an Amateur, and Brown could remain in the shadows until the issue was taken up by the Competition Committee after the season was over. When the protest was heard in September, it was William Davidson who made the motion that the protest be upheld, and that Woodman's Matchless be disqualified as illegal. Representatives of all three brands appear to have worked in concert to get rid of the G50 Matchless, banning it by a vote of 26 to 1.

That BSA and Triumph were the driving forces behind the campaign is confirmed in a letter from Hansen to Lin Kuchler, dated February 26, 1963, following the decision to ban the Matchless. Hansen states, "To put it very mildly, Lin, I feel absolutely crushed! I knew that Rod Coates had planned to bar my machine (and all those like it) from racing AMA this coming year; but I couldn't believe that he could actually do it. Even with the full support of BSA, Inc., I couldn't believe it would come off. It looks like they have done just exactly that, and I cannot lift a finger to prevent, forestall, or even delay it! . . . Rod told me both at Watkins Glen and Indianapolis that I wouldn't be able to run my machine in 1963. This at the same time he approved it to run then!"

Ironically, the rules interpretation that was applied to ban the G50 soon became a point of contention, breaking up the so-called iron triangle when Harley-Davidson's racing boss, Dick O'Brien, found himself in a position similar to that of Matchless, hoping for a more liberal rules interpretation for approval of an accessory frame. Serious bad blood developed between O'Brien and Rod Coates over the issue. In reporting on conversations with Lin Kuchler, Hansen wrote to Walt von Schonfeld in March, 1963, "Lin said that he was afraid that O'Brien was going to slug Coates at the San Francisco meeting on the frame episode." When the issue was next considered in October, 1963, the vote against the Matchless slipped to 15 to 11, indicating that the iron triangle was no longer intact.

It appears that the anti-Harley conspiracy theorists were wrong in trying to point the finger at one brand. It was Triumph's Rod Coates, supported by BSA's Walt Brown, who actively worked to keep their British racing counterpart—the G50—out of AMA racing during 1963, and all William Davidson ever did was place a motion on the table, to which the Committee responded with near-unanimity. This kind of ganging up and piling on by the dominant brands against upstarts and hopefuls may not have happened all the time, but it characterized the AMA's old-boy structure and its rule-making process at its very worst. A similar frame approval gambit was attempted a decade earlier—then with Indian as an active participant—to keep Dick Klamfoth's Norton off the track at Daytona.

Although the Committee reaffirmed the ban on the Matchless as late as October 1963, when Daytona 1964 rolled around there were several on the starting line though, again, no written record exists of the Committee reversing its decision. Dick Klamfoth finished fifth aboard Bob Hansen's machine, and Everett Brashear finished sixth aboard the bike owned by Dick

Mann. Over the winter Mann had already made a commitment to ride a Norton for Paul Dunstall. Looking back on the whole affair, Mann remains philosophical. Refusing to take it personally, he says, "Rod Coates was a tremendous team player. If you cut him, he would probably bleed Triumph engine oil. I always said that if Rod Coates had not already been tied to Triumph, he is the first guy I would want on my team."

Nevertheless, the decision-making process that hazed Dick Mann over his Matchless G50 was a system that would not prevail. The broad social reform that took place throughout America during the 1960s arose out of a distrust of the system of old-boy politics that was typical of so many American institutions formed early in the century. Before the decade was out, the AMA would undergo radical democratic reform, and Dick Mann would be one of the most influential players in that revolution.

6

The Innovative Mann

Bugs was never satisfied with his bike. He was always trying to make it better.

– Tom Clark, racer

Maybe it was the role-modeling in self-reliance of Rayola Mann, or the rejection of his high school football coach, or the mentorship of Bud Hines, or the tutelage of Al Gunter, or his austere upbringing that taught him to make do, or his own deep curiosity and quick wit. Or maybe it was all of the above. But some combination of nature and nurture invested Dick Mann with a compulsion to tackle problems and improve the performance of everything he becomes involved with, whether it is motorcycles, clothing, machines, or organizations. Dick Mann has a highly critical mind, but he is critical in the most positive and productive sense. He does not see fault and sit back and complain about how things are not what they should be. Rather, he envisions how things can be better, then he sets out to find the way.

In this sense, Mann is similar to John Penton, who envisioned in 1965 what the future of off-road motorcycling should be. But unlike Penton, who often relied upon the diverse talents of family and friends to realize his visions, Dick Mann both sees and realizes. He gets right in with his hands and his mind and builds what he can imagine. There is a reason he once said, "I have more dirt under my fingernails than anybody

Dick Mann puts the prototype Yankee through its paces. *Photo courtesy of John Taylor and the Yankee Motors archives.*

I know." Dick Mann's friend Jim Dour, the owner of Megacycle Cams, says, "Dick doesn't like to settle for the status quo. He cannot accept it when someone excuses bad performance or inferiority by saying, 'You can get used to it.' " Dour grins and continues, "I once heard Dick say, "Yeah, you can get used to a turd under your hat, too. But that doesn't make it good!' "

There is no doubt that the manual and technical skills taught by Bud Hines, Walt Kreft, and Carl Huth have served Dick Mann well. He is a practical engineer without an engineering degree. He has the capability of analyzing performance, identifying problems, designing potential solutions, fabricating parts, and testing his product. Mann gives much credit to Al Gunter for helping him develop his thought processes for what is described in today's jargon as the ability to "think outside the box." But it is more likely that Gunter's quick and free-ranging intellect only served to stimulate and give permission to the creative bent that already existed in Dick Mann.

Mann's creativity is manifested in innovation. He can rarely leave well enough alone. He sees large structures as components, and zeroes in on whether or how to improve each little component. Claude McElvain, who worked for John Lund, says, "I always got excited when Dick Mann arrived, and I always wanted to go out and help him unload his truck. I always wanted to see what he had done in the off season. He invented adjustable foot pegs, and things like that. His bikes always incorporated some new ideas." Gunnar Lindstrom, who raced head to head with Mann at the AMA's first professional motocross in Ohio in 1970, says, "Dick was not a follower; he was an innovator. He had the initiative to experiment and do things on his own. He was riding an OSSA, and he had modified it in ways that made him competitive with my Husky."

Just how creative Mann could be was demonstrated early on when he was a teenager in Richmond. He and his buddies started talking about what they could do to make a trials bike as light as possible. Dick removed everything except the footpegs and handle bars from a trials bike. He even removed the fuel tank and replaced it with a small tire inner-tube containing gasoline around his neck, with the gas line running from the valve stem to the carburetor. Mann rode and won the trial. He recalls, "My mother wanted to kill me. She didn't like the idea of me riding around with a gas tank around my neck."

Dick Mann could rebuild an engine, but, unlike many riders and tuners, he never became obsessed with finding more power. He knew that more races were won with reliability than with speed, and that a good-handling bike with an inferior engine and a smart rider could beat an overpowered and foul-handling machine any day of the week. He had proven that time and again throughout his own racing career. Johnny Hall puts it simply, "He knew geometry, and he always said it didn't

The Yankee prototype, left side. *Photo courtesy of John Taylor and the Yankee Motors archives.*

matter how fast it would go if it wouldn't turn a corner." So Mann concentrated on the chassis and its relationship with the rider. He thought about rake and trail and length and traction and weight distribution. He thought about ways to make a bike easier to adjust and set up at different tracks and under changing conditions. Tom White, who began his career in dirt-track racing, switched to motocross, then built a successful business as a co-owner of White Brothers, says, "Dick was always so smart about the whole motorcycle. He understood that power didn't always win." Mann's understanding of frame geometry also had a practical benefit that went beyond racing. While working at Walt and Carl's he developed a way to straighten frames without removing the engine, which significantly reduced time and labor costs.

Mann always questioned the fundamentals of dirt-track motorcycle design. Dirt-track bikes had no rear suspension because Class C rules dictated that they evolve from street machines in an era when almost no motorcycles had rear suspension. When the plunger suspension arrived on street machines, it worked horribly on dirt tracks because it let the axle twist from its horizontal position, so everyone simply concluded that

The Yankee prototype, with chassis designed by Dick Mann. *Photo courtesy of John Taylor and the Yankee Motors archives.*

rear suspension was bad on dirt tracks, period. Mert Lawwill, who became a chassis design and suspension wizard who revolutionized the bicycle industry after his motorcycle racing career, says, "The only reason we used rigid frames was because we didn't know better, not because they were necessarily good."

Some attribute the introduction of rear suspension in dirt-track racing to Dick Mann's unwilling use of a road-racing frame when the AMA banned his Matchless in the BSA chassis in 1962. But this is not the case. Mann says, "In 1954 Gunter and I were wondering how to put a rear suspension on a dirt tracker. We raced on terribly rough tracks, so why *shouldn't* a properly suspended bike work better?" The stock Gold Star frame was not an option because it was heavy and the wheel base was too long for a dirt tracker. Mann continues, "We reasoned that we needed to build a whole new swingarm frame for a Gold Star dirt tracker that was lighter and shorter, and that's what we did." Mann and Gunter experimented with the idea, but the rules would not let them test a prototype frame under true racing conditions. Mann concludes, "Under the rules, we would have had to get BSA to go through the paperwork of getting the frame approved by the AMA, then they would have to

Wearing coveralls and no face shield, Dick Mann tests one of his frames. Mann earned a reputation as the best chassis expert on the AMA Grand National Championship circuit. Through experimentation with chassis geometry, he could make his motorcycles handle better than any others. *Photo courtesy of the Dick Mann collection.*

be manufactured and made available to anyone who wanted one." The idea went no farther because conventional wisdom of the day was so strongly opposed to anything but a rigid frame in dirt-track racing. The dirt-track community would not come to accept the idea for at least another decade. However, by 1968 when the rules became more liberal toward frames, Dick Mann and Mert Lawwill showed up with swingarm frames. By 1969 they were fairly standard on the championship circuit.

Dick Mann also experimented with wheel camber, which was a critical factor in racing car design, but unheard of on a single track vehicle. By canting a wheel slightly off of the vertical, one could improve traction coming out of a corner, or turning into a corner. Mann says, "I got my Gold Star set up so I had to apply some steering pressure to run down the straightaway, but when I let up on the handlebars, it would turn left on its own." Mann also was the first person to make a Gold Star engine achieve racing performance with an air filter. Prior to his adaptation of a Clark fork lift air filter, Gold Star owners just sucked in the dirt and did more frequent engine overhauls.

When racers started using two-stroke engines in short-track machines, there was always a problem with where to route the large and awkward expansion chamber. Chicago-based racer Gene Hartline says, "You had to route the expansion chamber out the right side of the bike so it wouldn't drag the ground when you were leaning to the left, and it was hard to hang the chamber so you could have the footpeg in the right place, and have everything tucked in so it looked good and worked right. Dick solved the problem by mounting his footpeg on the exhaust system. It was such a simple and obvious solution, but nobody ever thought of it." Hartline continues, "That's the way Mann is. He just doesn't let conventionality limit his thinking."

Dick Mann had a friend in the Bay Area named George Curtis who was working on the leading edge of polycarbon and composite materials technology. Curtis was experimenting with materials that were tough and flexible, and Mann began

Using an OSSA engine, Dick Mann built a short tracker that was so successful that Yankee Motors put it into production as the OSSA DMR (Dick Mann Replica). *Photo courtesy of John Taylor and the Yankee Motors archives.*

Dick Mann tests the Yankee, whose big 500cc two-stroke, twin-cylinder engine is well displayed in this photograph. Mann was responsible for designing not just a frame that could handle the power, but one that could be easily replicated in mass production. *Photo courtesy of John Taylor and the Yankee Motors archives.*

to collaborate with him on applying the technology to racing motorcycles. The result was Mann's G50, featuring a one-piece seat/rear fender/number plate section that could be quickly removed with three bolts, leaving the entire motorcycle from the engine back exposed and easy to work on. Today the design is standard, but in 1963 it was a totally fresh idea conceived by Dick Mann. As for the use of flexible materials, Mann and Curtis manufactured a batch of dirt-bike fenders and field tested them. Riders said, "I don't want one of those. It will make my bike look funny." A decade later Preston Petty bought a personal jet from selling flexible replacement dirt-bike fenders. And looking "funny" was no longer an issue, because riders invariably chose the brightest and most conspicuous colors Petty could manufacture.

When Mann started his racing career, standard foot protection was a pair of tall lineman's boots. They were tedious to get in and out of, provided little protection to the shin, and their heel could catch the ground on a rough dirt track and twist your ankle, throw you off the bike, or worse. By the time Mann completed his professional career, motorcycle racing boots had improved considerably, incorporating quick-release straps, shin protection, and a flat sole. Still not satisfied with the standard products, many of which were slightly modified skiing boots, Mann designed a rebuildable boot that incorporated a quick lacing system and a shin-protecting flap to keep dirt out of the laces. It also had the arch recess moved forward so the rider's foot would rest level on the peg. Mann explains, "The location of the heel notch on normal boots makes you ride with your toes pointing down. That is what causes people to so often break their feet and ankles when they hit something." Using removable parts and padding, the boot could be adjusted for fit, and actually rebuilt for longevity. He found a company in the Pacific Northwest that made logger's boots to build a prototype. He says, "After we perfected the design, we concluded that they would cost $100 a pair to mass produce, and that would have put their retail price way out of the market, so we gave up on the idea." The decision to scrap the project was based in part on the fact that everyone, including the Japanese motorcycle manufacturers, had jumped big time into the boot business, flooded the market, and begun dumping their inventory at bargain basement prices. Mann says, "I was naive enough to believe that a product could succeed strictly on the basis of quality and design. But that's not how it works, especially in the motorcycle industry. It's all about style, fashion, marketing, and pricing."

In an article that appeared in *Cycle Guide* in November, 1977, Mann said, "I've got really bad timing. I don't know whether I'm ahead of my time or behind it, but I get some good ideas that never seem to go anywhere." Paul Dean, the author of the story, concluded, "Whether he is ahead of or behind his own time is a moot point; because he is a legend *in* it . . . Mann is unquestionably a thinker, an innovator, a unique person

Production manager, Jim Corpe, Yankee CEO John Taylor, and Dick Mann examine a Mann-designed Yankee frame. What is Dick Mann doing in a white shirt and tie? This was an official Yankee publicity photo, taken for a presentation to investors. *Photo courtesy of John Taylor and the Yankee Motors archives.*

with the ability to quickly see through all the extraneous bullshit and get right to the heart of a seemingly complex problem."

Dean's analysis of Mann's innovative ability nicely describes the approach Mann took when he became involved—sometimes reluctantly and sometimes willingly—in the politics of racing. To revert to his own colorful terminology, Dick Mann doesn't like a turd under his hat in any respect, whether it is the motorcycle he rides on or the motorcycle organization he rides for. This image of pungent unpleasantness is apropos of the AMA Competition Committee's G50 Matchless fiasco. While Dick Mann may have been ahead of his time in creating material objects such as boots and fenders, he was the man of his time in overhauling institutions. Dick Mann became a powerful architect of change in the evolution of the modern AMA. His motive was as it always has been: to make something better.

7

Losing The Combination

I thought I was in people's way. I just pulled off and quit. It was the only race I ever quit.
– Dick Mann, 1965

Among AMA Experts, the National Number is a badge of honor. At one time there were so many licensed riders, the AMA set up a system of numbers and letters, based on the regions of the country. For example, if you had 22F, you were from Ohio; if you had 22J, you were from Iowa; if you had 22X, you were from California. But those who carried no letter designation were the National Numbers. They were assigned to the big dogs, the overlords, the winners, the men to beat. Although there was no hard and fast rule, the lower numbers were often conferred by AMA Competition Director Jules Horky on the most outstanding riders, thus the lower numbers carried greater prestige. When a National Number holder retired, his number was not immediately reassigned, because racers are racers and often decide to come out of retirement. Of course, Number One was displayed each year by the AMA Grand National Champion.

Although he had a profitable off-season during the winter of 1963, dominating a weekly short track at Portland as well as the half-mile races in the Bay Area, Mann's 1964 national program began poorly with a 58th place at Daytona, where he rode the Dunstall Norton. Though he earned points in 11 of the first

Aboard the Dunstall Norton at Daytona in 1964. *Jerry West photo, courtesy of the Dick Mann collection.*

15 Nationals, his best finish prior to September was a third at Columbus. Then he caught fire, winning three road races on three consecutive weekends at Windber, Pennsylvania; Greenwood, Iowa; and Meadowdale, Illinois. At Greenwood he finished over a minute ahead of Roger Reiman, and at Meadowdale he lapped the field. These victories, and a second at the Springfield Mile behind BSA teammate Sammy Tanner, catapulted him to the top of the points standing with a narrow margin of 466 over Roger Reiman's 461.

At one time Daytona and Laconia were the only road races on the AMA circuit, and until it was relocated to Daytona International Speedway, Daytona was a road race in name only. AMA racing was so grounded in its dirt-track tradition that streamlining was not allowed on motorcycles—including those used in road racing—until 1963. However, by the 1960s, road racing was becoming more prominent, based on the proliferation of sports car racing circuits that took place in America after the Second World War. Many of these courses were low-investment, narrow asphalt roads, snaking over undeveloped rural land, constructed by people affiliated with the Sports Car Club of America. They had not been designed with the needs of motorcyclists in mind, as is still the case with most road courses. Barriers designed to stop cars were common, and planned runoff areas were an idea that had not yet come. Windber, which was a road through a forest in a public park, was especially unnerving for motorcycle racers. The surface was not even asphalt, but a crushed shale that had the abrasive force of a good bastard rasp if a rider were to fall on it. Mann says, "There was one place where the course made a sharp turn at the top of the hill. It was dark, and all you could see as you raced up the hill was a wall of trees in front of you. We painted some of the trees white so we could tell where we were supposed to make our turn. If you missed and went between the wrong two trees, it could be disastrous." George Roeder concurs, "At Windber you actually had to be careful not to lean too far off the motorcycle on the inside of a turn, because you might hit your head on a tree!" Roeder knew, because on one occasion he hit a tree and broke his bike into two pieces.

Returning to the dirt tracks, Reiman won the Santa Fe short track and Mann finished 11th on a Parilla, but he stormed back to win the Peoria TT on his Matchless. Then he had a front tire go flat while running at over 100 miles per hour at Sacramento, dueling with Ronnie Rall in a qualifying heat. At this time hay bales were not even used, and Mann ended up against the outside fence, shaken and with broken ribs. Mann explains, "Safety was not part of the game. It was not until Chris Draayer lost his arm and Gary Nixon shattered his leg that we started thinking about hay bales." Consequently, the 1964 Ascot TT almost seemed a repeat of the 1963 event, with Mann racing hurt and in contention for the Grand National Championship. However, he could not repeat the miracle of 1963. He was running second when he was knocked down by Dave Palmer, who went on to win the event. Mann finished the season second, behind Roger Reiman.

With the title relinquished to Reiman, Mann got a call from Jules Horky, asking if he would like a different national number. Mann says, "I liked 64 just fine, and wasn't looking to change my number, so I said, joking, 'Sure, but only if it is lower than Gunter's (Gunter carried number three).' Immediately Horky replied, 'Okay, how about number two?' " Number two had been that of Dick Klamfoth, who was retired, so Mann's joke became reality, bringing him the prestigious number two for the 1965 season, the number for which his fans still recognize him today.

Reiman celebrated his championship with a commanding victory at Daytona in 1965, lapping the entire field in the rain, except for second place Mert Lawwill. Mann says, "Roger Reiman was the best rain rider I have ever seen. We always heard and read so much about how good the British were in the rain. I don't think any of them could have held a candle to Reiman." Mann finished a creditable fifth on his Matchless. However, he proved he was still the road racer to beat in the 250cc combined race for Amateurs and Experts. Riding a Yamaha, he won with a scorching pace of 91.606 miles per hour, breaking Dick Hammer's old record by over three miles per hour. In fact, Mann's average speed was over a mile per hour

Sammy Tanner and Dick Mann celebrate a BSA sweep at the Springfield Mile in 1964. Mann's second place finish to teammate Tanner moved him to the top of the AMA Grand National Championship point standings with a margin of 466 to 461 over Roger Reiman. In the background are BSA President Ted Hodgdon, C.R. Axtell, Walt Brown, and Hank Westra. *Photo courtesy of the AMA Archives.*

faster than Reiman's average in the 200 aboard his big 750cc Harley. This is not an entirely fair comparison, because Reiman's time was over twice the distance under wet conditions, still, Mann's little Yamaha set a blistering pace, which was a harbinger of things to come from the Japanese two-strokes.

Following his fifth in the Daytona 200, Mann finished third at the next three races to gain leadership in the Grand National points chase. Reiman had slipped to fifth, and Lawwill was nearly 100 points behind Mann. Then Mann won the 120-mile road race at Wentzville, Missouri, finished fifth at Columbus, and third at Laconia. But consistent performance by Bart Markel, with victories at Heidelberg and Hagerstown, moved Markel slightly ahead of Mann in the championship.

AMA rules required riders to make a pit stop at road races, whether they needed gas or not. Mann's Matchless had a large tank, and he knew he would not need gas at Wentzville, so he instructed his pit man, John Lund, to prepare just a small container of gasoline. Mann would rush into the pits, flip the gas cap open, Lund would toss in the small cup of gas, and Mann would be gone. With this plan, they would avoid losing time by fumbling with a big refueling can. Lund says, "I said, 'Okay, what do you want me to use.' Mann didn't even have a container with him, and said, 'I don't know. Get some kind of cup.' " Lund got a wax and paper Pepsi cup, put in a little gas, and sat it on the pit wall. By the time Mann came in for his pit stop, the gasoline had eaten through the wax and the cup was misshapen, soggy, and leaking. To make matters worse, the fuel cap did not open easily, and Lund had to sprint alongside the moving Matchless, both men fumbling to open the gas cap. Lund says, "Finally, we got the cap about half open and I just kind of threw the cup at it, presumably splashing some of the gas into the tank." Mann roared back onto the track and to victory, having completed a legal pit stop!

Mann with Markel and Resweber at Peoria. Exhaustion from the sweltering heat is evident in the faces of the riders. *Photo courtesy of the AMA archives.*

At Nelson Ledges, Mann again rode a Yamaha, winning the event to become the first person to bring Yamaha a victory, and the first to win an AMA National aboard a two-stroke (this event, incidentally, was the only time the AMA ever awarded national championship points at a road race for 250cc machines). He finished 18th at the Castle Rock TT, placed fifth at Greenwood, then repeated his victory at Meadowdale in one of the strangest and funniest races of his career. Mann recalls, "John Lund was working as my pit man again, and I asked him to give me information on the pit board every single lap. I was in second, but George Roeder was just storming away, and there was little likelihood I was going to catch him. Lund kept holding up his pit board every lap, showing me the split times between me and Roeder. Then Lund made a mistake and held up an erroneous number that made it look like I had gained on Roeder. Roxy Rockwood, the announcer, was near our pit, and it turned out that he was announcing from our pit board, not from official timing information. Roxy went crazy and started yelling about how Mann was reeling Roeder in, blah blah blah. Lund thought that was really funny, and kept putting up bogus split times, just to screw with Roxy. Roeder's team, who were not keeping times, started listening to Roxy and got all flustered and excited, and when Roeder came in for gas stop, they were in such a hurry they did not give him enough fuel, so he ran out of gas on the last lap and I won the race!"

From his perspective, Roeder recalls, "I was just flying that day. Meadowdale had what they called the Monza Curve, a big bowl where you could run really fast up near the wall. I was taking that turn flat-out every lap, running right up next to the wall. No one else was doing it that way. The G-forces on the bowl were so great that the shocks on my Harley bottomed out all the way, making the rear tire rub a hole right through the seat. Pretty soon it rubbed through the seat and through my leathers too, and started burning my butt. I had to keep scooting around on the seat a little every lap so it wouldn't burn me in the same place." Being a true racer, it never would have occurred to Roeder to slow down a tad and save his bottom!

Dick Mann with Bart Markel and Sammy Tanner at Heidelberg in 1965. After carrying the Number One plate in 1964, Mann entered an uncertain period of his career, briefly retiring in 1966. Statistically, 1964 and 1965 were good seasons for Mann, but he was losing enthusiasm for the grueling pace of the professional circuit. Bart Markel was just coming into his own. *Photo courtesy of the AMA archives.*

He continues, "When I came in for fuel, my crew failed to open the vent cap on the filler can, and very little gas got into my tank. The next thing I know they were holding out a pit board that said 'Slow Down.' I was winning and couldn't figure why I would want to slow down, and I just kept storming around the track as fast as I could. I was having a great day. Later I learned they were trying to tell me to conserve fuel, because they knew they had made a mistake and not given me much gas. If they had just stuck out a board that said, 'Gas,' I would have understood what was going on. But I didn't and I ran out of gas on the last lap and Mann beat me."

Mann failed to qualify at Springfield, got a fourth at Peoria, and a third at Sacramento. Then, trailing Markel by a little more than twenty points, Mann pulled off the course and quit at the final road race of the season at Marlboro, Maryland. Although he gave it little thought at the time, he realized later that had he just finished the race, he would have again won the AMA Grand National Championship. He says, “I wasn’t even thinking about that. All I knew was that I was having a lot of trouble with my vision, I was going slower and slower, and I felt I was becoming a danger to myself and everyone else.”

But Dick Mann—to his own astonishment—was actually getting fed up with the grind. Battling the AMA over what kind of equipment he could race, and finding the struggle harder and harder against young, upcoming riders was beginning to wear him down. The national championship series, which had consisted of less than ten events when Mann started racing, had grown to nearly twenty races, and the pace was grueling. Furthermore, he had been having a problem with his eyes for several years. Sometimes he could not change his focus quickly, and on some race courses this became very hazardous. He tried time and again to explain it to eye doctors, but no one seemed to understand the condition. At one point he tried racing with eye glasses, but that did not help. He says, “It’s funny. My vision has never been very good, but this problem would kind of come and go. Sometimes I could kind of ignore it and overcome the problem, but other times it really got the best of me.”

Dick Mann, unsuited at Tulare. *Mahony Photo Archive.*

In his 1972 memoir, Mann describes his feelings at the end of the 1965 season: "I was 32, and even though I could scarcely believe it myself, I was becoming fed up with racing. I wasn't slowing down, but my desire to work hard was starting to slip. Apparently I was looking for ways to ease out of racing. I thought that after all those years, maybe it was time for me to open up a motorcycle shop of my own." Statistically, 1964 and 1965 appeared to be the best seasons of Dick Mann's career. He was at the top of his game, still able to beat anyone, and atop or near the top of the Grand National Championship ladder. But an emotional appraisal of oneself can be much more convincing than statistics, and Dick Mann clearly believed that he had lost The Combination. Worse yet, he thought he had lost the will to find it.

Not only did Mann get an opportunity to open his own shop, but he got an offer to open it in paradise. A friend named John Fields wanted Mann to run a motorcycle dealership in Honolulu, Hawaii, and offered him an arrangement that would make Dick the owner of the shop after four years as manager. Mann renewed his AMA license in 1966 with the plan of commuting to the mainland for selected races, and moved to Honolulu to become a motorcycle dealer. It didn't take him long to decide he may have made a mistake. Mann says, "I discovered I didn't like retail. The business in Hawaii was really competitive, and everyone had these smarmy used car-type guys on the sales floor. Sometimes I had to just walk away from the show room because I could not bear to listen to the kinds of lines these salesmen were handing people."

Dick Mann had enjoyed a 12-year professional racing career. He had finished in the top ten every year since 1957, and he had overcome all kinds of adversity to become AMA Grand National Champion. If anyone deserved a rest and had earned the right to retire with pride, he had, and at age 32 he was handed an opportunity that most aging racers would have killed for. Not only could he stay involved with the business he loved, but he could do it in Hawaii. It sounded like Easy Street. But Dick Mann hated it.

8

The Hard Road Back

If you made up your mind to race, then by God you raced. If you were worn out or detuned or healing up, or your bike wasn't running right . . . well, these were just obstacles to overcome.

– Frank Conner, Cycle, 1972

Dick Mann returned to Daytona in 1966, riding a BSA. Both Triumph and Harley-Davidson were beginning to invest heavily in their road-racing programs. The machines were no longer just geared-up dirt trackers. The rules had been relaxed to allow more modifications, and the Triumphs especially stretched the Class C rules right to the limit. Cal Rayborn was top qualifier on his Harley at 134.148 miles per hour. Mann qualified a full 15 miles per hour off that pace, and began the race in 59th position. Buddy Elmore won on a beautifully prepared factory Triumph. But it was a finish mired in controversy. Daytona International Speedway has a tall tower with lights that display a leader board every lap. George Roeder was leading the event, and recalls, "You could see the leader board as you came through the tri-oval and headed into the first turn. Elmore's number did not even appear on the leader board for almost the whole race, then suddenly, near the end, there he is at the top, and they credited him with the win. The scoring officials said they missed him a lap after his pit stop, and he was

Dick Mann and his friend and teammate Jody Nicholas were two of the riders who put Yamaha on the map in American road racing. Nicholas gave the brand its first AMA victory at Meadowdale in 1963. This photo of Mann was taken at Daytona in 1965, where he won the lightweight race and beat the track record by over three miles per hour. Later that year he won at Nelson Ledges, which was the one and only time the AMA awarded Grand National Championship points at a 250cc road race. *Jerry West photo, courtesy of the Dick Mann collection.*

supposed to be there all the time. I should have protested, but I didn't." Mann's BSA blew up early, and he finished in 71st position. However, in the AMA's annual top rider contest, which was announced each year at Daytona, clubs throughout the nation elected Dick Mann the most popular rider of the year.

Upon returning to Honolulu, Mann received a call from Suzuki with an offer to ride a local road race at Carlsbad, California. With Yamaha doing so well in the 250cc class, other Japanese manufacturers started taking an interest in road racing in America, and were looking for talent. Mann teamed up with Elmore on the Suzuki team, but it turned into a bad day for both. Both riders crashed and both broke a collarbone. By now Dick Mann could not count the times he had broken his collarbone, and this time it had to be pinned. He flew back to Hawaii hurting, and recalls, "Honolulu was everything I'd expected it to be. The people were warm and friendly, the climate was out of this world, and the dress was casual. The spill had changed my thinking a little about racing. If I was going to fall down and hurt myself, I was much better off away from the tracks and trying to make a really decent living for the first time in my life. Every time I thought about racing, I'd reach up and finger that lump that the pin made in my shoulder."

Mann recalls that he met some really great riders in Hawaii, the most notable among them being Cobra DeSoto, the father of motocross star John DeSoto. Mann says, "Everyone called him Johnny Boy, and he was only about 12 years old at the time." On Sunday mornings, Mann and his buddies would take their bikes out to whiz across the pineapple fields. He says, "Cow trailing in Hawaii is great fun, even though there are no cows!" Then one Sunday he hit a hole and crashed, launching himself off the motorcycle and re-breaking his collarbone. The collarbone had to be re-pinned, and, oddly, that injury made him realize again how much he missed racing. To make matters worse, he received a phone call from his buddies, Nixon and Keen, who were hanging out at Lund's in Decatur. Keen said, "Hey, Bug Man, don't you realize what a terrible thing you're doing to us, not racing with us? We miss you. When are you going to stop this foolishness and throw your leg over a flat tracker again?" Nixon chimed in, "Yeah, Bugs. When you gonna get off that island and do some racing again?" They were like the little devil on Mann's shoulder, whispering in his ear to remind him what he really wanted and needed to do.

A short time later, after thanking John Fields and apologizing for letting him down, Mann was back in Richmond, getting into Johnny Hall's pickup with a BSA dirt tracker and a Matchless road racer in the rear, heading for the Midwest to go racing. As for his old eye problem that convinced him he was over the hill just a few months before, Mann says, "What eye problem? I was ready to race." Hall said, 'That old BSA had been on the market for $500 ever since Bugs left for Hawaii. It's a good thing he couldn't sell it, because within 30 days of his return he earned $2,000 with it." Mann confirms, "I had the Matchless up for sale for $1,500, and two BSA's for $500 each, and luckily, none of them had sold." Today the Dick Mann Matchless is valued at over $60,000.

However, Mann still had a collarbone problem, and it had gotten worse because the pin worked its way through the skin. Like many of the riders, Mann suffered through breaks and sprains and trusted his own healing processes. He never had a good attitude about doctors, especially in towns on the road where you were getting the luck of the draw, might never see the guy again, and both of you knew it. He once told Bart Markel, "They need to make doctors carry numbers like us racers. Then we could tell how good they are." Racing every week left the protruding pin an open and active wound, and eventually the dirt and sweat caused it to become infected. Mann persisted, but finally admitted at the end of a race one day that when they got back to Lund's, he was going to have to seek medical help. He was weak and sick and could barely stand, and it was later learned that he had blood poisoning.

John Lund knew just the doctor for the job. Dr. Marvel was familiar with broken-up racers and also practiced some large-animal veterinary medicine. Dick says, "Dr. Marvel gave me some antibiotics and some really dark, sticky salve to dob around the infected wound where the pin was protruding through my shoulder. He had no problem with my continuing racing." Mann hung around Lund's during the week to rest and work on his equipment, then on weekends he would go racing, then return to Decatur and pay a visit to the doctor. Lund says, "Bugs was really sick. He spent a lot of time sleeping, but every weekend he would gather himself up and head off to some racetrack. To me that is the measure of a true professional, to do the job even when you feel too bad to do it." Lund adds, "To make himself work harder, he would give almost all of the cash he had to my wife, ask her to write a check to his mother, then head off to the races with about 40 bucks in his pocket. He told me he would try harder if he was broke!" Mann says, "Every week the wound was getting better, but the doctor knew I needed to get the pin out for it to clear up entirely. Every visit he would take a pair of pliers and wiggle the end of the pin, and say, 'Hmmm. Not ready yet.' Then one week he says, 'I think it's ready,' and he grabbed it with the pliers and pulled it out just like yanking a skewer out of a shiskabob."

Mann jokes, "One of the reasons the other guys were happy to see me was that I wasn't much of a threat at the races. When you miss several months, you lose your sharpness, and it takes time to get it back. Also, in the months I had missed, a lot of the guys had found ways to make their bikes go faster." For example, the big Triumph factory commitment behind Gary Nixon had provided him the fastest mile-track motorcycle on the tour, and Nixon was really coming into his own as a top-flight racer. He continues, "At Springfield I hooked onto Nixon in practice and drafted him around the track. Later I went out on my own, and I was a half second slower. That's when I realized how tough it was going to be to remain competitive with these guys." He adds, "With Lawwill it was as bad or worse. I could not believe how fast he had that Harley running."

Mann and Nixon went to some local races in Kansas, and Dick slowly started getting his confidence back. Then they went to Sturgis, and Mann won. At Greenwood he qualified in the front row on his trusty Matchless, and finished sixth. At the Springfield 50-miler he won the fastest qualifying heat in a wheel-to-wheel battle with Sammy Tanner, then finished fourth in the final behind Nixon, Markel, and Reiman. Apparently, the old man still had it, and could still run with the young dogs and the big dogs. However, for the first time in a decade, Dick Mann fell out of the top ten, finishing 12th in the nation. This was still a remarkable feat, considering he missed the whole first half of the 1966 racing season.

At this time, BSA was developing a new scrambler. It was based on their works motocross machines, and became marketed in America as the 441 Victor. However, Pete Colman was not sure whether the bike was right for the United States, and brought in two examples. He gave one to Charles "Feets" Minert in Southern California, and one to Dick Mann, and asked them to test the bikes and get some exposure. Colman says, "The reaction was tremendous. The bike looked sensational, and we started getting calls from dealers wanting to know why they didn't have them to sell. Of course, we brought it in and sold a lot of them, and the bike became a legendary model. I credit Dick Mann for playing a big part in the success of the Victor."

The 1967 season opened with a big announcement that the Hap Jones Distributing Company would sponsor Dick Mann. It also appeared in the press that Mann was creating a new business in Richmond called Dick Mann Frame Specialties. Other riders had taken note of his skills in chassis design, and there was a demand for his products. By now, AMA Class C rules had been relaxed to the point that racers were free to use aftermarket frames, and several companies sprang up with designs using the latest light alloys and aerospace welding technology. Mann's talents also earned him a position at Yankee Motor Company in Schenectady, New York. Yankee was the distributor of OSSA motorcycles from Spain, and also had embarked upon the development of a new American motorcycle, for which Mann was hired to design the frame. Mann moved to Schenectady in April of '67 where he set up the research and development department for Yankee. Out of that collaboration also came the OSSA-powered Dick Mann replica (OSSA DMR) short-track racing motorcycle. Mann says, "Yankee was in a big, old, former General Electric factory. I had a great big room with one light bulb hanging from a cord from the ceiling. I set up my frame-building jig, welding equipment, and tool box. Then I went out and found a used cot for five dollars, and put it right next to my tools. I lived right there in my R&D department, and was gone most weekends to races." One evening, late at night during a semi-social gathering, Mann designed the DMR chassis with chalk at 100 percent scale around an OSSA engine lying on the floor of the factory. It started as a project to build his own short-track racer, but the bike worked

Dick Mann aboard a Gold Star in 1967. Mann was one of the last championship riders to continue to race the venerable old BSA single. *Jack Hall photo.*

so well that it went into production without so much as a change to a single feature.

At Daytona in 1967, Ralph White became Mann's teammate on factory BSAs. The bikes were not running well, and Mann was told they would not have his bike ready for qualifying. Under the rules, he would have to start at the back of the pack. Unfazed by adversity as usual, Mann went off to ride a hare scrambles organized by John Penton. By four in the afternoon, Mann's bike was ready, but there was no Dick Mann to qualify. Ralph White, who was considerably taller than Dick, squeezed into Mann's leathers and put on a dark face shield to hide his face. He rolled Mann's BSA through tech inspection without uttering a word, and took it onto the track to qualify. White says, "I qualified Mann's bike on the grid farther forward than mine, then when he found out about it he got upset because he was afraid the AMA would get word about our trick and disqualify him." White laughs, "He complained, 'Why didn't you just let me start at the back of the grid?' "

Dick Mann chases Cal Rayborn at the Portland Mile in 1968. Between 1959 and 1972, 1966 and 1968 were the only seasons during which Mann did not win a championship race. However, in 1968 he still finished in the top ten. *Photo courtesy of the AMA archives.*

As in 1966, Mann's BSA let him down, finishing only 12 laps to leave him in 75th position. After an eighth-place finish at Loudon, Mann won Reading and finished within the top five at the next four Nationals. After a dry spell where he failed to earn a point at the subsequent four events, Mann won Peoria. With similar inconsistency through the remainder of the season (Mann seemed to either finish in the top five, or not qualify for the final—usually due to mechanical problems), he finished fifth in the national standings, with his friend Gary Nixon winning the Grand National Championship.

In 1968 George Roeder announced his retirement, and the AMA championship series moved indoors with a short-track event at the Houston Astrodome. Dick Mann finished second aboard his new DMR OSSA at the short track at Daytona in March, but failed to collect championship points either at Houston or at the Daytona 200. The composition of the AMA circuit had changed a lot in two years. Many of the road races where Mann excelled had been replaced with mile ovals, on which new Expert Fred Nix was king. But Gary Nixon's greater experience and versatility prevailed, and Nix was unable to edge him out of a second Grand National Championship. By this time the venerable old BSA Gold Star was near the end of its life as an AMA Class C racer. Mann was one of the few riders still campaigning such a machine, and he failed to win a single national event during the 1968 season, finishing eighth in the Grand National points standing.

During 1968 the AMA undertook a monumental overhaul of its rule-making process. The old Competition Committee was abolished in favor of an expanded legislative body called the AMA Congress. Many members of the old Committee continued as delegates in the Congress, but they found themselves outnumbered by a sea of new faces elected by the AMA-chartered clubs from across the nation. Right away, the new AMA Congress slew one of the sacred cows of Class C racing. For many years, the rules had provided that 500cc overhead-valve machines would race against 750cc side-valve engines, based on the fact that side-valve engines are less efficient. This meant that the Harley-Davidsons were 750cc while the British imports were 500cc, which had long been a point of contention with British brand partisans and probably the single biggest cause of the criticism that Harley-Davidson was favored by the AMA. Triumph was ready for the new rule with a 750cc version of its Bonneville engine. BSA came in with a new 750cc engine a year later, and Harley was caught off guard with no new competitive equipment for nearly four years.

In 1969 the Astrodome program was expanded to include two nights of racing, with a short track on Friday night, and a TT on Saturday. Dick Mann finished 11th at the short track, and did not qualify for the TT. He fared little better than he had the previous year at the Daytona road races. In the 200 his Yamaha fouled its spark plugs, leaving him in 41st position, and in the Amateur/Expert combined race he finished 45th. The Daytona short-track races went better, however. On Friday night he finished second on an OSSA, and on Saturday night he won.

Dick Mann with Gene Romero and Mert Lawwill at Cumberland in 1969. Between Romero and Lawwill is race promoter John Barton. *Photo courtesy of the Dick Mann collection.*

The AMA rule changes, the rapid development of quick Japanese two-stokes, and the general penetration of the Japanese into the American motorcycle market sent the traditional brands on a quest to introduce some exciting, powerful new models. With the British, it took the form of new three-cylinder 750s: the Triumph Trident and the BSA Rocket 3. To create some good publicity around the new machine, BSA's Don Brown dreamed up the idea of making high-speed endurance runs at Daytona on bikes certified by the AMA to be stock models, not souped-up racers. He rented Daytona International Speedway and conducted the runs in secret, with the AMA's executive director Bill Berry on hand to certify the integrity of the operation. Secrecy was required, because if something went wrong, it was better that the world not know. If the event was successful, secrecy would enable BSA to make a big splash by publicizing it through a major, carefully coordinated advertising campaign.

Brown hired Yvon DuHamel, Ray Hempstead, and Dick Mann as his riders. He thought, rightly so, that the diminutive DuHamel would be quicker, but he wanted Mann for his experience. Mann set 100- and 150-mile records of 125.99 and 125.72 miles per hour, respectively. Then DuHamel upped the numbers to 127.65 and 127.53 miles per hour. The bikes ran so well that Brown soon realized that even higher speeds over longer distances might have been possible, had tires not become the limiting factor. DuHamel was on his way to a 200-mile record in the 127 mile per hour range when he blew a rear tire. So successful was the project, within weeks all of the motorcycle publications were carrying big two-page ads about the speed and performance of the stock Rocket 3s. Furthermore, the program demonstrated that the new British triples had tremendous potential, and work was begun in England later that year on a full-blown road-racing version for both Triumph and BSA.

Back on the national circuit, Mann got third places at both Cumberland and Terre Haute. At Nazareth he finished 16th, but failed to qualify for the final at Reading after having a flat tire while leading his heat race. At Loudon he rode a Yamaha, finishing 11th in the National and 6th in the Amateur/Expert combined race. Back on his BSA for Louisville, Mann won his heat and finished second in the main event. He was leading at the Santa Fe TT when he threw a chain, then finished third at Columbus. At San Jose, Mann was fourth. He finished 21st at Ascot, got third at Castle Rock, and sixth at Santa Rosa. Then Mann won both the Santa Fe short track and the Peoria TT, proving he still had the ability of a champion. Though Mann was an accomplished short tracker who often dominated the off season local races in northern California and the Pacific Northwest, Santa Fe in 1969 was the only national short-track win of his career. Describing the madness and intensity of a short track at the national level, Dick Mann once said, “Short-track racing is kind of like conducting a symphony orchestra while you’re in a fight in a phone booth!” Mert Lawwill won the

Grand National Championship in 1969, and Dick Mann finished in sixth place.

Now 35 years old, Mann maintained a position in the top ten, but the field was becoming more crowded and the contenders younger. Five of the nationals during 1969 went to first-time winners Eddie Wirth, Chuck Palmgren, Larry Palmgren, and first-year Experts Jim Rice and Mark Brelsford. Brelsford, Rice, and Chuck Palmgren were just some of the new generation of talented and highly-motivated Experts (tragically, the brilliant comer Fred Nix died in a highway accident), and riders like Ken Pressgrove, Dave Aldana, Don Castro, and Frank Gillespie were building big reputations in the Amateur ranks, and would be moving up to further crowd the Expert class the following season.

In the trade there were significant changes as well. Triumph and BSA were no longer competitors, but had merged into a single American sales and marketing organization. This company had new leadership—Felix Kalinski in the United States and Peter Thornton in England—and they were spending money like crazy to position the company to deal with the rapidly growing threat from Honda. Big advertising budgets were established, and a whole stable of special road-racing triples were being prepared for Daytona—five blue ones under the Triumph brand and five red ones with the BSA label—but Dick Mann was not on the list to get one of the bikes. All of the BSAs were assigned to younger American riders (Dave Aldana was born the year Dick Mann won his first scrambles race), except one which was assigned for Daytona to the legendary world champion from Britain, Mike Hailwood. Road racing had become so big, it was quite impossible for a privateer to have any chance at all at Daytona, and the old twin-cylinder equipment available to Dick Mann was no longer in the hunt, no matter how skillfully it had been prepared. He could still have a chance at earning points at Houston with his BSA and his OSSA, but Dick Mann approached the 1970 season with no plans to attend Daytona . . . until he got an eleventh-hour phone call from American Honda.

9

Daytona and the Honda

I had heard BSA thought Dick was over the hill, and didn't have a bike for him. But Dick Mann would have been my first choice, no matter what."

– Bob Hansen, team manager

There is a legend that during the early 1960s, the head of one of the leading European motorcycle importers said to American Honda's Mr. Kawashima during an industry cocktail party, "We are happy that your cute little motor bikes are bringing in so many new customers who will eventually graduate to big motorcycles. But, of course, Honda will never be able to build a real motorcycle." This arrogant and condescending remark was accepted with a characteristically Japanese nod and a smile. But it was understood to be a stinging insult against Honda's engineering capability, and it was duly reported back to Mr. Honda in Japan. Less than a decade after entering the American market, Honda unveiled its awesome and revolutionary 750 Four, bristling with the kind of technical features more reminiscent of a Grand Prix bike than a street machine. In addition to its overhead cam technology, multiple cylinders, and disc brakes, it had a busy and somewhat brutish appearance that declared that Honda's days of cuteness were a thing of the past.

Mann's Honda stormed away from the Triumph and BSA triples at the start of the 1970 Daytona 200, serving notice that Honda was out to modify its "nicest people" image in America. *Jerry West photo, courtesy of the Dick Mann collection.*

Although Honda established its worldwide reputation through racing in Europe, it had scrupulously avoided involvement in the American motorcycle racing scene. America had called for a different approach. Honda bought pages in national magazines and cultivated a squeaky-clean image as it sought to sell its products to a totally new market of America's nicest people. It had carefully avoided meeting the established manufacturers on their traditional terms of flash, brash, and machismo. But the Honda Four threw down a whole new gauntlet, and its palm bristled with rivets. It was time to go racing in America.

It is impossible to overstate the risk and courage involved in this decision. One of the contributing factors in Indian's plunge into shame and bankruptcy was a brazen effort in 1949 to introduce a new product by entering a team of twelve untested bikes at the road race at Laconia. Not a single Indian finished the event, and by 1950 the dying company was under the control of British investors who had bought it for a pittance. Why should Honda be less likely to fail in an era when the stakes were considerably higher and the competition tougher? They were stepping into the ring under the critical gaze of an industry that thought them incapable of building a "real" motorcycle. The likelihood of their failing on the tough battlefield of the Daytona 200 was far greater than the likelihood of refuting that belief.

Bob Hansen—then working for American Honda—had struggled through the Matchless G50 fiasco with Dick Mann and was deeply experienced in the American racing scene. The Japanese really didn't understand Class C rules, so he explained to them that with the introduction of the 750 Four it was almost imperative that they begin to race. They feared failure, so he explained, "That is the *best* reason to enter a team. There will be private owners who will enter 750 Hondas against the other factory teams, and they *will* fail. We must have a factory team and do it right to protect the reputation of the brand." Still, no one could have been more surprised than he when his Japanese bosses called him to a director's meeting one day late in 1969 to inform him that Honda would go racing in America. Hansen relates, "They explained to me that Honda would enter a team of Honda 750 Fours at Daytona. They wanted me to help the company wend its way through the paperwork and procedures of AMA racing, but they made it clear the effort would be officially managed by Mr. Nakamura, Honda's racing boss in Europe. The motorcycles would be prepared in Japan, and Mr. Nakamura would choose the riders and support personnel from their pool of European talent. However, they also realized it would be prudent to have an American rider on one of the Hondas, and it was my job to find a rider and mechanics and manage that small portion of the program."

Hansen recognized that his role amounted to little more than American Honda's gesture toward political correctness, but Bob Hansen never failed to take any racing effort seriously. The best single term to describe his skill is "wily." Quiet, observant, and calculating, he is the Frank Williams of American motorcycle racing. His long experience as a successful private team owner in the shark tank of factory racing had taught him that speed, power, and a quick wrist on the throttle may be the least important aspects of winning. Once he told the Kawasaki engineers that he would give them back five horsepower if they would give him three more miles per gallon! They were simply astonished that anyone would want to race with less horsepower, rather than more, and, of course, they refused to take the deal.

Valuing experience, maturity, intelligence, and an understanding of mechanical complexity, Hansen immediately picked up the phone to call Dick Mann. Mann, who had been cut from BSA's sponsorship program at the end of 1969 in favor of foreign or younger riders, did not even have plans to attend Daytona in 1970—not even with a private effort. Hansen asked him to come to Honda's headquarters in Gardena to work out the details, since Daytona was less than three months away. Under Hansen's coaching, Mann asked for a reasonable fee to ride, full expenses, and $10,000 to win. The Japanese were more than happy to agree to the big bonus to win, because there was slim chance they would have to pay. They were going to Daytona to win, but that task had already been assigned to British riders Ralph Bryans, Tommy Robb, and Bill Smith. What chance did this grizzled pair of American racing veterans—Hansen and Mann—have of upstaging Honda of Europe, where they knew how road racing was really done?

When Speed Week began, Ralph Bryans, chief of the British superstars, promptly threw his Honda away in practice, turning it into a smouldering pile. His crew set about rebuilding the machine from parts, but they had no spare frame, so they began building around the frame that had been in the flaming crash. There were magnesium engine castings on the bike, which had generated tremendous heat in the fire. Hansen thought it ill advised to use the frame, and said so, but was told to keep his opinions to himself. Furthermore, Hansen's mechanics were angered by Bryans, who would wander in and handle their parts and tools while they were trying to work. It became clear to Hansen that his team was regarded as less

The Honda wrecking crew at Daytona in 1970. Mann is the sole American rider among British imports Bill Smith, Tommy Robb, and Ralph Bryans. With the European-managed bikes all failing, Honda won the race thanks to a survival strategy expertly executed by Mann and Hansen. *Photo courtesy of the Bob Hansen collection.*

than an American token effort. It was regarded a nuisance by the visiting Brits, so he segregated his crew to their distinct portion of the garage, and everyone started behaving like what they really were: two separate and unrelated teams.

The bikes were strong during practice—so much so that Hansen was disappointed when Mann qualified fourth. It earned Honda an impressive front row start, but based on practice times, Hansen had expected better. Then Bob Jameson, his chief mechanic, came to him and said there was foreign matter in the engine oil. It was not metallic, but made of tiny rubbery bits that clearly indicated something was coming apart inside the engine. It turned out to be the cam chain tensioner, which was being rapidly hammered into oblivion by the quick rise and fall of the radical racing cams. The engine would have to be entirely rebuilt, and there was serious doubt

Racing to victory on the Honda Four at Daytona, 1970. *International Speedway photo, from the AMA archives.*

that it would last 200 miles. Hansen told the British team what the Americans had discovered, and warned that their cam chain tensioners were probably damaged. Again, they dismissed his advice.

Jameson told Hansen that a careful, total rebuild would require as long as two days, which would take them right up to race day. Hansen went to Mann, explained the situation, and told him he might as well go to the beach or find some other way to relax for a couple of days. He apologized that there would be no time for additional practice. Mann shrugged off the situation and said, "Hey, I never won practice yet!"

When the machine was finally ready to go, Mann took it out for a lap and returned excited and enthusiastic. He declared it a jet—much quicker than the original engine set up in Japan—and thought their chances good, provided the cam chain tensioner could survive the 200 miles. Mann's appraisal of the machine proved right when the green flag fell and he streaked away, initially leaving a field of BSA and Triumph triples far behind. The British Honda riders all disappeared in no time, falling out with engine failures and leaving only Dick Mann to finish playing Honda's doubtful hand at the high-stakes table of the Daytona 200. Mann could tell when the Honda began to lose its edge, and he throttled back, letting Nixon's Triumph, Mike Hailwood's BSA, and Ron Grant's Suzuki pass. He settled in, riding only hard enough to keep the leaders within his reach. Eventually all three retired, moving Mann back into the lead during the waning laps of the race.

As the race wore on, so did the cam chain tensioner, but Mann and Hansen had the experience to deal with it. Hansen began posting lap times and split times between Mann and the second place rider each and every lap. Mann knew exactly what to do with this information. He deliberately slowed his pace to reduce the stress on the engine, sacrificing his lead by approximately a second a lap. But he knew how many laps were remaining, and he knew exactly how much advantage he had to play with. Gene Romero's Triumph was coming on strong, but he had a lot of ground to catch up, having run off the course earlier in the race. Mr. Nakamura either didn't understand or didn't agree with the strategy when he confronted Hansen and said, "You are losing a second a lap. Tell him to go faster!" It was the last straw. Hansen and Mann had been treated like second class citizens all week by Nakamura's team of imports, who had ignored Hansen's advice and subsequently only shamed the brand with engine failures and miserable rider performance. He was running three stop watches and trying desperately to help Mann nurse an ailing motorcycle home to a win. He turned on Nakamura and replied, "You get back over that wall (meaning the pit wall)! We're trying to win a race here!"

Mann breezed across the finish line with eight seconds to spare over the Triumph of Gene Romero, who had been fast qualifier at 157.342 miles per hour, and was gaining on the leader at a blistering pace. Don Castro finished third on another Triumph Trident. Even while throttling back in the declining laps of the race, Mann's performance on the Honda significantly raised the bar at Daytona, surpassing Cal Rayborn's 1968 average speed by more than a mile per hour (102.697 versus 101.290). About the victory, *Cycle Sport* reported, "You knew it was a popular win, the way the crowd gathered round at Victory Lane, . . . and later that evening in the plush surroundings of the Victory Banquet at the Desert Inn, when nearly one thousand of motorcycling's most involved people stood and gave the modest little man sitting alone at one end of the head table a standing ovation, you knew that Dick Mann's day had finally come." Mann had given Honda what is arguably the most important victory in America in its history, even to the present day. It left no doubt that Honda had arrived, and that it would be a far tougher future for the traditional dominators of the big-bike performance market, Harley-Davidson, BMW, Triumph, and BSA.

The victory also served notice that Dick Mann was still a viable and valuable talent on the American motorcycle racing scene. Those who counted him out as too old and over the hill had to reconsider. It was an enormously popular win among the fans. Dick Mann had been a respected racing star for more than a decade, but his achievement at Daytona in 1970 raised his popularity immeasurably. He had become more than a racing legend. He had become a living legend, earning adulation from fans representing several generations. The win likely proved something important to Dick Mann as well, propelling him forward in a long career extended several more years by virtue of this victory.

Ralph Bryans later whined in the British press that the European contingent had received no cooperation from Hansen and American Honda, a claim that was belied by an unsolicited letter to Hansen from Tommy Robb that stated, ". . . we all realize the effort you personally put into the race arrangements and in particular our personal comfort during the whole of our trip. I am sorry we could not have furnished you with better results from our part, but I can truthfully say that having met Dick Mann I got as much satisfaction seeing such a nice guy take the chequered flag, as I would have done had I been fortunate enough to be in that position myself. Your choice in this man as both a rider and a character could not have been better."

When Dick Mann and Bob Hansen left Daytona, Dick had no ride, and Bob Hansen had no job. He had left Gardena as Honda's National Service Manager with seventy-five people under him. When he returned his name did not even appear on Honda's organization chart. Apparently, within the context of Japanese face and honor, all of the prestige he brought the

Dark horses, for sure. Dick Mann had lost his BSA ride because he was thought to be over the hill. Bob Hansen was instructed to keep out of the way of the Europeans, who planned to win the race. Thanks to Mann and Hansen, Daytona 1970 became Honda's glorious debut in AMA road racing. *Photo courtesy of the Bob Hansen collection.*

Dick Mann in the winner's circle at Daytona, 1970. The unlikely and much-celebrated victory rekindled Mann's career and changed the mind of BSA, which had declined to renew his support after 1969. *Dave Friedman photo, courtesy of Don Emde Productions.*

company through the skillfully executed Daytona debut and victory was canceled by his confrontation with Nakamura. But both Mann and Hansen landed on their feet. Bob Hansen was snatched up by Kawasaki, who hired him to develop their new Formula 750 racing program around the three-cylinder H1R. Hansen gave them their first National victory a little over a year later when Yvon DuHamel won Talladega. As for Mann, BSA had inked a one-race Daytona deal with Mike Hailwood, and when he returned to England, they had a spare Rocket 3 available. They immediately reconsidered their decision to terminate America's grand old man of AMA racing. BSA/Triumph racing chief Pete Colman contacted Mann to offer him sponsorship, consisting of dirt-track parts and salaried, full factory road-racing support. It proved a smart decision, since Dick Mann delivered his second Daytona victory to BSA in 1971.

10

The Determined Mann

Dick Mann is tenacious. He never gives up.
– Brian Slark, AHRMA director

Physical stature notwithstanding, Dick Mann probably would have become a professional linebacker, had his high school football coach only given him the chance. If his racing career is any example, he would have done it through sheer, stubborn determination. Dick Mann has won with lesser equipment than most national champions, and he has ridden hurt more than anyone else. Jim Dour recalls, "In the weeks before Ascot in 1963 when Dick was recuperating from his terrible injury at Freeport, I kept him company in the evenings. He was wearing a bandage on his ass, and he had to put down towels so he wouldn't get the couch bloody." The fact that he even rode the 50 lap TT—regarded by most as the toughest race on the circuit—is hard to fathom. To have won the event is simply beyond comprehension. Fantastic stories arose from the feat. People who were not there claim he rode the entire 50 laps standing on the pegs. Some say he went to the Gardena hospital just before the race and talked a nurse into pumping his butt full of Novocain. Neither story is true. The only thing Mann was filled with that night was determination, which, for Dick, was standard operating procedure. Dour says, "I remember the look on his face after he won. He was totally drained,

Dick Mann on the starting line at Sacramento in 1970, trying to concentrate through his pain. This was the legendary event featured in the motion picture *On Any Sunday* when Mann cut away his cast to suit up and ride with a broken ankle. *John Gola photo.*

and you could tell he was in immense pain. He has determination like no one else I have ever known."

In the early 1960s, just when Honda was entering the U.S. market, they approached Mann at Watkins Glen and hired him to ride a little 250cc four-cylinder around the course. Mann says, "It was similar to one of the Grand Prix machines, and all they wanted me to do was ride it around and make some noise and get some attention. Although Mann was not running at racing speed, the front brake on the bike locked and threw him to the pavement, breaking his collar bone. His friend Digger Helm recalls, "It was bad. The bone was sticking through the skin, but Dick taped a sanitary napkin over it and went ahead and raced that day. At the end of the race his T-shirt was red with sweat and blood."

When Mann entered Sacramento in 1963 with a broken hand, he won his heat, but was in severe, debilitating pain by the final. Johnny Hall claims he taped Dick's left hand to the handlebar because he knew he could not hold on for the length of the race. In 1966, he rode much of the season with a broken collarbone and a pin sticking out of his shoulder. He cut a hole in the shoulder of his leathers so the pin could stick through. Ted Davis says, "Racing with that pin sticking out had wallowed a hole in his shoulder as big as a quarter. Before a race, I would squeeze puss out of the wound, put some gauze on it, then help him tug his leathers up over his shoulder so the pin could stick through." In the movie *On Any Sunday* there is a famous scene at Sacramento in 1970 where Dick Mann cuts a cast off his leg, grimaces in agony while he pulls on his boot, and goes racing. If you ask Dick to list his broken bones, he'll give you the short answer: "I've never cracked my skull or broken a femur." Eddie Mulder states it simply: "Bugs, Brashear, Leonard, and Markel were the real cowboys. They were just plain tough!"

Not all riders will ride hurt, but those who make it to the top of the sport usually do. Different riders deal with it differently. Some say that no matter how much pain they are in, when they begin racing, much or all of the pain will disappear. Some attribute the phenomenon to the mind-focusing and pain-killing effects of adrenaline; some say it is a kind of self-hypnosis. For example, Ted Davis broke his ankle just before the Daytona 200 in 1967. Neil Keen helped him tape it up with duct tape, and he rode the event. Davis says, "I figured out I shifted gears over 2,000 times with that leg, and I didn't feel a thing. But you can bet the next day I was in pure agony!" Other riders experience the pain, but just deal with it. Babe DeMay says philosophically, "You can only hurt so much. If you can handle that, then you can go on racing." Mann seems to agree: "If you race bikes for a living, and need the dough, and your injury isn't going to kill you, I say ignore it!" However, Dick Mann's determination to prevail, continue, and finish seems to be unrelated to whether he is getting paid or needs the money. Carl Donelson, a successful St. Louis motorcycle dealer who has known Dick Mann since 1971, says, "I saw Dick at an AHRMA race in Flat River, Missouri, break his foot and go on to win!"

Other riders recognized Dick Mann's determination and respected it. They respected the fact that he ran his own program, prepared his own equipment, and usually traveled alone. Johnny Hall says, "I don't know anybody but Dick Mann who could win Number One with nothing but a hammer and a screwdriver." Mert Lawwill was the only other rider who even came close to Mann's level of self-reliance. Mert built his own bikes and engines and, like Dick, was good at designing a chassis, but Mert had more support from Dudley Perkins and the Harley factory than Mann ever received from any of his sponsors. Mann was a loner and intensely focused on his racing. John Hateley recalls, "Dick showed up, did his business, then went on his way. He didn't hang out and party like a lot of riders."

Some riders, especially the younger generation who had not known Dick in the dusty days of the Kansas circuit, thought him aloof or unfriendly. But he wasn't. He is a shy man, and, like any rider, there were times when he put on his race face. As Neil Keen explains it, "Racing people are different. They can train their faces so you don't know what they're thinking." When riders have their race face on, they move mentally into a kind of zen zone of self-imposed isolation, a coma of concentration, shutting out the chatter and distractions in order to concentrate on the job at hand. Mann was not unfriendly, but he was—and is—a man of few words. Ted Davis says, "Dick didn't have a lot to say, but if you listened to him, you could learn a lot. About Mann's taciturn race day demeanor, Johnny Hall explains, "Most people don't know there are two different Dick Manns who ride motorcycles. The one at the professional race track is quiet and rarely smiles. But the Dick Mann who went cow trailing in the hills of Richmond never stopped grinning. He laughed all day and had a ball." On the occasions when Dick Mann returned home to Richmond during the Grand National season, he refused to enter amateur events because he wanted to maintain a clean boundary between racing for money and riding for fun. Rather, he would support his club as a rank-and-file member, working races as a flagman. Cow trailing and off-season scrambling was done for fun. Professional racing was his job, and he approached it with sobriety and fierce determination.

In his 1972 memoir, Dick Mann said, "As far as I am concerned, most pro racers fall into two categories: the naturally talented guys who can do it all and don't have to learn a thing, and the less talented guys who have lots of desire but have to learn as they go along. Most of the motorcycle racers I've known, including myself, fall into the second category." Mann is right, because the true naturals are few and far between.

Dick Mann probably missed opportunities because he was so determined to run his own program and maintain his equipment as he saw fit. One who stuck with him through much of his career was Hap Jones, distributor of NGK spark plugs. *Photo courtesy of the Dick Mann collection.*

A long career shows in the furrows of Dick Mann's forehead. *Rick Kocks photo, courtesy of the AMA archives.*

Names like Kenny Roberts and Carroll Resweber will come to mind, but racers and fans will always argue about what constitutes a true natural. About Resweber, Neil Keen says, "What he could do on a half mile was just hard to believe. We all tried to figure out how he could slide the turns with his feet up the way he did, but we just couldn't figure it out. I always thought we should protest Resweber for having a gyroscope up his butt!" Yet there are types of competition where Resweber did not excel, and his career ended so early, he was never fully put to the test. He was doubtless a tremendous talent, but never showed the versatility of Dick Mann. Kenny Roberts is thought of as a natural. He clearly had an incredible gift, but so much of his achievement came from hard work and learning. Just like Dick Mann, Roberts rode and rode and rode as a child. The talent he may have been born with was polished and honed by training and hard work.

Dick Mann believes—and many from his era will agree with him—that the greatest natural talent he ever knew was Dick Dorresteyn, the buddy from his childhood paper route. Mann recalls, "He was a big, heavy kid, funny and friendly as a bear, and he never realized how good he actually was. Tricks that would take me weeks to learn, Dorresteyn could do the first try. He had no idea until he was 25 years old and racing bikes professionally that the other riders couldn't do the stunts he could." Dorrestyn's versatility and talent were best exhibited during TT racing. Sammy Tanner says, "I would try my best to do what Dick Dorresteyn did, and I could just not make it work. He would come out of a turn and just sit up and slump back on the seat like a big sack of potatoes, like he was taking a relaxed ride down the street. We called it his 'sack of potatoes' style. When he did that he would get traction like you couldn't believe, and just roar past everyone, his front wheel gliding along and barely touching the ground. We couldn't figure out how he could steer the thing." Ralph White adds, "Dorresteyn would dive into a turn and throw his motorcycle so far onto its side that he would literally lift the rear wheel off the ground and pivot the bike around on its engine case. Then he would sit back and dig the rear wheel in, and be gone like a shot. You would think he had gone too far into a corner to make it, then suddenly he would pivot and spin and be going the other direction."

Unfortunately, most motorcycle racing fans today have never heard of Dick Dorresteyn. Dorresteyn had rheumatic fever in his late 20s which affected his career. But, beyond that, he simply did not have the desire and determination of his childhood riding buddy, Dick Mann. Dorresteyn did not like the grit and inconvenience of life on the road, and he did not like getting hurt. He did not deal well with defeat, yet even the best riders lose more than they win. He simply did not have the fire in his belly to make it to the top, though he was more than capable of doing so.

Eddie Mulder is a similar example. Dick Mann regards him as one of the greatest natural talents he has ever known, and Mike Jackson, who was the American Norton and AJS importer, says, "Eddie Mulder was smoother than any other rider I have ever known. He and the motorcycle flowed like they were one and the same." However, while Mulder went back East a time or two, he never seriously campaigned the national circuit. He says, "I was enjoying my life too much to take on that kind of punishment." And he adds, as if to validate the wisdom of his decision, "And I never broke a bone on a motorcycle until I got out of racing and into the movie stunt business."

Determination to learn and train and overcome adversity in a brutal, hardscrabble sport like motorcycle racing is a greater contributor to success than natural talent. In an article about flat-track racing published in the 1968 *Cycle Racing Annual,* Dick Mann said, "I was a clumsy kid, never able to do anything better than anybody else, a complete athletic wash-out. But I tried to become a racer, and tried, and tried some more, and finally made it. A willingness to just plain work hard is as good, if not better, than natural ability." Everett Brashear says, "Dick Mann usually didn't have the fastest equipment. But he was a real scrapper who could outride his competitors rather than outrun them."

Dick Mann's determination did not end when he ended his professional racing career. It is an integral aspect of his personality, and has sustained him through every chapter of his life, including his choice to continue to contribute to the motorcycle sport even after suffering a recent brush with cancer that affected his ability to speak. American Historic Racing Motorcycle Association legal counsel Ted Bendelow describes Mann's service on the AHRMA board of directors: "We saw his agony as he came back from the disease. He was sometimes embarrassed that he could not speak, but he continued his service to AHRMA and continued to make his contribution, even when he was obviously in misery."

11

Back On Top

Dick Mann was the quintessential motorcycle racer. There was nothing he could not do, and do well.

– Don Brown, marketing consultant

Despite a second at the Astrodome short track and his fabulous victory at Daytona, 1970 proved a frustrating season. There was no doubt that Dick Mann was still competitive with the best, because by June he was holding first place in the points in a fierce battle with Jim Rice, who was closely followed by Gene Romero. Aside from the points earned at Daytona, Mann achieved his lead through dogged consistency, with a string of mid-pack finishes. Then he delivered one of his stunning victories, shattering previous records at the 30 lap TT race at Castle Rock, Washington. But the summer went downhill when Rice ran over Mann's foot at the Sedalia mile. The accident broke Mann's leg, and it was announced in *American Motorcycling* that he was out for the season. Then, to everyone's surprise, Dick Mann, limping badly, suited up at Sacramento and reentered the fray. However, too much of the season was lost to injuries, and Gene Romero won the Grand National Championship, with Mann finishing fourth.

By 1971 Dick Mann was beginning his 18th season of professional racing. He had almost retired in 1966, but came back to hold a place among the nation's top ten riders every year

Dick Mann rode the triple with an unspectacular ease, appearing to be out for a casual ride as he maintained a pace with world champions, such as Kel Carruthers. *Jerry West photo, courtesy of the Dick Mann collection.*

thereafter. Yet, by 1969, the smart money would not bet on him. BSA and Triumph were embarking on the biggest spending spree in the history of AMA championship racing, but had nothing to spend on Dick Mann. 1970 was going to be the year for the British duo to make their big splash, and Triumph came to Daytona with a film crew hired to document their expected victory. Then Dick Mann, riding on Honda's second string in the shadow of imported foreign riders, pulled off a stunning victory, setting a pace that would have left Cal Rayborn, the previous race record holder, running two miles behind. BSA would have looked foolish not to offer Mann their spare road-racing bike after that, but still, his victory might have been a fluke. As they say, even a blind hog can find an acorn now and again. Those who might have said this were about to be embarrassed again, because Dick Mann was about to prove in 1971 that he was better than ever.

The 1971 season began with Dick Mann winning the Astrodome TT before a crowd of 35,000 people, benefitting from the misfortune of his friend Jim Odom, who broke an axle while leading. At Daytona, British champion Paul Smart declared his intentions with a qualifying time of almost 106 miles per hour. Mann qualified 11th at 104.019, then defeated Triumph's Romero for the second year in a row. The victory circle was all British, with Mann's BSA followed by Romero's Triumph, and Mann's BSA teammate Don Emde taking third.

From Daytona the series went on to Road Atlanta, where Mann finished second behind Kel Carruthers. At Louisville, a swingarm pivot bolt broke while Mann was leading the race. He says, "I ran five laps with the swingarm flopping around in the frame, then finally retired because the chain came off." At Terre Haute he had to qualify through the semifinal on a borrowed machine that was visibly down on power, but finished eighth. At Loudon, Mann and Carruthers battled most of the race, but were nipped at the line in a spectacular drive by Mark Brelsford on his Harley. Mann finished third.

At Columbus, Ohio, Mann failed to qualify for the National due to oiling problems in a BSA with an experimental 180-degree crank—despite having won at Troy the previous evening. He finished 12th at San Jose, and fifth at Castle Rock, then achieved another road-racing victory over Kel Carruthers at Kent, Washington. It was becoming clear that Dick Mann and his three-cylinder BSA were the most formidable combination in road racing. A broken rear axle kept Mann out of the final at the Ascott TT. At Corona, poor flagging affected several riders including Dick Mann. Mann filed a protest, and, to his surprise, an appeals board ruled in his favor, awarding him valuable additional championship points. In the meantime, an AMA review of its licensing files resulted in a suspension of several riders for falsifying medical records. One was Gene Romero, who was one of Mann's biggest rivals in the championship chase, and Romero was suspended from competing at Ascot. Whether this would have affected the championship is conjectural, since Dick Mann also failed to earn points at Ascot. The points race between Mann and Romero tightened as

Romero won Oklahoma City and Nazareth, with Mann finishing fifth and second, respectively. In spite of several poor dirt-track performances with his BSA twin, which was giving away 100ccs to the new 750 Triumphs, Mann held a lead of 1002 to 924 points over Gene Romero as they moved into the final weeks of the season.

Statistically, Romero could have pulled it out with a victory at the final road race at Ontario, California. He and his Triumph triple had been good on road courses all year, but not as good as Mann and his BSA. Ontario was a unique event, run in two segments. With the heat on, Romero crashed in the first segment, further relieving the pressure on Mann. However, Mann still had to finish the event to win the championship. In the second segment, a back marker blew an engine, spilling oil in one of the turns. Seven riders crashed, including Mann. Mann says, "I knew I had to get that big BSA going and back into the race. It had spun around when it slid off the track, and all kinds of dirt and gravel were packed behind the fairing and around the carburetors. First I pulled the bike backward as hard as I could and dropped the clutch, causing the engine to puff some of the dirt out of the carbs. Then I pushed it with my hand over the dirty carb, and when it started running I revved it up and released my hand. I could hear the engine clattering with dirt and gravel, and for a second I held my breath. But it blew the stuff on through and didn't stall or break anything, and I was able to get back into the race. Englishman John Cooper won the race, and Dick Mann cruised to ninth to win the AMA Grand National Championship. It had been a spectacular season for Mann and BSA. Less than 24 months before, he had been counted out of the running due to his age. Now no one talked about "age." Rather, the press praised Dick Mann for his "longevity." No rider prior to Mann had ever won the AMA Grand National Championship twice in seasons nine years apart. Indeed, the careers of many notable riders are over in less than eight years. Mann celebrated his championship by hopping on an airplane and flying back east to race the Inter-Am motocross series on a 500cc BSA. Even the young kids on the AMA circuit didn't do that!

Dick Mann at Houston in 1970. *Mahony Photo Archive.*

By 1970, motorcycle racing had changed enormously since Dick Mann had gotten into the game. Although he continued to run his own dirt-track program, for road racing he had one of the best machines on the circuit, with a salary large enough to hire the mechanic of his choice. Becoming Number One was no longer simply an honor and a new jacket at Daytona. In addition to higher purses and special televised races on ABC Wide World of Sports, the AMA offered a $400,000 point fund to be divided among the riders, and Mann's share of that fund was more than he earned annually during his early years as a professional racer. Instead of a pickup or dilapidated trailer, he traveled in a motor home, and at road races BSA had the big triple there waiting for him when he arrived.

However, at Houston in 1972, the future was made clear by a new young kid named Kenny Roberts who won a National during his first weekend as an AMA Expert. Only Brad Andres

Dick Mann on his factory BSA triple at Daytona, 1971. Following his 1970 victory aboard the Honda, BSA quickly invited Mann to return to its factory team. It would prove a wise decision for the British firm. *Dave Friedman photo, courtesy of Don Emde Production.*

had previously performed such a feat, winning Daytona in 1955 at the beginning of his rookie Expert year. Roberts was emblematic of a hot, fresh, new crop of riders, ready to displace the old guard. When Dick Mann and his colleagues started, they bought inferior street bikes—like Mann's BSA Bantam—when they were 14 to 16 years old. They modified them, fabricated their own parts, and did the best they could. They really did not begin to learn the trade until they arrived in the company of Experts, so it was not unusual for a young professional to struggle for three or four years before winning his first national championship. The new kids, like Kenny Roberts and John Hateley and Gary Scott, had grown up in an entirely different world. Motorcycling had become big business during the 1960s, based to a large extent on the performance and appeal of small, quick, reliable, inexpensive Japanese motorcycles, many of which were purpose-designed for young people. The new generation had been going like hell on good motorcycles since their childhood years, giving them a decade of experience by the time they bolted on their Expert number plates.

Mann finished fifth at the Houston TT, and again failed to qualify for the short track. At Daytona he had ignition problems and finished 22nd. Daytona 1972 was further evidence that the world of racing was quickly changing. Don Emde beat the big 750cc Harleys and Brit bikes on a little 350cc Yamaha, becoming the first two-stroke to win Daytona and beginning a 13-year winning streak for the Yamaha brand. The mighty BSA and Triumph triples that had dominated the American road racing scene over the past two years were already on their way to the scrap heap or the museum. Gary Nixon and Paul Smart had abandoned the big British four-strokes for rides on factory Kawasakis. Dick Mann says, "One year Romero and I were battling it out for first place on our big British triples, the next we were battling it out for last place."

Dick Mann's rewards at Daytona 1972 came in another form. As reported in *Cycle Sport,* "A round of activities Thursday, March 9, in Daytona Beach, Florida, has demonstrated

In the victory circle at Daytona in 1971, Mann is flanked by Triumph rider Gene Romero and BSA teammate Don Emde. *Dave Friedman photo, courtesy of Don Emde Production.*

Dick Mann on the mile at Arlington Park in 1971. *Dave Friedman photo, courtesy of Don Emde Productions.*

Dick Mann of Richmond, California, to be the most celebrated motorcyclist in the history of the sport. Mann's exciting evening began when *Cycle* magazine named him as man of the year at a Plaza Hotel cocktail party honoring the 35-year-old professional racer. Accompanying the announcement was a gift of a Datsun 240Z sports car." Later that evening the American Motorcycle Association announced that Mann had again been named its most popular rider of the year, and *MotorCycle Weekly* announced that its readers also had named him man of the year.

DuHamel and Smart finished first and second on their Kawasakis at Road Atlanta, and Romero and Mann finished third and fourth respectively. Colorado Springs was the kind of deep cushion Dick Mann loved, and he was leading by a full straightaway when a $2 set of points broke. Young riders Jim Rice and Mark Brelsford won at Colorado Springs and Ascot, where Mann finished 19th and 15th respectively. Rice and Brelsford repeated again at San Jose and Louisville while Mann got a third at San Jose, but failed to qualify at Louisville. Gary Fisher—another new face—won Loudon and Dick Mann finished sixth. Cal Rayborn won Indianapolis, and Mann finished 10th. Mert Lawwill won Columbus; Mann finished fifth.

Then came a bad patch for Mann, who got a sixth at Castle Rock, but failed to qualify at San Jose, Salem, and Laguna Seca. He was leading his heat at Roosevelt Raceway on Long Island when a rear shock failed. It was somewhat reminiscent of the bad patch Mann went through in 1964, followed by three victories in a row. This time Mann came back to win the first mile event of his career at Homewood, Illinois, near Chicago, then won again the following week at Peoria. The Homewood victory was especially stunning, and may be ranked as one of the greatest races of his career. Mann rode like a man on fire, lapping the entire field up to third place. Chuck Palmgren says, "It was a rough track, and Dick Mann was always his best on a rough track. He was so fast that night, it was like he was in a different race from everyone else." It was the kind of track where Mann's deep experience became his best asset. 1970 Grand National Champion Gene Romero recalls, "One time I was complaining about rough track conditions, and Bugs said, 'Gene, if the track is perfect, even the slow guys can go fast.

Dick Mann sees the checkered flag at Daytona in 1971 for a second consecutive year. The combination of his skill and experience, and the brief but sterling domination of the BSA triple, established Mann as one of the greatest road racers America has produced. *Jerry West photo, courtesy of the Dick Mann collection.*

Dick Mann accepts the checkered flag for his victory lap at Homewood, Illinois in 1972. It was one of Mann's greatest moments in racing, lapping a field of much younger riders up to third place, and becoming the first man in history to win every category of AMA Grand National Championship racing. *Photo courtesy of the AMA archives.*

When it's really rough, only the best guys go fast.' " But Homewood and Peoria were Mann's Grand National swan song; they were the last AMA championships he would win. The final standings for the season showed that the new kids had truly arrived, with Mark Brelsford winning the Grand National Championship, and Gary Scott finishing second. Gene Romero was third, Roberts fourth, and Chuck Palmgren fifth. Dick Mann, the highest-ranking member of the old guard, finished sixth, followed by another youngster, Jim Rice.

Astonishingly, BSA, which had won Daytona and the Grand National Championship in 1971, was out of business by the end of 1972. However, the American distributor still stuck with Dick Mann, offering him a Triumph triple road racer for the 1973 season. Dick says, "In fact, it was my old BSA triple repainted blue and given Triumph logos." At Houston he failed to qualify for the TT, then finished 11th at the short track. He qualified poorly at Daytona in 62nd position on the grid, but rode his Triumph to a fourth place finish. *American Motorcyclist* declared his ride the best showing of the day, and Mann regards it as one of the finest races of his career, having started in the second wave and finishing almost on the podium. At the Dallas road race he ruptured a brake line and failed to earn points, then failed to qualify at both San Jose and the Ascot TT. At both Louisville and Loudon he finished ninth, at Columbus he got a seventh, at San Jose a fourth, at Ascot sixth, and at Laguna Seca a 13th. The season continued with Mann getting mixed results, sometimes not qualifying, and sometimes finishing as high as third.

Dick Mann finished the 1973 season in 10th position in the point standings, despite the fact that it was the first season since 1959—except for 1968 and his partial season in 1966—that he did not win a national championship. Mann says, "I was very proud of my 1973 season. It was important to finish in the top ten. Furthermore, I qualified to ride the International Six Days Trial, and I qualified and rode the international motocross races on my 420 BSA." Although Mann continued to race professionally into the 1974 season and beyond, he could see it was finally becoming time to retire from the Grand National wars. Going out still in the top ten was something to be proud of. Over 17 seasons, he had finished among the top ten 16 times, and that is a record that no other rider could match in the AMA's Grand National Era.

Dick Mann entered Daytona in 1974 aboard a Don Vesco-tuned Yamaha TZ700. He thought it was a brute of a bike, far less civilized than his BSA or his Matchless. Vesco confirms that they had problems with the bike all week, and on one occasion during practice Mann was charging into the banking at close to 170 miles per hour when the gearbox locked up. Vesco says, "How he kept it on its wheels I'll never know, but that's an example of the kind of rider Dick Mann was." Nevertheless, Vesco and Mann got the bike sorted out by race day, and though Mann started far back on the grid, he caught up with the top guys and was working his way through the top ten when the TZ pealed off a large chunk of its rear tire. Mann says, "The bike had tremendous potential, but I could see that I would have to start a whole new development program, and an independent like me could no longer keep up with the rate of factory development. I knew that no matter how rapidly I developed the bike, the next year the factory would have an updated model that would be light years ahead of me, and it would be available to only very few sponsored riders." With the introduction of the TZ Yamahas, the collapse of the BSA/Triumph organization, and Harley-Davidson's technological atrophy in road racing, the whole economic fabric of racing in America changed. The departure of the British left a terrible vacuum, and Yamaha had production road racers to sell by the hundreds, so they had no incentive to help more than one or two of the very best riders. Many more riders than Dick Mann found themselves facing a famine of support.

A similar phenomenon took place in dirt-track racing at about the same time with the introduction of Harley-Davidson's alloy XR. It became a superb dirt-track machine, but was expensive to maintain. Like Yamaha, with the British gone, Harley-Davidson found it unnecessary to continue the broad-based program of support through dealers that had sustained its dominant presence in dirt-track racing. Almost everyone was on a Harley, so the factory could maintain an edge by providing only one or two riders with first-rate, factory sponsored equipment. American racing was becoming rather monochromatic, confined to the yellow of Yamaha on road courses and the orange of Harley on dirt, and very little green anywhere except for a small number of riders. The days when a rider like Dick Mann could build his own program, develop and maintain his own equipment, and win enough to earn a living were suddenly over. Darrel Dovel, who met Mann on the Kansas circuit in the late 1950s, says, "Dick Mann never lost his ability and his competitive edge. Even at the end of his career he could race with the best. But everything changed, and there was very little support to be had, and what there was was given to the younger guys."

Dick Mann had raced through a very special time in the history of the AMA. Prior to 1954, the rider who won the

Springfield Mile was awarded the Number One plate. Springfield was the most prestigious race in the series, but, still, a rider could win the coveted plate by having a good day. The system did not really determine who was the best rider of the season. In 1954, the AMA set up a system of awarding points at every national championship race, and the rider with the most points at the end of the season was declared the Grand National Champion and given the Number One plate. This difficult and varied points chase gave the Number One tremendous prestige and meaning. The system also awarded versatility, since the championship series included five different types of racing: short track, half mile, mile, TT, and road racing. It was a system that encouraged riders to master a wide range of skills. Specialists in one form of racing or another—no matter how good they were—could rarely make it into the top ten under the AMA's Grand National system. The Grand National era began the same year that Dick Mann burnt the sole off of his boot winning the Amateur final at the Bay Meadows Mile. It came to an end in 1986 when the AMA created a separate national championship title for road racing.

Dick Mann at San Jose in 1972. *Mahony Photo Archive.*

Dick Mann riding the Triumph triple in 1973. *Photo courtesy of the Dick Mann collection.*

No man will ever match Dick Mann's record of 16 top ten finishes in 17 seasons under the demanding conditions of the Grand National system. Steve Morehead finished in the top ten 18 out of 26 years during a career extending from 1974 to 1999. Scott Parker performed the remarkable feat of finishing in the top ten 20 out of 21 years between 1979 and 1999. Jay Springsteen, one of the most popular riders in AMA history, finished in the top ten 21 out of 26 years between 1975 and 2001, and he's still going. Chris Carr has finished in the top ten each and every year of his 15-year career, from 1985 to the present, and there is little doubt he will be a top ten finisher many years to come. However, none of these men have actually equaled Mann's performance, since all of their top ten finishes since 1986 have been in dirt-track racing only. This is not to diminish their remarkable careers, but it must be recognized that none of them has approached Dick Mann's record in road racing, and their results likely would have been very different had they raced entirely during the Grand National era.

Within the context of the Grand National system, a special recognition called the "Grand Slam" was created to describe the achievement of a rider who had won a national championship in each of the five categories of competition. The Grand

Slam was never an official title, nor was there a trophy or a monetary award conferred on anyone who could complete the Grand Slam. That may be because it was such a rare achievement; it was a feat accomplished only three times in the history of AMA racing. Dick Mann was the first rider to complete the Grand Slam, winning his first TT at Peoria in 1959, his first road race at Laconia in 1960, his first half mile at Heidelberg in 1961, his first short track at Santa Fe in 1970, and his first mile at Homewood in 1972. The only other men to have completed the Grand Slam were Kenny Roberts, Bubba Shobert, and Doug Chandler.

Yet, none—not even Roberts or Shobert—can add to their record a victory as a professional motocross rider, which Dick Mann achieved in 1970, beating Swedish star Gunnar Lindstrom. Add to this the fact that Dick Mann finished and earned a medal at the International Six Days Trial in 1975, and it becomes indisputable that, on the basis of breadth and versatility, Dick Mann is the greatest motorcycle rider America—and perhaps the world—has ever seen.

Looking back over his long and remarkable professional racing career, one might wonder what was his most memorable victory. Was it his Amateur championship at the Bay Meadows mile or his first Expert victory at Peoria, both won on borrowed machines? Was it the 1963 miracle aboard a Matchless at Ascot, riding fifty grueling laps with a wound in his crotch the size of his fist? Was it his celebrated Honda victory at Daytona in 1970, beating the best that America and Europe could deliver on their Harley-Davidsons and powerful, new BSA and Triumph triples? Or was it that blazing ride at Homewood late in his career, when he sped away and lapped nearly the entire field? If you ask Dick Mann the question, the answer will be none of these. He will tell you, "My greatest race was the first time I beat Gunter at Tulare in 1963." It was a little local race that paid no championship points, and that none of the magazines reported.

Dick Mann's answer to the question speaks volumes about the man. He is a person who has always had his own method of measuring success and failure. He has never evaluated his

At the age of 37, Dick Mann earns his second Grand National Championship. *Photo courtesy of the AMA archives.*

performance based on whether he won or lost. Dick Mann says, "Some of my best races were those where I didn't end up very high in the results. And sometimes I rode badly, but won because all the fast guys dropped out." Finally beating Albert Gunter—the man he admired and who taught him so much—was far more important to Dick Mann than those many, many achievements that the motorcycle press has chosen to celebrate. Living up to his own standards has always been more important to Dick Mann than meeting the expectations of others. As his friend Jim Dour said, "Dick Mann has integrity."

12

The Politics of Racing

In the bad old days it was practically impossible to get any kind of rule change pushed through the AMA.

– Dick Mann, 1972

Ascot Speedway is a legendary name in American motorcycle racing. In fact, since 1920 there have been four racing tracks named Ascot in greater Los Angeles, but the Ascot where so many riders earned fame and developed their skills in the post-war era was created on a landfill in Gardena by Harrison Schooler and Tom Haynes in 1957. In 1958 J.C. Agajanian, a local motor-sports personality and Indianapolis race car owner, made a deal with Schooler to rent the track every Friday night to promote motorcycle races and periodic events for USAC sprint cars. Agajanian set up a system whereby the riders got a percentage of the purse, which was audited and verified each week by an AMA official, and Ascot's weekly program began to grow and prosper. By 1973 Agajanian took over the lease to manage the track on a full-time basis.

Ascot became famous throughout the nation as a tough track that bred good talent. It was a tight oval—less than a half mile, but much too large to be considered a short track—with a hard, tacky surface that provided excellent traction and quick handling for those who had the skill and nerve to take advantage of it. Around the turns was a wooden crash wall with big

Dick Mann with Joe Bolger, Charlie Vincent, and Ron Jeckel at Pepperell. The riders in this photo—including Mann—were suspended by the AMA for racing an unsanctioned motocross. The controversy that arose from Mann's suspension caused changes in AMA personnel and rules-making procedures. *Photo courtesy of the Joe Bolger collection.*

diagonal white stripes that amplified the noise and enhanced the perception of speed and excitement for the spectators, the white stripes creating a kind of strobe effect when the riders sped around the turns, just inches from the wall. Ascot was wild and wooly and dangerous. It was a killer, generating several fatalities each season. Just across the street was a cemetery that spawned lurid urban legends about Ascot's dark and fearful reputation. For example, it was whispered that the dirt from the graves of fallen riders was hauled across the street and spread on the front straightaway. It is true that surplus dirt from the cemetery was used to replenish the surface of Ascot, but any connection between those graves and Ascot fatalities is doubtful. Nevertheless, it was the opinion of many that Ascot caused too many deaths and injuries.

Because Ascot ran professional motorcycle races 39 times a year (29 half miles and 10 TTs) and got more than 150 riders per night, exposure was very high. Novice riders were over-represented among the casualties, and the more experienced Experts were sure they knew why. In that era, Novices competed on the same big 500cc and 750cc motorcycles used by the Experts. In 1962, knowing too well how the big engines on Ascot were challenging enough for even the best Experts, Dick Mann, Neil Keen, and Al Gunter decided something needed to be done.

In 1956 an organization called Motorcycle Riders Incorporated was established. It sought to elevate the motorcycle sport, hopefully by working with promoters and the sanctioning body to everyone's mutual benefit. It was a progressive organization that founded the first benevolent fund for motorcycle racers in America, and Dick Mann and Donnie Smith were elected MRI rider representatives. At a local race at Fresno in 1958, Mann had his first experience at confronting authority, and it did not go well. The promoter made no effort to provide a good racing surface, and decided to pay a lower purse than advertised. Dick Mann is not a hothead. He had raced on terrible tracks in Kansas, and was always willing to cooperate if he believed the promoter was being fair with the riders and doing the best he could. But he could not abide dishonesty and what he saw as exploitation of the riders at Fresno, and he and Smith organized a boycott. As a result, the AMA suspended their racing license for a few weeks. Given this unhappy experience, Mann favored a non-confrontational approach to the Ascot problem, and sought an audience before the AMA Competition Committee, which was meeting near Dick's home in San Francisco that November.

Keen reports that the three riders met at Mann's house in Richmond to prepare their presentation. On the morning of the meeting, they dressed in white dress shirts and neckties, the better to be accepted by the committee as serious professionals. Keen says, "When Mann walked into the room, Gunter and I simultaneously started howling with laughter, because you could see a big, red BSA logo through his dress shirt. When we pointed it out to him, he said, 'What are you laughing at me for? You look just the same.'" Keen continues, "He was right.

Gunter and I had BSA logos showing through our shirts also. Our dress shirts were not as thin as Mann's, and it was less conspicuous, but you could see the logos through all of our white shirts." The three riders knew this wouldn't do, and decided to change, soon discovering that no one owned a T-shirt that did not have a big motorcycle logo on the front. Keen says, "Finally, we took off our T-shirts and turned them wrong-side-out so the logos wouldn't show, then got dressed again in our white shirts and ties."

A number of rules and issues were addressed that day, but mainly the three riders appealed to the committee to require Novice riders to use smaller engines. Such a decision was made, and the injury and fatality statistics at Ascot, as well as throughout the nation, began to improve. It was a victory for open dialogue and cooperation between the professional riders and the leaders of the governing body, and the first time riders had been given a say in the determination of their own safety. The riders had proven they knew their business and how to improve safety, and the leaders of the AMA demonstrated that they knew how to listen. Unfortunately, it was at the same meeting, following Mann's departure, that the committee voted 26 to one to ban the G50 Matchless, thereby setting the stage for serious conflict between Dick Mann and the AMA at Daytona in 1963.

Motorcycling achieved a popularity in the early 1960s that would not have seemed possible a decade earlier. More and more motorcycles were being sold, more and more fans began to attend the races, and more and more promoters stepped up to request a sanction for an AMA National Championship. The series began to expand and the riders and teams were traveling more and working harder to chase coveted points for the Grand National Championship. On a cumulative basis, more money was available, but individual purses were not keeping pace with the increased crowds at the events. During 1964 the riders began to discuss their situation. They did not understand why the promoters of the major events throughout the nation could not adopt a system like that used by J.C. Agajanian at Ascot, wherein the riders earned a percentage of the ticket income at the event. This, it seemed, was a fair and equal partnership for the betterment of the sport. When a promoter had a big event, he shared his good fortune with the riders on whom he relied for the show. If he had a bad day, the riders earned little, but could not complain, because they understood the promoter was sharing the loss. The national championship promoters, however, only wanted to post fixed purses which were, in reality, small enough to protect their profit margins if they had a mediocre turnout of spectators. The AMA accepted their position, and would not push for rider compensation based on a percentage of the gate.

In addition, the riders wanted more consistency in officiating at the events. At that time there was a system of appointed regional referees, and each referee ran his region like a fiefdom. He selected his own crew of officials, and while he had the AMA rule book to guide his decisions, he pretty much ran things as he saw fit. There was no recognized training program for officials, and sometimes the regional referees even defied the AMA national headquarters to interfere in their work. It was the riders who suffered from this kind of provincial and egotistical leadership. This lack of consistency resulted in danger, confusion, aggravation, and low morale. The riders also wanted to see the clubs and promoters do a more professional job of organizing and promoting the events. They wanted to see more televised races and better race coverage in local newspapers, and felt that those profiting from racing were not adequately reinvesting in the sport.

Finally, the riders wanted to participate in the rule-making process, not with a one-hour audience before the AMA Competition Committee from time to time, but with full-time elected representation. They felt that the Committee did not understand the realities of campaigning the series year after year, and they felt there were too many abrupt or unjustified rule changes that forced the riders to make costly corrections in their plans and equipment at the eleventh hour. It was standard operating procedure for the Competition Committee to meet in September or October—and sometimes as late as November—and make rule change effective with the upcoming season. The minutes of the meeting would not appear in *American Motorcycling* until its January or February issue when the riders were already trying to prepare their equipment for Daytona.

Dick Mann, Gary Nixon, and Mann's friend, Jim Dour, emerged as the leaders of the movement to improve the working conditions of the professional riders. Dour prepared a firm but polite statement of needs that was circulated among the riders, and approximately 300 riders signed a postcard and mailed it to the AMA, stating:

1. I want direct rider representation on the Committee.
2. I want to get 40% purse whenever possible.
3. I want to see the clubs do a more professional job of promoting.
4. I want a one-year notice before all major equipment and classification rule changes.

Three-hundred signatures represented only 15 percent of the roughly 2,000 licensed professional riders, but the point still had been made. Everyone on the Competition Committee realized that these 300 were the cream of the cream who provided the show for the Grand National Championship Series, and Dick Mann and Gary Nixon were invited to meet with the committee to make their case concerning these issues, and to comment on the rule changes currently under consideration. After addressing the committee for an hour and a half, the idea of permanent rider representation was discussed. It was pointed out that only the AMA Trustees could alter the composition of the AMA Competition Committee, so William Davidson made a motion that the Competition Committee members recommend to the AMA Trustees that the licensed rider group be given some type of representation in all business of the AMA Competition Committee. The motion carried 22 to 3. This was a major step in democratizing the AMA and altering the system of government under which it had functioned for forty years.

In June, 1966, AMA Executive Director Lin Kuchler announced he was leaving to take a position with NASCAR, and William T. Berry was selected to fill the post. Berry had a motor

Dick Mann, celebrating with Gunnar Lindstrom in 1969 at the first professional motocross ever sanctioned by the AMA. Mann won the 250 class; Lindstrom won the open class. In part, it was Mann's persuasive lobbying that got the AMA involved in motocross. *Rick Kocks photo.*

industry background, having been a district manager with Dodge Trucks and Willys Jeep. He was executive director of the American Motor Scooter Association, which merged with the Motorcycle and Allied Trades Association in 1965, and seemed a logical choice to head up both the trade and the sport-governing organizations. Berry headed the AMA for less than four years and he was generally not a popular leader. He was an intelligent man who was abrupt and sometimes abrasive, and was condescending to those he considered not his intellectual equal. Unfortunately, these generally bad public relations have obscured the good he did for the AMA. Berry was a good systems and infrastructure man. He thought about strategic and systemic issues that no one else in the AMA had ever paid much attention to. He saw the extraordinary expansion of the motorcycle sport, and understood that the AMA was poorly positioned to maintain a leadership role. Under the capable leadership of Bob Hicks, the New England district was already setting up its own governing bodies in the form of the New

England Sports Committee and the New England Trail Rider Association, and talking about seceding from the AMA. With the exception of the annual national championship at Laconia, AMA sanctioned activity in New England dwindled to almost nothing. Some of the California districts were not far behind in their disaffection with the AMA. In some cases, the districts were driven by grievances and discontent with what seemed to be an aloof and remote home office. In other cases it was not necessarily discontent, but the AMA just seemed no longer relevant to the good governance of the sport at the local level.

Berry overhauled the AMA's business operations and installed a plastic embossed card-based event registration system, and a computer-managed membership system that remains intact and still effective today. He realized the sport was fragmenting and that leadership at the local level was drifting away from the AMA. In response, he supported a project to study the organization to identify where changes should be made in its political structure. The old-boy system of having everything dictated by relatively small committees of industry-appointed people had run its course, and was out of sync with the times. In fact, what needed to happen within the AMA was going on throughout the nation. It was an age of revolution when a new generation was demanding more openness and accountability from government, and a greater say in how important decisions were being made.

What was happening in the AMA was a microcosm of changes in American society. The baby boomers, the first generation of Americans raised in relative leisure and prosperity, were becoming young adults. They had the education, the resources, and the time to question what they saw going on around them, like unwinnable ideological wars in faraway Korea and Vietnam. With the advent of television news coverage—which the federal government had not yet learned how to manage—the realities of war could no longer be hidden from Americans, and a vocal segment of the public was becoming angry. The youth and anti-war movements reached their zenith with riots at the Democratic National Convention in Chicago in the fall of 1968, and at Woodstock in 1969. America was truly in a state of revolution, though no government was overthrown. Instead, the government and its relationship with the people had to change quickly, and sometimes radically, and this change came in the form of beefed-up civil rights and voter registration laws, the Freedom of Information Act, and the Supreme Court's Miranda ruling. It was the same with the AMA. The old-boy system had to go, and be replaced with a system that was more forthcoming and more democratic.

By the time the Competition Committee met in October 1966, rider representatives had been brought into the body, with Dick Mann and Bart Markel named to serve. The minutes reveal that Dick Mann took an assertive role in the process. Along with AMA Director of Competition Jules Horky, Mann proposed that a category of true amateur competition be created at the local level where payment to the riders would be prohibited, and that purses be increased at the professional level. Mann was trying to bring greater logic and order to the AMA's growing but confused program of sanctioned events, where true professional events were being eroded by clubs paying small purses at low-level, poorly-promoted local races.

Mann also moved that the AMA home office create and distribute training materials to AMA officials on how to conduct national championship events, and that the AMA Board of Trustees clarify the role and authority of regional officials at the race meets. His motion further recommended that the AMA hire a national referee and a national starter who would attend all championship events, and requested that the Trustees clarify the role and authority of Competition Committee members when they were working in the field, and provide them with training materials with guidelines for their behavior. It was a comprehensive and well-thought-out proposal that addressed many of the concerns of the riders. It drove toward consistency and improved professional performance among officials, and there is little doubt that when Mann raised the issue of guidelines over the behavior of Competition Committee members, he was thinking of the machinations of Rod Coates, Walt Brown, and others who had used their positions within

The controversy over the approval of Dick Mann's Matchless in 1963 brought disfavor to the decision-making procedures of the old AMA Competition Committee, eventually bringing about internal changes that transformed the AMA into a more democratic organization willing to listen to the advice of professional riders. This photo of the Matchless features the innovative body work designed by Dick Mann and executed by George Curtis. *Photo courtesy of the Dick Mann collection.*

the AMA to advance their brand-related commercial interests. BSA's Pete Colman seconded the motion, and it was approved.

In the meantime, Bill Berry's studies of the operation and structure of the AMA were coming to fruition, leading to a historic decision by the Board of Trustees. In a report published in the April, 1968 issue of *American Motorcyclist,* Berry announced that in the coming October, a new legislative body called the AMA Congress would be convened. The old Competition Committee would be abolished, but its members would be invited to participate in the new body. In addition, delegates would be elected by the clubs from every district throughout the nation, providing representation for those who organized AMA sanctioned events. Furthermore, the Competition Congress would include six of the current licensed professional riders, elected by the riders. While the plan—probably wisely—provided for the old group of appointed delegates from the AMA's roster of corporate members, they were vastly outnumbered by the district delegates and professional riders, selected through democratic processes.

In retrospect, it is astonishing how quickly the AMA reinvented itself in response to the criticism of its clubs, members, and professional riders. Within weeks of the Chicago riots that rocked the nation, nearly 70 members of the Association—most of whom were democratically selected—met in a quiet and orderly fashion in Worthington, Ohio, to help chart the future of motorcycling in America. Dick Mann and Neil Keen, who had first taken their safety concerns to the AMA Competition Committee in 1962, were among the professional rider delegates present. That the Congress was prepared to forge a new, forward-thinking, and more democratic AMA was demonstrated without a doubt when the body promptly abolished the old 500cc overhead valve/750cc side valve formula that had stood since 1926 as one of the sacred cows of American motorcycle racing. In addition, the Congress decided that motocross would be incorporated into the AMA's professional racing rule book, and Dick Mann and John Penton—men previously punished by the AMA for participating in international motocross races—were selected to help draft those rules.

Shortly before the convening of the first AMA Competition Congress, Bill Berry announced that Tom Clark—National Number 66—had retired from racing and been hired by the AMA to fill a new position entitled Supervisor of Professional Racing. It would be Clark's job to improve quality and consistency in promoting and officiating. With this announcement, and the creation of the AMA Competition Congress, the AMA had made an honest attempt to address every one of the nonmonetary issues raised by the professional riders in 1966.

Over time, the AMA Congress has been restructured and expanded on several occasions, and now consists of more than 150 delegates. All are democratically elected, and none is appointed by the motorcycle industry. Dick Mann remained an active delegate until 1974 when the Congress was put exclusively in charge of all amateur racing and road-riding activity, and the job of professional rule-making was delegated to special advisory committees focusing on each aspect of competition: dirt track, road racing, and motocross. This was one reorganization with which Dick Mann did not agree. He explains, "While the Congress was big and cumbersome, there were many good minds and a lot of different ideas. That many dedicated people working on the problems was, in the long run, the best and quickest way to get to the best solutions. I think moving parts of the rule-making process back into committees with industry ties was a step backward."

Some people get into politics for the power and prestige. Some get involved from a sincere desire to make a difference, and later some of these are corrupted by the lure of power and prestige. Dick Mann got into AMA politics for the same reason he built a frame or designed a boot. All he ever wanted was to see things work better, and the same motivation drove his efforts within the politics of the AMA. He wanted to see races promoted better and run better. He wanted to see riders get better pay and suffer fewer injuries. With these clear and simple goals in mind, Mann served for eight years on the AMA's rule-making bodies. It is doubtful that in 1962 Dick Mann had the slightest notion he would become a key and influential player in the overall growth and success of the AMA. Yet his desire to see professional riders have a voice on the AMA Competition Committee led eventually to a massive political reorganization, without which the AMA would certainly not be the powerful organization it is today. When Dick Mann and Gary Nixon spoke out on behalf of the professional riders in 1966, the AMA had approximately 60,000 members, and its clubs and district organizations had begun to defect. Today the AMA has over a quarter-million members and is the center of a sophisticated network of district and club volunteer leaders who organize over 3,000 sanctioned events a year. Dick Mann's desire to see the AMA work better has brought results that are surely beyond his wildest expectations.

13

The Golden Age of Flat Track

If you want to be a racer of motorcycles in the United States, you have to have a flat tracker. It's as simple as that.

– Dick Mann, 1968

When technology outstrips the sport, pretty soon the sport goes away.

– Dick Mann, 1983

Historically, flat-track racing is the bedrock of the American motorcycle sport. Prior to 1970, it was the kind of racing to which all young would-be American racing stars aspired. Unlike Europe, where road racing evolved as a distinct style of competition early in the history of the sport, in America flat-track racing was the crucible out of which road racing evolved, and through which America developed its best road-racing talent. Whether it was around a frantic, lightning-quick, tacky short track; a wide, cushioned half mile; or a big, long-winded mile, going fast and turning left is as characteristically American as Merle Haggard and apple pie.

At the dawn of the twentieth century, motorcycles evolved from bicycles, and motorcycle racing evolved from bicycle racing on small, banked, plank ovals called velodromes, typically about one-third mile in length. When used for motorcycle

Dick Mann, flanked by Gene Romero, Chuck Palmgren, and Mert Lawwill at the start of the Sacramento mile in 1970. *John Gola photo.*

racing, these types of steeply-banked tracks were called motordromes, and were incredibly dangerous. The machines were little more than engines chain-driving a wheel. They had no gears, no clutches, little or no brakes, and often no throttles. Riders simply got them running, then went like hell, letting the engine run wide open and regulating the speed with nothing other than a kill switch to the ignition. Like an electric light, the engines were either off or full on. Spectators hung over the upper edge of the track, watching the motorcycles speed by. Motordrome racing was denounced by the media and fell into public disfavor after an accident in September, 1912, when Indian factory star Eddie Hasha lost control of his machine at a race near Newark, New Jersey. By the time the noise ended and the smoke cleared, Hasha, a fellow rider, and six spectators were dead or dying. News reports claimed that some of the spectators were decapitated by Hasha's careening eight-valve Indian. Even after the Motordromes fell into disuse, motorcycle racing on big, outdoor board tracks, some as big as two miles in length, continued into the late 1920s, but the board tracks, exposed to the elements, proved not to be economically viable. Built from untreated lumber because wood preservative techniques had not yet been invented, many of the big board tracks lasted less than three years, and rarely more than five. They were expensive and difficult to maintain, and had a relatively short useful life.

American motorcyclists developed a keen taste for going fast and turning left, and fans loved it, in part because the whole exciting, noisy spectacle was played out right there before their eyes, with the smell of fuel and oil hanging pungently in the air. The demise of the board tracks was no great inconvenience, because motorcycle races had been taking place simultaneously on dirt tracks originally designed for horse racing, and one thing America had in great abundance was horse tracks. Every county had several, and at least one really good one at the county fairgrounds, with grandstands, outhouses, and grassy lawns for picnickers. These facilities served as the county's main status symbol. Rural counties with small budgets built a nice half mile. Counties with urban centers, more people, and more money might build a big, beautiful mile, sometimes with fancy art deco ironwork on the grandstand. In an agrarian society before the advent of television and mass-marketed entertainment, the county fairground was the social center of the community, and the dirt track was where the excitement happened.

At one time the American Motorcycle Association had only two types of professional competition listed on its sanction application: hill climbs and race meets. Everyone knew what a race meet was. It was a bunch of guys speeding around an oval track, or over a meandering and less formal closed course later known as a scrambles track or a TT. There was little room for confusion, because true road races (typically over dusty country roads, not modern paved circuits) were few and far between, and motocross did not yet exist in the United States. Flat-track racing began to grow in popularity in America in the early 1930s when the AMA introduced Class C rules. Based on these rules, anyone who owned a Harley-Davidson or an Indian could ride to the racetrack, join the AMA for a dollar, sign up, take off his lights and mufflers (if he had any to start with), and compete. With lots of horse tracks available, and lots and lots of motorcycles suitable for racing under the Class C rules, the sport began to grow, hampered only by the economic malaise that prevailed throughout the Depression years. Then flat-track racing really took off after the Second World War, when a growing prosperity and high public morale caused people to seek more excitement and entertainment.

With Excelsior going out of business in 1931, flat-track racing became the arena in which Indian and Harley-Davidson punched it out for glory, fame, and bragging rights in the American motorcycle market. With the proliferation of cheap Model Ts in the late teens, both companies realized that motorcycles had lost their niche in the transportation market, and they made the strategic decision circa 1920 that the only way they could survive would be by positioning their product as a sporting vehicle, a source of pleasure and excitement. Thus, both factories sponsored racing teams and built a significant number of special racing machines corresponding to the Class C rules, and encouraged their dealers to become involved in racing by sponsoring teams and riders, or by promoting races. At this time, the AMA national championship races numbered less than a dozen, but there were hundreds of events promoted on the local level, sometimes on a weekly basis throughout the summer; and these events drew significant numbers of participants and fans.

The golden age of flat-track racing began in 1954 when the AMA created a Grand National Championship title, based on points awarded at a series of leading events across the nation. This system caused the series of national races to grow, bringing the stars and the spectacle of the sport to many more major urban population centers. The golden age of flat track began to wane in the 1970s when the AMA created a national championship title for motocross, and the Trans-AMA international series brought to America a host of spectacular riders from Europe. The golden age of flat track ended in 1986 when the growing popularity of road racing resulted in the creation of another separate AMA national championship title, thus bringing to a close the true Grand National Era. The peak was in the early 1970s when Bruce Brown's *On Any Sunday* made movie stars of the leading personalities on the Grand National circuit, and when Camel cigarettes signed on as a series sponsor with big tobacco money. Brown pioneered on-bike cameras with stunning results, especially the film's opening shot of Mert Lawwill shuttering, shaking, rattling, and vibrating at a hundred miles per hour, looking straight into the camera, then casually throwing his Harley into a graceful, dirt-spurting slide as he entered the turn. At the time *On Any Sunday* was filmed, the AMA issued licenses to nearly 3,000 professional dirt-track racers per year, and some meets got as many as 150 and 200 entries. Skip Van Leeuwen recalls, "So many Experts turned out for the Ascot weekly show, more than two-thirds of them knew they were not going to qualify for the main event. There was so much good talent, the 48 riders who made the show would have qualified within a half second of each other."

The flat tracks of America produced some of the greatest legends in motorcycle history: Ed Kretz, Joe Leonard, Carroll Resweber, Everett Brashear, Paul Goldsmith, Al Gunter, Neil Keen, Eddie Mulder, Skip Van Leeuwen, Dick Klamfoth, Bart

Dick Mann earned championships in every category of dirt-track racing, including short track, half mile, mile, and TT racing. *Dave Friedman photo, courtesy of Don Emde Productions.*

The golden age of dirt-track racing arrived when Bruce Brown heavily featured the AMA Grand National Championship series in *On Any Sunday.* Pictured here are Mark Brelsford, left, Dick Mann in the straw hat, Mert Lawwill, and Cal Rayborn, behind Lawwill, conferring for a shot in the movie. Behind Rayborn with the camera is Bruce Brown. *Photo courtesy of the Bruce Brown collection.*

Markel, Gary Nixon, Mert Lawwill, Gene Romero, Kenny Roberts, Scott Parker, Chris Carr, Jay Springsteen, Ricky Graham, and, of course, Dick Mann. But the golden age of flat track came to an end, and today America's most revered racing stars are earning their fame and fortune in road racing and motocross. In retrospect, the steadiness of the decline of flat-track racing is shocking. In the early 1970s, 40,000 fans were watching AMA short track and TT racing inside the Houston Astrodome. By the early 1990s, grandstands were 40 to 60 percent full, and national championships were drawing crowds not much larger than a high school football game. For the media, the fans, the motorcycle industry, and the sponsors, road racing and motocross had become the motorcycle sports of choice. How could a type of racing so uniquely American and so avidly followed as flat-track racing lose its place so quickly to what were, essentially, European imports?

Under its original Class C rules, flat-track racing motorcycles were required to use frames and engines from road-going, production motorcycles. Lights, fenders, and mufflers could be removed, but very little else could be changed, and the bikes were not allowed to carry brakes. Even the tires were supposed to be road bike tires, readily available through motorcycle dealerships. In a long series of changes over the years, these rules were relaxed so that today, flat-track racing motorcycles are the least faithful to the Class C concept of any type of motorcycles used in AMA national championship competition. Today, the flat-track motorcycles used in the Grand National class sport brakes and special frames, the tires are produced in very limited quantities from a super-sticky compound reminiscent of road-racing tires, and the engines are assembled from expensive parts and castings by skilled builders and machinists. The series is supported by only about two dozen teams, and equipment is so limited and expensive that relatively few aspiring newcomers can find a ride. The engines produce in the neighborhood of a hundred horsepower and are troublesome to maintain, requiring frequent overhauls. In short, it has become an elite and costly program that few riders have the ability to break into. In fact, not many do, because the road to other forms of professional motorcycle racing is so much smoother, wider, cheaper, and more inviting.

Diehard enthusiasts and pundits in the media frequently place the decline of flat-track racing at the feet of the AMA. They will point to this or that particular decision that supposedly sent everything to hell in a handcart. But it isn't that simple. Flat-track racing declined through an evolutionary process that included rule changes, product development trends in the motorcycle industry beyond the AMA's control, and broad cultural changes evident in every aspect of American society. And even if flat-track racing were the victim of its rules, we must remind ourselves that each and every change was undertaken with the judgment, guidance, and best intentions of experienced individuals deeply involved in the sport. No one sets out to change rules for the purpose of screwing things up. We all do the best we can, then suffer later from the simple perfection of 20/20 hindsight.

Professional flat-track racing today is largely the product of rule changes involving suspension, brakes, and tires. Dick

Mann was one of the biggest advocates of adding brakes to flat-track motorcycles. His motive was safety, and he and his fellow riders envisioned brakes being applied only under dire and emergency circumstances. Today he believes this was a mistake, and says, "We never envisioned riders using the brakes on a dirt track, as they do in a road race. But that is what has happened." The inclusion of brakes might not have been so bad if the rules had not also been changed to permit the use of purpose-built, soft-compound, racing tires. Like brakes, better tires seemed like a good idea at the time, but no one really understood what the two changes would do in concert. Soft tires started laying down a tacky path of rubber around the turns, creating something like a narrow road-racing course. Dick Mann explains, "Today every Expert goes out in practice and sacrifices $100 to take rubber off his tire and deposit it on the surface of the racetrack. By the time the race begins, there is a narrow groove around the turns made of the same rubber that the tires are made of. The traction of rubber on rubber is just tremendous, but if you get off the narrow rubber groove, you are in serious trouble. So riders can no longer pass in the turns." While the phenomenon of "grooving" had always existed, it was vastly exaggerated by the combination of brakes, suspension, and special racing tires.

Not only was racing changed by the evolution of equipment, but the tracks have changed as well. In the 1950s and '60s, half of the tracks were grooved. By the 1970s that number increased to 75 percent. Even tracks built as cushions cannot hold up under the battering of big horsepower and wide, sticky tires, which blow the surface away and take the track down to base clay, where they groove up quickly.

A new generation of young riders who had not honed their skills without brakes by broad sliding the turns were inclined to charge into the turns at top speed, grab the brakes, slow the bike down while deliberately staying in tight on the rubber groove, then road race the turns in single file, waiting for the next straightaway where more racing would begin. The fact that the bikes now have a rear suspension, which provides smoother, more consistent traction, only further facilitated this new style of riding. As early as 1972, Dick Mann realized that the combination of suspension, brakes, sticky tires, and increased horsepower had taken flat-track racing down the wrong road. At that time he said, "Nowadays, you ride very deep into the corner, apply your brakes, then more or less hold the bike straight up and down. Brakes have made dirt-track racing much safer, which is good, but to my way of thinking they have damaged the show. Before brakes, if you were blasting around a mile track, you had to gas it into the corner really fast, then heave the bike sideways into a chattering, tire-burning skid to slow it down. We're going much faster today, but we don't *look* faster. The spectacle is missing." Another rider from Mann's era has stated, sarcastically, "The only reason we use oval tracks any more is so the riders will go past the grandstand, because there certainly isn't any racing going on in the turns."

Dick Mann demonstrates a classic cushion track broad-sliding style at the Charity Newsies at Columbus in 1972. While the national championship statistics would suggest that Dick Mann's forte was TT and road racing, in fact, he got more than half his earnings at non-national short-track and half-mile races throughout the nation. Mann was one of the few riders who made the transition from the old no-brakes style of riding to the modern machines featuring brakes, rear suspension, and sticky tires. *Rick Kocks photo.*

The necessity today to get on the brakes, slow down, and play follow-the-leader in the turns, has encouraged tuners to develop engines that pump out twice the power they were designed for. Winning or losing depends upon accelerating out of the turns quicker and drag racing down the straightaway faster, so horsepower has become king. In an interview that appeared in *Cycle Guide* in 1977, Dick Mann said, "Almost all the problems can be directly related to one thing: the bikes are too fast. The expense of running them is directly related to how fast they are; the difficulty in finding riders capable of riding them is directly related to how fast they are; the inability of tires to finish races is directly related to how fast they are." Yet there is one other factor directly related to speed that Mann did not mention, and that is the problem of quality track preparation. Flat-track racing has become so fast and the bikes are so fragile, it is not possible to race on the rough and pitted tracks that once were standard fare. Today the national championships have become long and tedious evenings of track preparation, punctuated from time to time by racing.

The depth of talent during the heyday of dirt-track racing is evident in this 1969 photo taken at Ascot. Included in the photo are Skip Van Leeuwen, Dusty Coppage, Mert Lawwill, Ralph White, Dick Mann, Gene Romero, Dave Palmer, Dan Haaby, Eddie Wirth, Gary Nixon, Bob Bailey, Jack Simmonds, Eddie Mulder, Dallas Baker, Jimmy Plain, and other championship-quality riders. The competition was so intense that the fastest to the slowest qualifiers in the final might be less than a half-second apart. *Dan Mahony photo, courtesy of the Skip VanLeeuwen collection.*

Flat-track enthusiasts will still tell you, "It is the best show in motorcycling!" If they are speaking of the closeness of competition that happens between the green and checkered flags, they may be right. But if you take into consideration the whole show, the show that the paying spectator in the stands is forced to sit through, the statement is not remotely true. As a nation we have become used to immediate gratification. We get upset if it takes a few seconds longer to shoot an E-mail across the planet than we think it should. We favor the sound bite and the video clip, and relatively few of us love motorcycle racing enough to sit through the tedium and down time of a flat-track race. This is why the crowds have thinned, and why flat track cannot get as much television coverage as other forms of motorcycle racing. Producers are not much interested in televising events that cannot function to a predictable schedule. It is simply too challenging, unrewarding, and expensive to do.

So where goes flat track today? This is a question that the AMA, the riders, and the teams constantly struggle with. Turning back the clock is not an option. No one would suggest that a return to rigid frames, no brakes, and rough and dangerous tracks is a reasonable solution. Besides, even if we could turn back the clock, it probably would not matter, because the decline of flat-track racing has been more the result of market trends and product design than of anything the AMA might have done through the rules, ill-advised or not. Quite simply, while flat-track enthusiasts hate to admit it, motocross delivered a better mouse trap. When European-style motocross was introduced to America in the late 1960s—along with a new generation of light, agile, two-stroke motorcycles—a lot of Americans began to fall out of love with flat-track racing.

The evidence is in the numbers. In 1965, the AMA sanctioned 156 dirt-track races and only 15 motocross races. Over the next decade, the AMA's program of sanctioned events exploded, in part because the motorcycle market was booming, and in part because the AMA's infrastructural improvements and political reforms of the late 1960s resulted in a revitalized, strong, more efficient, and more responsive national organization. By 1975, the AMA's calendar of sanctioned dirt-track races had grown to 660, but sanctioned motocross events had skyrocketed to more than 1,500! Dirt track had increased five-fold during the decade; motocross had increased a hundred-fold! The motorcycle industry and America's riders simply went nuts over motocross in the early 1970s. Not only was it cheap and easy to buy a competitive racing bike at any dealership, but motocross tracks were easier to build and maintain than dirt ovals; thus the clubs and promoters were quickly attracted to motocross. From the late 1970s until the end of the '80s, motorcycle sales declined precipitously in America, due to a poor domestic economy, environmental issues, and increasing prices for Japanese imports caused by an unstable dollar/yen relationship. By 1985, the AMA's calendar had settled back to about 1,100 sanctioned motocross events, but dirt track had slipped back almost to 1965 levels, with only 191 sanctioned events. Sadly, the situation has not significantly improved for dirt-track racing, despite the fact that motorcycle sales began to rebound in the early 1990s. In 1995 the AMA's calendar of sanctioned motocross had grown to just under 1,300 events while only 140 dirt-track races were sanctioned nationwide.

So, the decline of flat-track racing in America was caused not so much from the top down by rule changes affecting the championship machines, but from the bottom up by a sea change in the tastes and preferences of a new crop of young competitors who chose motocross over flat track. This was understood by Dick Mann as early as 1977 when he stated in an article in *Cycle Guide,* "The sport is dying . . . it is like a tree with healthy leaves, dying at the roots."

Unfortunately, something else disappeared with the decline of flat-track racing, and that was the schedule of races that sustained the working-class professional racers of Dick Mann's era. While the glamor resided at the Nationals, the true earnings remained at the many weekly shows that ran throughout the nation. Dick Mann estimates that more than half of his lifetime earnings as a professional racer came from these small, local events. And the same is true for a great host of others, men like Babe DeMay, Eddie Varnes, Art Barda, Billy Lloyd, Larry Williamson, Bob Sholly, Larry Palmgren,

Dick Mann at the Houston Astrodome short track with Bart Markel (inside) and Walt Fulton (outside). *Photo courtesy of the Walt Fulton Collection.*

Sid Carlson, Charlie Seale, Jimmy McMurren, Darrel Dovel, Neil Keen, Sammy Tanner, Jim Corpe, Moon Buchanan, Ronnie Rall, and many more. Thanks to the creation of a thing called the "pro-am" or "semi-pro" event, as motocross emerged in America, it did not generate a calendar of races that paid enough to sustain a professional rider. For a few years in the early 1970s, a strong calendar of professional races began to develop, but it quickly collapsed with the advent of semi-pro races. Basically, promoters figured out they could get a new generation of riders to pay to ride, rather than vice versa, while subsidizing their absurdly small semi-pro purses. As a result, professional flat-track racing has been replaced by a system where there is no middle class, either in modern flat-track racing or motocross. There is amateur racing, and national championships where only a few riders earn a lot of money, and nothing in between.

This is a lamentable tale for those who love traditional American flat-track racing. Some of us might love to remain in the past, but that is never an option. Rather, we might take a lesson from the resilience and versatility of Dick Mann. Traditional Class C racing was his life and livelihood. Most of the hours he spent earning a living were on the flat tracks of America. Rather than simply lament the decline of flat-track racing, Dick Mann devoted a great deal of time and energy to trying to

Dick Mann and his buddy Neil Keen on their Bultaco short trackers in the early 1960s. *Photo courtesy of John Taylor and the Yankee Motors archives.*

help the AMA update its rules, doing the best he could to protect and keep flat track alive. Yet, as he saw the sport changing, Dick Mann moved on to become one of the most enthusiastic supporters and proponents of motocross.

Not including TT championships, Dick Mann won only four flat-track races in his long championship career. These included one mile, two half miles, and one short track. However, his perennial standing in the AMA's top ten was derived from consistency of performance on the dirt ovals. More often than not he qualified for flat-track Nationals, and garnered valuable national points by finishing third to eighth. Consequently, his reputation as a great flat-track racer overshadows the fact that he had relatively few championship victories. For example, in 1994 *American Motorcyclist* assembled a panel of flat-track experts and posed the question, "Who is the best dirt tracker of all time?" The results placed Dick Mann in the all-time top ten, finishing ninth behind Jay Springsteen, Scott Parker, Ricky Graham, Kenny Roberts, Carroll Resweber, Bart Markel, Joe Leonard and Bubba Shobert. Surprisingly, this subjective but interesting exercise placed Mann ahead of such flat-track luminaries as Chris Carr, Gary Scott, Steve Morehead, Mert Lawwill, Everett Brashear, Albert Gunter, and Steve Eklund.

14

TT—A Footnote

The Peoria TT was the site of Dick Mann's first national win. It would also be where Mann won his final national 13 years later.
– Motorcycle Hall of Fame web site

Class C racing—initiated in 1932—may have come about in part because of the vision of Indian advertising department employee Ted Hodgdon, who traveled to Somers, New York, in April, 1931 to see a new event being staged by the Crotona Motorcycle Club. With the idea of conducting a miniature British Tourist Trophy, the club carved a meandering track through an apple orchard and over a hill. Because this kind of course was entirely unsuitable for powerful and fragile works track-racing machines, the competitors that day rode production street motorcycles. It was an event designed to appeal to motorcyclists at large, to come out and have fun on their everyday machines. The event had little resemblance to the Isle of Man TT, but it was a great idea. Hodgdon immediately recognized the sales and marketing potential of this new kind of American TT racing, and he returned to Indian's headquarters in Springfield, Massachusetts to convince general manager Joe Hosley and AMA President Jim Wright that this idea needed to be explained and promoted to other motorcycle clubs throughout the nation. Wright agreed to publish TT rules in the 1931 AMA rule book, including a diagram of a TT course sketched by

Dick Mann on the jump at Peoria, 1970. Mann won the Peoria national championship TT five times. It was the site of his first national win in 1959 and his last in 1972. *Photo courtesy of the Mert Lawwill collection.*

Hodgdon (Incidentally, this is the same Ted Hodgdon who, as a BSA executive 26 years later, was called upon to bail bad boys Dick Mann and Al Gunter out of jail so they could race in the Daytona 200).

TT became one of the categories of dirt-track competition within the AMA Grand National Championship series, with venues—depending upon the year—at Castle Rock, Washington; Ascot, in Gardena near Los Angeles; Peoria, Illinois; Houston, Texas; and Santa Fe Speedway, near Chicago. A typical TT course had a relatively smooth surface and was based on a half mile or less oval track, incorporating a dog leg—creating both right and left-hand turns—and a jump. As conducted in the AMA Grand National Championship series, it was also known as TT Steeplechase. What Hodgdon witnessed at Somers, New York in 1931 would probably have later been called a rough scrambles. The term "scrambles" was also commonly used in England as synonymous with the Continental term, "motocross." TT equipment differed somewhat from flat trackers from the outset. While they were consistent with basic Class C rules, TT bikes were allowed to use brakes.

Some of the great names from the Grand National Championship era earned their fame as TT specialists. These included Skip Van Leeuwen, Eddie Mulder, Sonny Burres, Chuck Joyner, and Sid Payne. Had he not developed a reputation for his remarkable versatility, Dick Mann might have been ranked among the top TT specialists, having won eight TT national championships during his career. In fact, he won more TT championships than any of the TT specialists mentioned above. The best among these were Van Leeuwen with five championship victories, and Mulder with four. Dick Mann's championship victories began and ended at the Peoria TT. He won his first AMA national championship there in 1959, and his last in 1973. Mann's other TT championships included Ascot in 1963, Peoria again in 1964, 1967, and 1969; Castle Rock in 1970, and Houston in 1971. Many will insist that Mann's greatest ride of all was his incredible performance at the Ascot in 1963 that earned him his first Grand National Championship.

Dick Mann at Ascot. Although Mann did not like the Ascot half mile, the TT was one of his favorite tracks. *Mahony Photo Archive.*

15

The Emergence of Motocross

Nothing affected the sport so much in my lifetime as the Europeans coming to America.
– Dick Mann, 2001

The first reference to motocross in the documents of the American Motorcycle Association can be found in the minutes of a meeting of the Competition Committee that took place in the fall of 1958. The reference was striking in its simplicity: "Motocross is a scrambles, except in the method of running and scoring the event." While it remained a little-known type of competition throughout most of America, clubs in both New England and California hosted motocross events as early as 1960, when Dick Mann won the District 36 (the AMA's northern California district) Championship by winning all three motos.

It would be almost another decade before motocross would catch on in America, thanks to an entrepreneurial free spirit named Mario Edison Dye. Motocross had been popular in Europe for decades, and it differed from racing in America in that it required a high level of physical fitness. Though motocross is flat-out racing, its essence is stamina and endurance, since riders are required to ride "motos" (in American parlance, "heats") from 20 to 45 minutes in length, and in order to win they must score well in every moto. When Edison Dye witnessed his first motocross races in Europe, the sport was

Dick Mann was sponsored by OSSA to race motocross late in his career. *Photo courtesy of the Bruce Brown collection.*

undergoing a technical revolution. Around 1960, the principle of the expansion chamber was discovered by East German engineer Walter Kaaden, vastly improving the power-to-weight ratio of two-stroke engines, and a new generation of quick, agile, lightweight two-strokes were beginning to displace the traditional big British and Swedish-built four-stroke singles. Dye found the British Greeves, Czechoslovakian CZs, and Swedish Husqvarnas—especially the Husqvarnas—thrilling to watch, and he decided he wanted to sell Huskys in America.

Husqvarna's main business was the manufacture of sewing machines and firearms, but it had a skunk-works operation that turned out a limited number of 250cc racing motorcycles

(In 1963 they produced only 200 copies of their potent 250cc works motocross machine). Dye negotiated an agreement to become an American distributor for Husqvarna. He understood that it would take racing wins to attract customers in America, and he found his winning racer in Malcolm Smith. The first in a decades-long series of advertisements publicizing victories by Smith and other great riders on Husqvarnas appeared in late April, 1966. Smith and other young Californians—plus John Penton and other leading mud runners in the East—probably could have eventually driven Husky's commercial success on their own, but the entrepreneurial Dye achieved a promotional coup in the fall of 1966 by bringing three-time world motocross champion Torsten Hallman to America.

Malcolm Smith describes his first impression of the Swedish star: "Hallman arrived at our dealership in Riverside. He had this funny little pudding-bowl helmet that everyone thought was kind of silly. Then he started putting on European motocross pants, which none of us had ever seen before. They stopped about mid-calf because they were designed to fit into tall boots, but they looked kind of like pantaloons. Guys were grinning and laughing behind his back. Then Hallman climbed on the Husky and fired it up. He lofted it right onto the rear wheel and went roaring off across the intersection, running it up through the gears without ever setting the front wheel down. He jumped a curb and took off across a rough field at top speed, and disappeared over the crest of a hill, still riding on his rear wheel. We had never seen anything like it. You can bet we all stopped laughing!"

Hallman dazzled the American fans. No one had ever seen the kind of acrobatic riding that Hallman did, and it was not just showing off. He was fast as hell and had the stamina of a bull. He demonstrated competitive riding at a level Americans had never seen and could barely comprehend. One simply could not believe his eyes when first witnessing the spectacular riding of the Swedish star. And although not everyone—possibly not *anyone*—could ride like Torsten Hallman, many wanted to own the kind of motorcycle Hallman was riding. Clearly, Dye had devised a winning marketing strategy, and the success of the Torsten Hallman traveling show gave Dye a radical idea. He would not simply import a man; he would import European motocross in its entirety.

During his travels to Europe in 1967, Dye offered world-class riders contracts to come to America at the close of the Grand Prix season. Among them were Husky riders Hallman, Ake Jonsson, and Stefan Enqvist. But Dye's fertile imagination had conceived of much more than a Husky road show. He also recruited the Swedish brand's top rival, the CZ wrecking crew of world champion Joel Robert, Roger DeCoster, and Dave Bickers. Dye's motocross road show debuted at Pepperell, Massachusetts on October 29th, 1967, then moved to Aztec Park in Sedan, Kansas, on November 5th, then to Hopetown, California, on November 11th and 12th. The response was incredible. *Cycle News* reported that the Hopetown crowd was estimated at 25,000, and publisher Chuck Clayton wrote a perceptive and penetrating analysis of the European riding style and why they were able to beat the Americans. The Americans, many of whom were on big four-stroke Class C machines, did wide, wheel-spinning slides through the turns, applying as much power as possible. The Europeans, Clayton noted, kept their bikes hooked up and vertical as much as possible, getting on and off the throttle as necessary to maintain as much traction as they could at all times. Echoing Clayton's observations, Torsten Hallman recalls, "The Americans overworked their riding, using more energy and hard work to ride the bike, so they got tired faster and went slower. We had a much more relaxed riding style, letting the bike do the work."

This new style of racing, it appeared, was not about power. It was about lightness, agility, responsiveness, and physical fitness. The extent to which the American riders as a whole found themselves outclassed by the Europeans was simply hard to believe. *Cycle News* wrote, "In the first 250 moto the visitors had lapped most of the U.S. riders by the halfway point, and *all* of them by the end." However, what *Cycle News* failed to note was that there were a few Americans who held their own in these early outings with the Europeans. At Pepperell, for example, Glenn Vincent finished seventh aboard

Riding an OSSA at Pepperell. *Photo courtesy of the Dave Latham collection.*

a Bultaco, and Dick Mann finished eighth on his trusty BSA, both edging out Swedes Steffan Enqvist and Lars Larsson, who finished ninth and 10th respectively, riding Husqvarnas.

Clayton also published in *Cycle News* an intense and exciting photo of Torsten Hallman, Ake Johnsson, Roger DeCoster, and Dave Bickers charging shoulder-to-shoulder off the starting line, leaning over their mounts and battling toward the first turn. It was captioned, "The Four Horsemen of the Apocalypse." In fact, what Dye introduced through his Inter-Am series, which continued through the early 1970s, eventually spelled apocalypse for traditional forms of American motorcycle racing. The Inter-Am was the beginning of a revolution in motorcycle competition that would see motocross become a huge sport at the expense of American flat-track and TT-style racing as clubs and promoters shifted their interest and resources toward motocross races, and as the industry—first the Europeans and then the Japanese—began to fill their dealers' showrooms with ready-to-race motocross machines at affordable prices. Edison Dye changed the face of motorcycling in America, and is rightly known today as the father of American motocross.

Dick Mann, riding the Inter-Am international motocross at Pepperell. *Dave Latham photo.*

The phenomenal success of Dye's Inter-Am was another example of the AMA failing to keep up with the rapidly changing American motorcycle sport. Dick Mann observed these developments, and expressed concern to his colleagues in the AMA Congress. Mann loved motocross, felt sure it represented the future of the sport, and believed strongly that the AMA should take a leadership role. When no one seemed to adequately share his concern, he decided to take action to shake the AMA out of its lethargy. Mann entered the first event of the 1968 Inter-Am series, in Pepperell, Massachusetts, which was promoted by Bob Hicks and the New England Sports Committee. Not only did Mann intentionally break the AMA's rules by entering an unsanctioned event, but he called the AMA to tell them what he was going to do. Mann says, "I wanted to get their attention. I wanted them to understand how they were missing out on something really important. I didn't care if they suspended me, because I knew the publicity would make them look bad, and maybe embarrass them into getting involved in the motocross movement."

Dick Mann got his wish. The AMA suspended his professional license for the remainder of the season, and also suspended John Penton's membership for teaming up with Edison Dye to promote one of the so-called "outlaw" Inter-Am events. In the December issue of *Cycle Sport,* publisher Bob Hicks wrote, "I think the gesture is in very poor taste, and ill-judged, for Mann has so far been the leading U.S. rider to face up to the European invaders, doing it with no guaranteed start or prize money, but just to carry out the courage of his convictions. Since the AMA has not offered him any opportunity to compete in motocross professionally, he entered the FIM sanctioned events. His thanks for upholding the U.S. rider in this series to date is suspension. With the exercise of this demeaning power taking place so selectively, the AMA is losing stature among its members and interested fans." Astonishingly, the AMA even suspended the membership of Bob Hicks, who was on the AMA

Mann raced against the Europeans at Pepperell in 1968 and 1969. His first competition against world champion Torsten Hallman took place at a hare scrambles race in California in 1966. *Dave Latham photo.*

board at the time. Allegedly it was because Hicks, like Penton, was an Inter-Am promoter, but undoubtedly his editorializing was a contributing factor. Hicks thought the absurdity of the situation was hilarious, and still laughs about the tension in the air when he attended his next board meeting as a "non-member." Mann didn't care, because he had no plans of riding professionally for the remainder of the season anyway. With John Penton it was another story. He made an issue of the whole affair in the press, and American fans responded with outrage toward the AMA, just as Mann suspected they would.

Mann and Penton were two of the most well-known and popular motorcyclists in America. Both had contributed enormously to the AMA, and it was a dreadful tactical error for the AMA to punish them. *Cycle News* published letters from angry readers, and Hicks turned up the heat, writing a series of editorials critical of the policies of the AMA. To the world it looked not only like the AMA did not want to change, but that it would punish anyone who wished to involve himself in the exciting, modern aspects of the sport. Of course, this was not the truth. AMA Executive Director Bill Berry had done more than any previous executive director to improve and modernize the organization, but all of that was lost when he unwisely carried out punitive action against Mann, Hicks, Penton, and others. The storm of protest from AMA members was intense, and a brief notice soon appeared in *American Motorcycling,* reporting that the board of trustees had unanimously accepted Berry's resignation.

The AMA sanctioned its first professional motocross in the spring of 1970 at a racetrack in Croton, Ohio. Former three-time Daytona winner Dick Klamfoth was the promoter of the event, and AMA Class C racing stars Ronnie Rall and Dick Mann were there to ride against imported talent in the form of Swedish Husqvarna engineer and international rider Gunnar Lindstrom. *American Motorcycling* reported, "As the race began, it was soon evident that the main competition was going to be between Mann and Lindstrom. The two were inseparable, and their constant challenging each other for the lead made for very exciting races." Lindstrom fell on the last lap, and Mann—

Dick Mann aboard an OSSA in 1969. In the late 1960s, Mann began to carry a motocross bike as he toured the AMA Grand National circuit, looking for opportunities to race motocross on open weekends. *Rick Kocks photo, courtesy of the Dick Mann collection.*

nine years the Swedish star's senior—won the event. However, Mann, who is always reluctant to take too much credit, says, "I only rode the 250 class that day. Gunnar rode both the 250 and the 500, and he won the 500, so it really isn't fair to compare my performance with his."

By Summer, 1970, the AMA board hired Russ March as the organization's new executive director. March was a motorcycle-industry veteran. He had worked as a district representative for American Honda; a marketing executive with American Safety, manufacturer of Buco helmets; and served on the AMA board of trustees. March was an aggressive, forward-thinking, publicity-conscious man with good leadership skills. It became immediately clear that it was his agenda to move the AMA rapidly forward and erase any residual doubt that it was still a regressive hidebound organization run by old-boy committees.

One problem impeding the progress of the AMA was the fact that it was not affiliated with the Federation

Dick Mann and Joe Bolger at Pepperell. *Photo courtesy of the Joe Bolger collection.*

Internationale de Motocyclisme (FIM), the worldwide governing body for the international motorcycle sport. At that time, the official FIM affiliate in the United states was MICUS—the Motorcycle International Club of the U.S.—a privately-held company owned by California businessman Wes Cooley. The AMA had been trying to obtain an affiliation with the FIM for more than five years, but couldn't seem to figure out how to open the right door. Year after year the AMA would politely submit its application, and the FIM would respond, without explanation, that the AMA's application had not been placed on the agenda of its annual meeting. It was ridiculous that the international governing body would ignore what had become the largest national motorcycling organization on the planet, but the situation was a direct result of the old AMA's isolationist policies and lack of interest in much of anything beyond America's shores.

Russ March was not a man to stand on ceremony. He, along with AMA board chairman Bill Bagnall, climbed aboard an airplane for Europe and did what March did best: sell himself and his product, the AMA. By the fall of 1970 the AMA was named the FIM's official affiliate in the United States, and March announced plans for an international motocross series called the Trans-AMA, with a commitment from Suzuki and BSA to bring their world-championship teams. Suddenly, the politics of racing had changed. There was a one-year transition period when both the AMA and Cooley enjoyed the privileges of FIM affiliation, but it was clear that in the future, Edison Dye would not be able to obtain an international sanction unless he obtained it through the AMA. Both Dye's Inter-Am and the Trans-AMA ran in 1970, but for all intents and purposes the Inter-Am series was dead, and the Trans-AMA would become the most prestigious motocross series in America, gaining the support of all of the international teams in 1971. After Dye's series ended, he was invited to become a promoter within the Trans-AMA, which he did until 1974.

The first Trans-AMA was an odd combination of European experience and American enthusiasm. It featured world champions Jeff Smith and John Banks on their works BSAs. Both the bikes and their riders had seen years of service campaigning the Grand Prix wars in Europe, and the American series was pretty much a busman's holiday for them. In stark contrast, a young kid out of Dick Mann's hometown of Richmond, riding a production CZ, captured the imagination of the press. He had long hair and a peace dove mounted on his handlebars, but he had the attitude of a Cossack, taking no prisoners and scorching the earth as he passed. While the Europeans were billed as the big show, it was Brad Lackey's flamboyance and charisma that landed him on the cover of *Cycle News* when the series debuted at LaRue, Ohio. He rode like a man possessed, leaping, sliding, crossing it up off the jumps, and doing everything in his power to beat the Europeans. He didn't beat them—not by a long shot—but race after race, the exuberant and youthful Lackey demonstrated the raw ability and determination that would one day make him America's first motocross world champion.

Lackey's story is a perfect example of why Class C racing gave way to motocross in America. When he was a young man learning to ride on the same hills around Richmond where Dick Mann cut his teeth as a motorcyclist, Class C racing was still popular, but motocross was just beginning to arrive at the amateur level. Brad says, "When we wanted to go racing for the weekend, we might have a choice of a short track and a scrambles and a motocross within driving distance. We didn't really care where we rode. We just wanted to ride. But it didn't take us long to figure out that if we went to a short track or a scrambles, we might not qualify out of our heat race, and when that happened you were done for the day after just a few minutes of riding. But in motocross, you got to ride a 20 minute moto, and if something went wrong or you broke, you could get it back together and ride the second moto, then the third. In fact, just one moto got you more riding time than a whole scrambles program, even when you qualified all the way through to the final. It's pretty easy to see why we liked motocross. It wasn't necessarily about winning. It was about riding, and motocross gave you a lot more riding for your entry fee."

Looking back on the introduction of motocross in America, Edison Dye recalls that he did not know Dick Mann prior to meeting him at the Pepperell Inter-AM in 1968, but he immediately realized that despite the fact that Mann was older than other riders, he was a great asset to the event. He explains, "The fans loved him. Dick had the drive, determination, and experience to succeed. He showed that he had the courage to ride against the world champions, and that made him very popular among the fans and riders."

Hallman remembers Mann from his first visit to America in 1966. At a hare scrambles at Wilseyville, Hallman's Husky would not start until the entire field of over 200 riders had sped away into the woods. Hallman recalls, "After a while the engine started so I could go after them. I passed rider by rider and finally after ten or 15 minutes I passed what I thought was the guy in the lead. Then I noticed tire tracks on the course and understood that it must be one more rider a long way in front of me. I had to go quicker, and finally I saw a rider on a BSA on a

Dick Mann beat Gunnar Lindstrom in 1970. Lindstrom raced two classes, and won the open class, while Mann won the 250. *Rick Kocks photo.*

long, long uphill. The rider was Dick Mann!" Hallman passed and beat Mann that day, but he says, "He was so much better than the rest of the Americans. Dick was surely one of the better riders I raced against during my first time in the States, in the same class as Malcolm Smith."

Motocross, however, came too late for Mann to be a true contender at the international level. Even the spectacular Hallman was in the twilight of his career, and Mann was five years Hallman's senior. While Mann's career is one of the most remarkable in the history of the American motorcycle sport, there is one aspect he would change if he could. Mann says today, "I wish the timing had been a little different. I like all kinds of motorcycle riding, and I loved what I did, but I would have loved also to have a full career of racing motocross."

When Dick Mann helped draft motocross rules for the AMA and competed in the first international motocross races in America, the visiting champions from Sweden, England, Belgium, and Germany were gods. Americans watched them in awe, and believed it would never be possible to compete at their

Dick Mann at the Delta, Ohio, Trans-AMA in 1971. *Rick Kocks photo.*

level. But motocross in America became a runaway train. Within a few years, 60 percent of all the events sanctioned by the AMA were motocross races, and literally tens of thousands of young children were honing their skills. Dick Mann was correct in 1968 when he tried to tell the AMA that motocross would be motorcycle racing's future. This was proven without a doubt in the fall of 1981 when Johnny O'Mara, Chuck Sun, Danny LaPorte, and Donnie Hansen beat the best Europe had to offer, winning both the Trophee des Nations and the Motocross des Nations, and setting off thirteen straight years of uninterrupted dominance by American riders in world team motocross championships. As Dick Mann predicted, the United States took to motocross with zeal, and within a decade the Americans were looked upon by the rest of the world as the gods of motocross.

16

Road Racing Comes of Age

All you read in the European press was that we were a bunch of cowboys, and we believed it. But when we finally went to England to the Match Races, we learned we could ride right with them.
– Dick Mann, 1998

Road racing in America and Europe emerged through two entirely different traditions. Racing over the mountainous roads of Europe provided an exciting challenge that attracted manufacturers and enthusiasts in the earliest days of the century. Early road races did not use closed circuits, but were point-to-point events aimed at demonstrating reliability. The appeal of the road was such that the British government passed a law against racing over public highways, and famous road courses were created in Ireland and the Isle of Man to satisfy the demand. Rules used in Europe, promulgated by the FIM, catered to nationalistic attitudes, where each country tried to outdo the other in engineering and technology.

Often money was no object in the quest to win world championships, and by the eve of World War II, supercharged works racers like the German BMW boxer twin and the British AJS V-four were competing for supremacy in the international Grand Prix. After the war, the Italians came to the fore with their beautiful overhead cam multis, as represented by the Gilera, the MV Agusta, and culminating with the awesome

Because BSA was out of business, Dick Mann raced a Triumph triple in 1973, his final full season on the Grand National Championship circuit. The bike was Mann's 1972 BSA, repainted in Triumph colors. *Photo courtesy of the AMA archives.*

Moto Guzzi V-eight. Even the Russians, Czechs, and East Germans built works prototypes to showcase their communist technology. Streamlining came early, and the Germans, benefitting from their advanced aero industry, created such efficient fairing designs that the FIM had to impose streamlining limitations for the sake of safety. Across the Atlantic, America provided a totally different environment for motorcycle racing development. With low population density and wide open spaces, the roads were straighter and not so interesting for sporting use. Rather, Americans took to track racing, based on the abundance of oval tracks throughout the nation. For example, during the 1940s there were over 1,200 oval tracks used for motor racing in the United States, and only 14 road courses.

Although Indian, which made a three-place sweep at the Isle of Man in 1911, was one of the most technically advanced motorcycles in the world during the first decade of the century, by the 1930s Europe had moved well ahead of America in motorcycle engine design, due in part to economic and political influences. Whereas Europe was gearing up for war and the Germans and British were attempting to outshine each other for engineering sophistication and industrial might, America's motorcycle industry competition was strictly intramural. Willingly constricted by the Class C rules they helped devise, Indian and Harley-Davidson seemed to stop time around the era of the old side-valve V-twin. Though Harley-Davidson introduced an overhead-valve design as early as 1936, racing remained devoted to low-tech, low-cost, and readily available technology, mainly because the American manufacturers believed racing should be used to sell motorcycles, not to show off their engineering departments. While the FIM was banning supercharging because 500cc machines had become too frighteningly powerful for the tire and chassis technology of the day, America continued happily along with its old street-legal, 750cc side-valve racers.

In the United States, where competition was steeped in the flat track and TT tradition, road racing after the European model practically did not exist. Prior to 1956, there were only two so-called road races on the AMA national championship circuit. The first was Daytona, which was nothing more than a huge oval comprised of a long, sandy beach connected to a straight, narrow, brutally rough strip of macadam highway. The other was Laconia, which was more in the style of a true road course, winding through the pines of a New Hampshire state park, but it too included a section of dirt road. Whereas one could ride the Daytona beach course like the huge oval track it was, the tight, short Laconia circuit could be ridden more like a TT, complete with dragging feet and sliding tires. The Harley-Davidson on which Dick Mann finished second at Daytona in 1958 and 1959 was practically indistinguishable from a TT motorcycle. In fact, its model designation was KRTT. With the press displaying photographs of such machines and America's top stars hanging a leg out in the corner and wrestling big, wide flat-track handlebars, it is no wonder that most of the world thought Americans knew nothing about road racing. In fact, AMA rules, which banned fairings until 1963, militated against the development of European-style, state-of-the-art road-racing equipment. Thus, road racing in America did not evolve in its own right as a separate discipline as it did in Europe, but rather had its roots firmly planted in the soil of flat-track racing, a uniquely American version of the motorcycle sport.

By the mid-1950s, motor sports as a whole were changing in America. The post-war popularity of small and agile British and Continental sports cars led to the development of purpose-built road-racing circuits all over the nation, and from 1950 to 1959 there was a ten-fold increase in paved road courses in the United States. This trend was stimulated by the formation of the Sports Car Club of America, incorporated in 1944. The California circuit at Willow Springs was added to the AMA championship series in 1956, then Watkins Glen in New York in 1958. Dick Mann won his first road-racing championship at Laconia in 1960, setting a new track record and lapping the entire field except for second-place Carroll Resweber. With road racing becoming more popular and road courses becoming more available, by the mid-60s a full third of the events on the AMA championship calendar were road races, which was beneficial to a strategic rider like Dick Mann, who developed special transmission gear sets for his Matchless for each individual circuit. Although still conducted under Class C limitations, American road racing was becoming more sophisticated and beginning to look similar in appearance to road racing in Europe, especially after the FIM began to control the aerodynamic qualities of fairings and impose technical limitations to discourage overdogs like the Guzzi V-eight.

Prior to 1966, 14 of the 24 races staged at Daytona were won by Harley-Davidsons. To beat the long-winded, 750cc side-valve Harleys at Daytona in 1966 and 1967, Triumph spent a lot of money and pushed the Class C rule book to the limit, upping the ante for factory involvement in AMA competition. Harley-Davidson responded with a vengeance with new motorcycles and a seven-rider wrecking crew in 1968. Arguably, Daytona '68 was the beginning of the modern era of road racing

Dick Mann on his way to victory at Daytona, 1971. *Dave Friedman photo, courtesy of Don Emde Productions.*

in America. The team Harleys had all new body work, designed by Dean Wixom. They featured a wide, rump-hugging seat that helped the rider's body become part of the streamlining. A beautifully sculpted gas tank provided recesses where the riders arms could be tucked in out of the air stream. The rounded fairing and wind screen were designed right to the dimensional limits of the rule book. The whole package, gel-coated in lustrous black and orange with white trim and number plates, was wind tunnel developed, leaving no reminder whatsoever of the dirt-track heritage of the KR power plant hidden inside. Cal Rayborn, Mert Lawwill, Fred Nix, Bart Markel, Dan Haaby, Roger Reiman, and Walt Fulton were chosen to pilot the fleet of Harleys. Rather than the usual hodgepodge of personally designed leathers, Harley-Davidson provided team leathers in a standard livery of black, orange, and white. Others, such as Yamaha, turned up with larger and better-appointed teams, but none so impressive and overpowering in appearance as the Harleys. That something had changed in American road racing was noted by *Cycle News* publisher Chuck Clayton, who wrote, "The new look at Daytona this year is factory team riders in bright leather uniforms and identical-looking bikes."

Harley-Davidson's big effort delivered victories by Cal Rayborn in both 1968 and 1969. However, these were the brand's last victories ever at the Daytona 200, as a change in AMA engine displacement rules unleashed in 1970 the new 750cc overhead valve multis from both England and Japan. Triumph, BSA, and Honda delivered four and five-rider teams, complete with matching bikes, matching leathers, small armies of mechanics, and, in the case of Triumph, a film crew to document its efforts.

The combination of the new 750cc engine rule, the AMA's newly-acquired affiliation with the FIM, and Russ March's visionary and aggressive leadership brought a major change to road racing in 1970 which would eventually launch America to prominence on the international road-racing scene. March and other leaders of the organization promoted a new concept called Formula 750. While it was grounded in some of the basic principles of the old tried-and-true Class C formula, it was

Dick Mann on his way to victory at Daytona, 1970. *Dave Friedman photo, courtesy of Don Emde Productions.*

America's best road racers at the Trans-Atlantic Match Races in England in 1972. Left to right are Cal Rayborn, Don Emde, Dick Mann, Jody Nicholas, Ron Grant, and Art Baumann. *Photo courtesy of the Dick Mann collection.*

designed to entice as many riders and brands as possible onto the racetrack, and to persuade the manufacturers to produce new, competitive road-racing machines in significant numbers. Although Formula 750 allowed the development of purpose-built racers, they had to be homologated (the FIM's term for "approved") and 200 had to be manufactured and available for sale to non-factory riders. The British were especially keen on the idea, because America was their largest market, and they needed something to stimulate sales and encourage sporting activity. Consequently, in February 1971, officials of Britain's Auto-Cycle Union (England's governing body counterpart to the AMA) traveled to America for the purpose of collaborating with the AMA to make Formula 750 an international racing class. It was a concept alien to the FIM, but American and British delegates agreed on a set of rules and lobbied them through the FIM's rule-making process, creating a place for 750cc serial production machines in world-class competition. No longer could America be seen as a nation behind the curve in motorcycle road racing. Not only had it exported a domestic racing concept to international racing, but American Steve Baker became the first Formula 750 world champion.

Although the new American Formula 750 rules delivered one more Daytona victory to a British brand when Dick Mann won on the BSA Rocket 3 in 1971, in the long run the plan proved advantageous to the high production capability of the Japanese factories. A dying British motorcycle industry had been going through a painful process of shrinkage and consolidation for more than a decade, wherein once-arch rivals merged to survive a few more years, only to inevitably fall by the wayside. It had happened to Douglas, Vincent, Velocette, AJS, and Matchless, and by 1970 the process of merger and consolidation took in the remaining major brands. Triumph and BSA consolidated marketing, engineering, and product planning, which would have been quite unthinkable only a few years earlier. Only Norton remained independent, and it too would be drawn into common ownership with Triumph within the decade. While the British remained proud of their engineering traditions and old-world methods of manufacturing, it was becoming ever more apparent that they didn't have a chance against the Japanese motorcycle-manufacturing juggernaut.

Perhaps it was just the pride showing, but you would not have figured the British were in trouble, given their behavior in the early 1970s. New leadership—Peter Thornton and Felix Kalinski—arrived in both Great Britain and America at about the same time, and they were a well-matched pair in their propensity for flamboyance and extravagance. Based on the big teams fielded by Triumph and BSA, the methods with which they operated, and the behavior of their executives, one might have concluded that the British industry was on top of the world, and that its American distributor had a bottomless pit of money. Thornton chartered helicopters and private jets to attend the races, and sometimes treated the riders like rock stars when it suited his public relations purposes.

To showcase their impressive new road racers and publicize Formula 750 racing, BSA/Triumph invested heavily in a spring promotion in 1971 called the Anglo-American Match Races. The American teams and their motorcycles were flown to England to compete with British stars on their home circuits. Don Emde recalls, "We weren't even aware this was being promoted as a big deal. We thought we were going over just for a factory tour and some exhibitions, and when we landed here was all this publicity about the big match races, like it was a big showdown between the best America and Great Britain had to offer. We were totally unprepared. Our bikes still had their big Daytona fuel tanks and seats, and the British team had a whole new generation of triples set up for the short circuits." Jim Rice and Dave Aldana, riding for BSA, and Don Castro, riding for Triumph had each done only one road race in their career, and that was Daytona, which was a far cry from the short, tight British true road courses. Aside from Dick Mann, the American's best and most experienced road racer was Gary Nixon, and he fell and broke his hand in practice. Mann, who was named American team captain, recalls, "Our team was a bunch of kids and an old man."

Dick Mann leading Jody Nicholas at Brands Hatch in 1972. *Photo courtesy of the Jody Nicholas collection.*

Dick Mann at Indianapolis, 1972. Although his BSA was dominant the previous season, by 1972 the British triples were already being made obsolete by the onslaught of Japanese two-strokes. *Rick Kocks photo.*

Predictably, the British team defeated the visiting Americans, but the fans and media were shocked by the skill and professionalism of the Yanks. Emde says, "There were people in England who thought we Americans were still racing with big, wide handlebars and dragging our feet in the turns." Dick Mann set a top lap time in the rain, and the Yanks won the first heat, proving once and for all that Americans knew more about road racing than the British fans had been led to believe.

The British fans were also exposed to a new kind of cowboy attitude toward road racing that would—in the person of Kenny Roberts some years later—revolutionize the sport. Classic European road racers simply did not slide the tires. They approached a corner on a predictable line, leaned with the motorcycle, and carried through like they were riding on rails. If ever they went in too hot and got a little loose, they usually just jumped off and threw it away. Recovering from a slide simply wasn't an accepted or practiced skill. Mann says, "I'm sure the fans couldn't believe their eyes. If Aldana or Castro ran off the course, they would just lock it up and skid and muscle those big triples around like they were TT bikes. Then when they got themselves under control and pointed in the right direction they would grab a big handful of throttle and roar back onto the course, squirting a big plume of sod behind them. You could almost hear the Brits muttering, 'Bloody Yanks!' "

What Emde recalls most about the week was the extravagance of the BSA/Triumph operation. The riders were placed in suites in London's Grosvenor Place and two hired limousines with drivers were posted outside the hotel, around the clock, for the convenience of the riders. Emde says, "Can you imagine giving a bunch of kids like me, Castro, Aldana, and Rice a limousine and the run of London? What were they thinking?" Mann recalls the culture shock of Aldana on London. He laughs, "The fad among the kids then was to wear a painter's cap. One evening Aldana strolled in the front door of the Grosvenor in his painter's cap, and the doorman stopped him and told him he would have to use the rear entrance. He thought he was some kind of tradesman!"

Thornton and his entourage arrived at the racetracks by helicopter, and the riders were given rental cars to travel from one circuit to another. Of course, the American riders showed the Brits what they did best with rental cars, racing around the circuit at Oulton Park. The motorcycles had not yet arrived, so the Americans took their rental cars out to try to learn the track. Jim Rice recalls, "They were some kind of little Fords, I think. They were really evil-handling cars." Dick Mann was in the back seat of the lead car, with Rice driving and Castro riding shotgun. Aldana, who was in the second car, says, "I knew we were having fun when I saw Dick put on his helmet." Moments later Rice rolled the car and sent it sliding down the tarmac on its top, leaving a trail of shattered glass and leaking fluids. Mann says, "When we started over I just rolled up and braced my feet on the ceiling. When the car came to rest upside down, I was just squatting there, right side up. Rice and Castro were still belted in, hanging upside down. Just as a joke I said, 'You know, this thing could catch on fire,' and instantly I heard 'click click' and both Rice and Castro crashed down on their heads and began scrambling out through the windows." Rice laughs, "Here were Castro and I, rolling around in broken glass, trying to crawl out the windows, and Bugs was already standing outside, just smiling at us. It was classic Bugs Mann. Even in a rental car crash he was a step ahead of us."

Mann continues, "The British officials were just horrified. We were getting out of the car, laughing and giggling, and there was glass and debris all over the place, and the stodgy British were really upset that we were having so much fun. Then here comes Pete Colman, and I heard one of the Brits say, 'They've had it now!' They were really stunned when Colman jumped out of his car laughing, and started joking with us about the big mess we had made." Rice adds, "I kind of got beat up by the British press. You know: ugly Americans, and all that." Bloody Yanks, indeed!

By 1972 the fun and games for BSA/Triumph were coming to an end. BSA's world championship motocross team was liquidated, the big triples had failed to blunt the market penetration of Honda's 750 Four, and a desperate effort to rush new overhead-cam 350s into production to compete with the Japanese middleweight motorcycles was terminated due to a lack of funds. By 1973 BSA was gone, and Pete Colman, who had controlled a ten-bike road-racing budget in 1970, had only two Triumphs available. He assigned one of them to Dick Mann. Gary Nixon, as great a loyalist as Triumph ever had, will still today send forth a flood of expletives at the mention of the name Peter Thornton: "That ******, ******, ****, ***** ruined a great company. The American Triumph organization was a great group of people, and that ****** destroyed it all!" In truth, the cause of Triumph's demise was the same as that of the entire British motorcycle industry, which included refusal to modernize its antiquated manufacturing techniques, self-destructive stubbornness among labor unions, and outright Victorian arrogance within the management. But Nixon was right that Thornton's profligate ways did little to help the ailing company.

In his last national championship road race, Dick Mann rode a Don Vesco-tuned Yamaha at Daytona in 1974, seen here with Kenny Roberts. Mann turned in one of the best performances of the event until his Yamaha ejected a large section of rubber from its rear tire. *Rick Kocks photo.*

In the meantime, the emerging Japanese took good advantage of the Formula 750 opportunity. At first Yamaha joined the fray with its little 350cc two-stroke, taking victory circle at Daytona away from the big boys with Don Emde in 1972 and with Finnish world champion Jarno Saarinen in 1973. Kawasaki and Suzuki also developed factory teams, but the real hammer blow to the era of four-stroke motorcycles came in 1974 when Yamaha introduced its stunning TZ700, on which Giacomo Agostini again won Daytona for the brand. Gene Romero won in 1975 on the updated TZ750, and Johnny Cecotto repeated in 1976 with Yamaha's OW31, which satisfied the Formula 750 rules, but was tantamount to a full-on Grand Prix racer. After Don Emde's victory in 1972, a four-stroke machine did not return to the winner's circle until Freddie Spencer rode a Honda to victory in 1985.

By the mid-1980s, the world road-racing scene had been turned on its ear by the rapidly developing Americans. Daytona was now the most important road race on earth, not the Isle of Man. And American riders were becoming recognized as the greatest pavement racers on earth, with Steve

Baker, Kenny Roberts, Freddie Spencer, Wayne Rainey, Eddie Lawson, and Kevin Schwantz winning world championships. Ironically, the first Americans to make their name on the world road-racing scene were men who learned their skills on dirt. Baker, Spencer, Roberts, Rainey, and Lawson were men who had no fear of breaking both tires loose at high speed, and sliding sideways. Taking this skill from dirt to pavement was only natural for them, and, gifted with rapidly improving tire technology, they introduced to the Grand Prix an aggressive tire-sliding style of riding that completely revolutionized the sport.

Dick Mann's career encompassed the era when American road racing came of age. Beginning with modified Harley and BSA dirt trackers on the beach course at Daytona, he progressed to the quick and well-handling Matchless, then twice won Daytona on big multi-cylinder Formula 750 machines. Mann's career also reached into the era of the two-stroke, winning a championship at Nelson Ledges aboard a Yamaha. He is a modest and self-effacing person, and will tell you, "I was never much of a road racer. The only time I won was when the good guys dropped out." This may be the way Dick Mann remembers it, but the record would indicate otherwise. No less than half of his 24 championship victories were on road-racing circuits. In addition to two Daytona wins, he finished second three times at Daytona. When he won Daytona in 1970 aboard a Honda with an ailing engine, he still broke Cal Rayborn's 1969 record. When he lapped all but one of the riders at Laconia in 1960, one of those he lapped was Roger Reiman. And in 1971 he won several wheel-to-wheel battles with world champion Kel Carruthers. Dick Mann may be doubtful about his road-racing skills, but he will always be remembered as one of America's greatest road racers. In naming Mann its Rider of the Year in March, 1972, *Cycle* magazine summarized his ability on pavement nicely: "As a road racer, both here and in England, he demonstrated that he can go as fast as the best, and sustain his speed and concentration."

17

World-Class Cow Trailing

I was amazed at the amount of skill, knowledge, and stamina necessary to succeed in this event, and the little acknowledgment our riders received because it was not an "American" sport.

– Dick Mann, 2001

Dick Mann earned his living racing motorcycles, but he found his bliss while cow trailing. From his earliest days on a motorcycle, Dick took to the hills around Richmond every chance he got, riding for the sheer joy of the experience. As with everything else he did in motorcycling, he became legendary for his off-road riding skill. AMA champion Jimmy Odom recalls, "I was a lot younger than Mann and his buddies, and one day Jim Hutzler, a District 36 AMA Congressman, asked me if I would like to go cow trailing with them. I was just beside myself with the opportunity. We met in a small group at the Richmond Ramblers club house, and took off toward a deep ravine." Odom describes how he watched Mann plunge over the edge and fly down the steep slope, then shoot effortlessly up the other side, where he stopped at the top and waited for the others. Odom says, "No one else followed, and they were all looking at me. I suddenly realized this was a test. Dick and his buddies didn't want to ride with some slug who couldn't keep up, and I had to prove my ability by making it through the ravine." Without a doubt, every rider in the group had gone through the same

Dick Mann at an ISDT qualifying event at Potosi, Missouri, in 1973. *Rick Kocks photo.*

experience. Odom continues, "I was sitting on my bike, looking over the edge, and Hutzler roars up behind me and runs into my rear tire and pushes me over the edge. I could hear everyone laughing as I started down, and I knew I had no choice but to just get on it and go. I made it down and up the other side without falling, and everyone else came in after me. When I popped up on the other side and stopped next to Dick, he just nodded his head and gave me a big grin. He sped off and we all roared off after him. Getting to cow trail with Dick Mann and his buddies was one of the best days of my motorcycling career."

Cow trailing is a casual and unstructured sport. The American version of organized cow trailing by the rule book is called Enduro. World class organized cow trailing is known as the International Six Days Enduro (ISDE), called during Dick Mann's competitive career the International Six Days Trial (ISDT). The ISDT is the most difficult and prestigious off-road motorcycle endurance event on Earth, frequently referred to by its followers as the Olympics of motorcycling. It first took place in Great Britain in 1913, and has run annually ever since except when interrupted by world wars. During motorcycling's glory days, when practically every industrialized nation had its own motorcycle industry, the Six Days was devised as a nationalistic contest to determine whose machines were the best designed and most reliable. National teams competed for two highly prestigious awards: the World Trophy, for six-member teams, and the Silver Vase, for four-member teams. In the early days of the event, the Trophy Team could ride only motorcycles made in its own country. To even ride in the Six Days is an indication that one is among his nation's best off-road competitors.

ISDT riders competed on 150 or more miles of difficult trail each day over a period of six consecutive days, trying to maintain a minimum speed, enforced at various points—called "checks" or "controls"—throughout the event. For arriving late at a check, the rider lost points. Although the rules have been modified from time to time over the years, during the 1970s the essence of the event was to test the reliability of the motorcycle as well as the skill and endurance of its rider. Certain repairs were allowed, but no one was permitted to touch the motorcycle except its rider. Unlike an American enduro, points are not lost for arriving at a check early, so emphasis is placed on speed over challenging terrain. Describing his first Six Days experience, American off-road endurance champion John Penton said in 1962, " You could call it a pure cross-country race. The idea is to get to the next control early enough to work on the bike. Every single day is tougher than the entire 500 mile Jack Pine enduro." The Jack Pine, conducted in the sand dunes and pine forests of Michigan, was one of America's most difficult endurance events.

While riders had to stay on time on the trail, it was also necessary for them to earn bonus points in special tests designed to measure racing—sometimes on pavement—and hill climbing skills. The ISDT was purely an amateur event, with no prize money awarded to the competitors. Rather, for recognition the riders received simple Olympic-style medals: a gold for a perfect score on the trail, plus requisite bonus points; a silver for less than 50 penalty points; and a bronze for finishing the event. Those small medals are the most cherished objects in the world of off-road motorcycling. To just finish the Six Days is no mean feat, and while Americans have dominated every other aspect of the international sport at one time or another over the past 30 years, American teams have always struggled with the ISDT. After nearly forty years of trying, America has won the Watling Trophy twice (in 1972 and 2001) and the Silver Vase once (in 1973), but they've never been in the hunt for the World Trophy, repeatedly losing to smaller nations with lesser resources. Dick Mann thinks he knows why.

From his teenage years, Dick Mann was fascinated by European aspects of the motorcycle sport. He read about and followed the progress of the world motocross and trials championships before most enthusiasts in America had even heard of such events. He considers the ISDT a superior and more modern form of competition than traditional American enduros, where the rules dictate penalties for arriving at a check point either early or late. It is a complex system wherein the rider receives a greater penalty for being early than being late. Mann believes that the AMA and other off-road organizations should have embraced the European rules for off-road competition years ago, as they eventually did with motocross. He explains, "Enduros are basically a 1906 event planned around belt-drive Harleys. They hoped back then that the belt wouldn't come off and that they could stay on schedule with a motorcycle that was pretty primitive. If a rider was really good he could win. Enduros are still operated under the same basic philosophy, but with motorcycles that are reliable and technically superior.

And guys use digital clocks and computer technology to handle the time keeping. Enduros are still a lot of fun, but today they are out of style. Kids today like to ride fast, and in enduros you can get penalized twice as much for riding too fast, so you have to learn how to keep time, which doesn't interest those kids in the least." Mann prefers the IDST because, as he says, "They are not trying to make you late at the next check point, so the trail does not have to be severe, and can be negotiated by riders of all skill levels. If the rider can negotiate the trail for six days, the event is won or lost in the special tests."

Most riders today, Mann points out, learn their basic skills in motocross. He says, "They do their two or three years in motocross and learn how to ride really well. But most guys seem to burn out. They get tired of going to a race every week

Dick Mann, ready to start the second day of an ISDT qualifying event. Mann qualified to ride on the American team at the ISDT several times in the early 1970s, but his only opportunity to make the trip came in 1975. *Rick Kocks photo.*

and doing a little practice and then sitting around for seven hours waiting for their next turn to race for 15 minutes. These guys still want to ride and go fast, but they are tired of motocross, and enduros don't appeal to them because they get penalized for going fast. They are really prime for ISDT-type riding." He concludes, "I think the ISDT is great, and ISDT-type riding is fun. But if we're ever going to win the ISDT and grow a healthy crop of ISDT riders, we'll have to change the system in this country. There is no grass roots program to encourage and develop ISDT riders." The only events in America conducted according to international rules are a handful of Six Days qualifiers for top-flight riders. Nothing similar to the ISDT is available for beginner or journeyman cow trailers and motocross riders, so there is little wonder that Americans have found themselves in alien territory at the ISDT, since it is fundamentally different from what they have been trained to do.

Mann's lifelong dream to ride the Six Days could not be fulfilled while he was campaigning the demanding and time-consuming AMA Grand National Championship series. He actually found time to enter some of the qualifying events and qualify for the American team on several occasions in the early 1970s, but by the time October rolled around and the professional racing season was over, there simply was not enough money or energy left to travel to Europe to compete in the ISDT. Finally, after he retired from professional racing in 1974, Dick Mann got the opportunity to qualify and ride at the Six Days at the Isle of Man in 1975. He received support from his old friend John Taylor at Yankee Motor Company to ride an OSSA in the event.

Marcia Macdonald, a journalist and photographer who had done marketing work for Yankee, was OSSA team manager for the event. Macdonald arranged for many of the team members to depart through Canada, where she obtained favorably priced tickets on Wardair. About that memorable departure, she recalls, "We were at the boarding gate in Montreal, and it was absolute chaos. Our bikes were already loaded, and they were in the process of boarding more than 400 passengers on a stretch 747. They actually came on the public address system and announced that they were making history by carrying more passengers than any airline had ever carried. I looked at Dick and he looked at me, and said, 'In other words, we have just qualified to become the greatest air disaster in aviation history!' "

The team made it safely to London, but there began the usual comedy of errors that always seems to haunt big international events. The truck that Macdonald hired to move equipment to Liverpool, where it would be loaded on the ferry for the Isle of Man, did not arrive. Macdonald and OSSA rider Don Cutler actually shanghaied a man at the airport with an open truck, and persuaded him to make the day-long trip to haul their bikes to Liverpool. With room for no more than three people in the cab, Dick Mann rode with the motorcycles in the back of the open truck, sitting on sacks of coal and breathing diesel fumes all the way to Liverpool. It had to be a reminder of some of his funny and miserable experiences on the road when he was campaigning the national series in the 1950s. Arriving at Liverpool after dark, the driver explained that he had to be back in London for work in the morning, and dumped all of the equipment on the docks. Macdonald says, "We slept on the pier and took turns staying up during the night to guard our stuff."

It was a difficult Six Days for the American team. The weather was wet and ugly, and Bren Moran, a well-liked Six Days veteran, crashed and died of head injuries. Furthermore, Trophy Team hopes were immediately dashed when Tom Penton's bike caught fire within miles of the start on the opening day. Then later that day, Trophy rider Jeff Gerber threw his Penton under a cement truck. The event was criticized by most of the participants because about 70 percent of the course was over public roads. Not only was this not in the spirit of the Six Days, but it gave the United Kingdom riders an advantage, since almost everyone else had to use up a lot of concentration just staying on the correct (left) side of the road.

Macdonald recalls, "Having Dick along was one of the bright spots of the week. Most of our team were young, green, aggressive, flamboyant riders, and they were a handful. They were always in a panic, grabbing tools, getting in the way, and stepping on other people's stuff. Dick, by contrast, was so calm and polite. He was helpful and courteous and always asked permission to get fuel or borrow tools. You would never have known that they were the greenhorns and he was a great champion of practically every form of motorcycling that exists." She continues, "I had gotten where I could identify almost every team member at a great distance, based on their body language and riding style. I could always tell which rider was Dick, and I just loved to watch him ride. He is so smooth and has such beautiful balance. He is a slight man, and doesn't have the body weight to throw a motorcycle around and make it do things it doesn't want to do. Rather, he has learned to ride with such a delicate touch, and never seems to use an ounce of unnecessary energy."

From Dick Mann's point of view, the week probably didn't seem so smooth. On Wednesday Mann was riding through dark woods, hit a rock, and broke a toe. In typical Mann fashion, he states, "That's no big deal for riding, but I didn't get any sleep that night because my toe ached so much." The next day the rear brake backing plate on his OSSA disintegrated. He recalls, "With no rear brake, I could barely get from one check to the next within my grace period. I had to work so hard to stay up, I rode 180 miles that day without ever getting off the motorcycle. I didn't have anything to eat or drink, and I didn't take a leak the whole day. I was still on gold near the end of the day when my chain came off, and I fell to silver. In the meantime, my front fork seals went away, and I had pumped all the oil out of the front suspension, so I was banging along with no suspension and the fork tubes bottomed out."

Mann recalls one little ray of sunshine in his otherwise disastrous day. He says, "I was on my knees working on the chain when I saw a little pair of shoes next to me. I looked up, and here was this British school boy, about 12 years old, impeccably dressed in his uniform, with a little cap on his head. He said, 'Mr. Mann, nice job at the motocross yesterday,' then he turned and walked away." I've often thought about that little boy, and I wish I could find him to tell him how much that meant to me."

Once a cow-trailer, always a cow-trailer. Dick Mann prepares his custom-built Triumph trail bike for a ride in October, 2001. *Ed Youngblood photo.*

Mann also remembers an amusing incident that resulted from his failed rear brake. He says, "The only thing I could do to slow down was use my compression release. In Europe, when you want to pass a slower rider you hit your compression release, he hears the loud sputtering, and gets out of the way. While I was desperately crashing along, trying to stay on time, two Czech riders passed me. They were as cool as could be, cruising along like they were out for a scenic tour. I was about to kill myself trying to stay with them, because I knew they were on time. Of course, every time we came to a turn, I had to hit my compression release to slow down, and they kept looking over their shoulders with a really annoyed expression on their faces. They were wondering who was this stupid American who couldn't ride worth a damn, but kept wanting them to get out of the way!"

The next day Dick Mann had to make a grim decision. He fixed his rear brake before departing in the morning, but he knew he could not finish the event with no front suspension. Consequently, he chose to sacrifice his silver medal by pulling off behind a barn and totally rebuilding his front forks. Dick Mann finished the ISDT and earned his bronze medal. He laughs and says, "If you want to hear about the Six Days, never talk to the gold-medal winners. Everything went right for them. If you want to hear the really great stories, go talk to the bronze-medal guys. Those are the ones that all the awful stuff happened to."

Macdonald was the first woman in history to serve as an ISDT team manager, and the press sought her out for interviews. She discovered that her gender was not the only attention-getter for the Americans that year. Dick Mann had been to England for the Trans-Atlantic Match Races in 1971 and 1972 and had already earned celebrity status in the British Isles. Macdonald says, "The press and fans all knew Dick Mann as one of America's greatest racers, and they were dazzled that among all of his other accomplishments, he was riding the Six Days, and finished to earn a bronze medal."

Without a doubt, a bronze medal at the 1975 ISDT fleshed out an already impressive resume for one of the most versatile champions ever to throw a leg over a motorcycle, but Dick Mann looks back on the experience with disappointment. He says, "I finished one of the toughest motorcycle events on earth, but it made me realize I was too old and beat up to do the Six Days, and I was just taking a place that could have gone to a younger and better rider." This is typical of the quality of character of Dick Mann. Rather than lament the Six Days gold medal he would never earn, Dick worried about the opportunities that his involvement might take from others.

After his experience with the ISDT, Dick Mann did what came naturally: use his knowledge and experience to try to improve the sport. In 1976, he and friend Jeff Hammond and the Richmond Ramblers organized a one-day event based on Six Days scoring and special tests. Mann says, "It was the best event I ever rode, and we tried to get the other clubs in Northern California to organize such events, but we could never stir up any interest." Reflectively, he adds, "It's a shame. I still believe such an approach could add another dimension to the American off-road scene."

18

America Goes Vintage

Dick Mann is America's ambassador of vintage motocross, and solely responsible for the vintage motocross movement.

– Fred Mork, AHRMA chairman

In 1954, the same year that Dick Mann went on the road with Al Gunter and won the ten-mile Amateur championship at Bay Meadows, Ted Hodgdon, Emmett Moore, Henry Wing, Sr., and Henry Wing, Jr. formed the Antique Motorcycle Club of America. The AMCA enjoyed slow but steady growth through the next two decades, then, toward the end of the 1970s, a great interest in the history of American motorcycling began to emerge. Some attribute this phenomenon to the fact that the baby boomers, who had fueled the greatest period of growth in the history of the American motorcycle industry, were turning 30 and waxing nostalgic about their motorcycling memories. Whatever the cause, the AMCA grew to more the than 9,000 members it has today, and local and regional vintage-racing clubs began to spring up throughout the nation. The American Motorcyclist Association began to sanction some of the activity organized by these clubs, and in 1982 it funded and founded the American Motorcycle Heritage Foundation. It is the purpose of the AMCA to encourage the preservation of antique motorcycles, and the mission of the AMHF to create a motorcycle museum, archives, and hall of fame. In September 1986,

Dick Mann aboard his Monark at Metcalf in 1996. *John Gola photo.*

a third national historical organization—the American Historic Racing Motorcycle Association—was formed for the purpose of promoting and bringing greater order to vintage motorcycle racing.

At the time of its formation, AHRMA was a for-profit corporation, solely owned by the New York-based Team Obsolete, an organization that restored and campaigned vintage road racers. As such, it was basically a promotional organization that hoped to bring together the various regional road-racing organizations under a single set of vintage racing rules. AHRMA quickly earned recognition and prestige by affiliating itself with the AMA and seeking the AMA's support in conducting vintage road races as support classes at the AMA's national championship events. Gary Winn, a former member of the AMA's government-relations staff who had left the association to pursue a graduate degree, was hired as AHRMA's executive director. His experience with the operations of the AMA was useful in moving AHRMA rapidly from a fledgling organization to the recognized leader in vintage motorcycle racing it is today.

However, AHRMA's owners soon recognized that it was not going to achieve its for-profit objectives. Money was pumped into AHRMA by Team Obsolete for a little more than a year, but conflict in the parent company resulted in a termination of funding. For all intents and purposes, the organization looked and behaved like a not-for-profit membership organization, and finally its founders realized that is exactly what it should become. AHRMA struggled on without investment capital for another two years, then in early 1989 was reorganized as a member-owned, not-for-profit organization governed by a democratically-elected board of trustees. At the time of this reorganization, the California Vintage Racing Group, a leading west coast club organized by Fred Mork and Mike Green, merged with AHRMA, bringing aboard leadership talent, additional members, and an interest in vintage motocross racing and trials, as well as road racing.

In the fall of 1990, the AHRMA board hired motocross world champion Jeff Smith as AHRMA's executive director. After the demise of BSA in 1972, Smith emigrated to Canada where he went to work for Bombardier in the development of the Can-Am off-road motorcycle, then after retiring from Bombardier, was hired by AHRMA. Smith brought to the job a lifetime of motorcycling experience, energy, and strong leadership and administrative skills. He also brought his wife Irene who has worked tirelessly by his side to develop the organization. Since its reorganization and the creation of an efficient central office, AHRMA has gone from strength to strength, establishing its own magazine, web site, and rider benevolence fund, growing to more than 5,000 members, and sponsoring programs for vintage road racing, motocross, dirt track, observed trials, and off road, which includes hare scrambles and enduro.

Dick Mann, who was on the rules committee of the CVRG, served also on the rules committee of AHRMA before its reorganization. Upon the reorganization of AHRMA, he joined its board of trustees, where he has served for more than ten years. Mann has embraced the vintage motorcycle movement just as he has dealt with every previous experience in his motorcycling career. He spotted the trend early, and took a strategic and studious approach in his involvement. Along with Jim McClinton, Mann joined an old-timers motocross organization strictly for people over 40. This wasn't just a senior class at the local races. They developed their own program with their own philosophy toward racing. Mann says, "In a typical motocross program, everything is geared toward advancement. You keep getting better and moving up through the classes until you become a professional. No one really thinks too much about most of the riders who can't keep getting better and better, and countless numbers of them drop out, or move to some other form of motorcycling where there is less pressure and emphasis on advancement."

Mann explains, "Every one of us in this club had faced the fact that we had seen our best days. We were not going to get any better. We were probably going to get worse, but we still wanted to have fun and ride." As a result, Jim McClinton and Dick Mann scrapped the advancement philosophy and created a program where competitors are observed by a committee of their peers, and placed in a class based on their ability." Dick says, "It can cause some hurt feelings from time to time, but no more so than having to drop out of the sport because you can't keep advancing. As a whole, it is a system that works well, and mature people like it because it keeps them involved, racing at a level where they are less likely to get embarrassed or hurt." The concept of classes based on ability is one of the ideas that Mann and McClinton brought to AHRMA, and it has probably contributed as much as any other single factor to AHRMA's growth.

However, creating a program for seniors based on ability seemed to Mann to address only the human factor. There were also big issues concerning motorcycles and racetracks in the development of a successful vintage program. Catering to the extraordinary demands at the highest level of AMA Supercross, the manufacturers began in the mid-1970s to

Dick Mann, motocrossing a BSA at Carnegie Park in 1995. *John Gola photo.*

design motocross bikes with very long suspension. The combination of long suspension and more powerful engines began to alter tracks, creating unnatural whoops and berms. Track design and suspension became a vicious circle. Tracks grew intentionally rougher and more artificial to challenge the modern bikes, and longer suspensions evolved to cope with the rougher tracks. Eventually, there were few tracks left in America using the natural terrain essential to pre-1970 motocross. Mann says, "You can have the best rules in the world for rider classification and vintage motorcycles, but a vintage program just won't work on the modern tracks. The bikes are not designed for it, and it is not fun." Consequently, the success of AHRMA's vintage motocross program depended upon the identification or development of purely natural tracks, and Dick Mann has become the nation's leading consultant in vintage motocross track design. Dick says, "Promoters and riders were interested in vintage motocross racing, but it just wasn't working to mix vintage in with modern motocross at tracks suitable for modern bikes."

His understanding of the bike/track relationship came straight from Mann's personal experience. As his Class C racing career began to wind down in the mid-1970s, Dick spent more time racing motocross. He says, "As the bikes evolved, I found myself enjoying it less. While I might be able to make better lap times as the bikes improved, I felt that I was less in control. At first I attributed this to age. I thought I was just getting old and that my skills were eroding. Then one day I got to ride a vintage motocross machine over natural terrain. It was marvelous, and suddenly the fun was back. I realized it wasn't me; it was the long-suspension motorcycles and the modern tracks that were spoiling the experience for me, and I knew there must be many more people like me. I started looking for ways to share this exciting vintage riding experience." In an interview in *Cycle News* Mann said in 1994, "It was fun again. After thinking about it, I felt it was very important to preserve

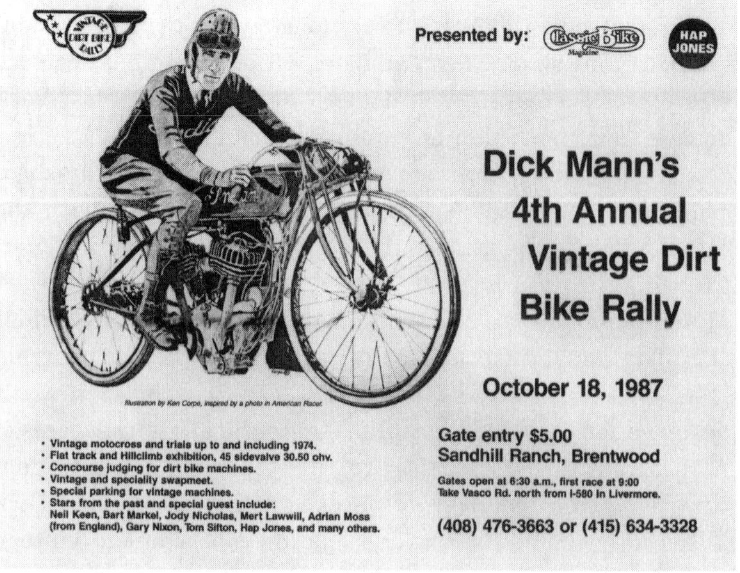

Promotional poster from the 1987 Dick Mann Vintage Dirt Bike Rally. *Courtesy of the Johnny Hall collection.*

a time that had come and gone, a time that I think was the biggest competition movement in the United States. It expanded our sport ten-fold in just a few years." He elaborated, "I wanted a chance to show riders what it was like when motocross was introduced to America, and revisit the strategy and techniques of those early Europeans. These are strategies and techniques that we are losing because they are no longer applicable on modern, man-made, and highly modified tracks. It is not just a matter of riding old machines. For true vintage racing, I cannot overemphasize the importance of recreating the kinds of natural tracks that existed when American motocross was young."

In 1983 Dick Mann started a vintage dirt-bike rally at Sandhill Ranch near Brentwood, California. With his own event, he had the control he needed to design the track and enforce his own rules, based on the motivation for senior riders and vintage-bike enthusiasts to just have fun without getting caught up in the craziness of all-out competition. Mann also understood the power of celebrity, and invited his old buddies, the great personalities of Class C racing, out to the event to sign autographs and conduct exhibition rides on old racing bikes. Some of the special guests were Hap Jones, Tom Sifton, Joe Leonard, Carroll Resweber, Neil Keen, and Mert Lawwill. The Sandhill Ranch events included vintage motocross, trials, hill climbing and dirt-track exhibitions, and a concours. It was a winning formula. With attendance doubling each year over a period of five years, the Dick Mann Vintage Dirt-Bike Rally grew in prestige and popularity, earning national recognition. Mann also began to seek vintage racing converts in other parts of the country, and in the southeast he found enthusiastic support in the persons of Barry Higgins and Beno Rodi.

In the meantime, Mann studiously followed the foreign motorcycle press, as he had throughout his career. He read about an event in England called the British Bike Bonanza, first organized in 1982 by a former scrambles rider named Adrian Moss. The event, designed for pre-1965 motorcycles, had grown in popularity at a rate similar to Mann's event in California, doubling in attendance every year and eventually drawing famous personalities such as John Draper and Dave

Bickers. In 1985 Team Obsolete's Rob Iannucci asked Mann to travel with him to England to help maintain his G50 Matchless that Dave Roper intended to ride in some vintage road races. Mann said, "Only if we can take my dirt bike along too." Iannucci agreed, and Mann traveled to England where he met Moss and competed in a scrambles at Donington Park. Then Moss returned the favor and came to California in 1987 where he raced and won at Sandhill Ranch on a Mann-built Matchless G50 scrambler.

Mann, Derek Wylde, and Moss spent a lot of time discussing rules, and they found themselves in agreement on the importance of limiting suspension to protect the integrity of vintage motocross racing (Incidentally, in England the term "Vintage" has a specific meaning, applying to pre-1930 motorcycles only. The British use the term "Classic" to describe the later era that Americans loosely call "Vintage."). During one of their trips to ride the British Bike Bonanza, Mann and Moss traveled on to vintage-bike events in Sweden, France, and Germany. In France Mann got to race one-on-one with his heroes, Ove Lundell and world champion Sten Lundin. Mann recounts that he was very flattered when he learned that Lundell and Lundin had sent Rolf Tibblin around the circuit to watch Mann and tell them about his lines. Moss recalls, "Everybody knew Dick Mann, and they flocked around him for autographs. People still phone me to ask if Dick Mann is coming over this year."

In 1985 Mann got a phone call from a vintage-bike enthusiast from Denver named John Sawazhki, asking what he could do to help. Mann says, "I was really impressed. It is not often someone just makes a cold call to offer their support. At the moment I did not know what to tell him, but soon we found a project at Steamboat Springs." Rob Iannucci began promoting a vintage road race at Steamboat in 1984, and Dick Mann wanted to add a motocross to the program in 1985. Mann says, "We had arranged for a piece of property, but there were some ownership changes, and suddenly we had no place to put a track. It was John Sawazhki who came to the rescue."

Sawazhki contacted a business colleague who helped locate another piece of land, and loaned them a riding lawn mower.

Sawazhki recalls, “Dick and his friends and I staked out a track in this field, then we got on the riding mower and started mowing down the foot-tall grass. It took us almost three days, and we pretty much wore out this guy’s lawn mower.” Sawazhki laughs, “That’s when I realized what kind of a guy Dick Mann really is. I was amazed at his dedication. What other two-time Grand National Champion do you know who will ride around on a lawn mower for three days to put on an amateur motocross for about 30 guys?” Sawazhki continues, “When I told him we must be crazy, he said, ‘ John, you gotta start somewhere. All we have to do is make sure these guys have fun, and there will be twice as many next year, and it will double every year after that.’ ”

Mann and the Monark, 1994. *John Gola photo.*

During that week Mann recruited Sawazhki to become AHRMA's first national motocross coordinator, motivating him with the same practical philosophy. Sawazhki recalls, "Dick said, 'Don't worry about it being perfect. Just call around and get some tracks and dates around the country. No one has ever done it before, so whatever you do, it will be better than what we have.' " Sawazhki did as Mann advised, creating the nation's first vintage motocross series. The first race took place at Dick Klamfoth's Honda Hills in Linnville, Ohio. Sawazhki says, "It was a big success, and a lot of fun. Mann and I both rode. Klamfoth made us start from a penalty box, and we still finished first and second." Sawazhki adds, "I really believe that if we didn't have Dick Mann, we wouldn't have vintage racing today. We might have something, but it would not be as successful as it is. Dick lived through it, and he paid attention, and has brought all of that learning and experience to AHRMA."

Consequently, when Mann joined the AHRMA board in 1989, he had already been involved in vintage road racing

Dick Mann with one of his BSA vintage motocross bikes in Colorado in 1990. *Photo courtesy of the Dick Mann collection.*

through Team Obsolete, and his ideas on vintage motocross were well thought out, based on experience with the CVRG and his study of systems in California, Great Britain, and throughout Europe. AHRMA, which heretofore had been devoted largely to road racing, found itself by 1990 benefitting from the knowledge and experience of Dick Mann and Jeff Smith, both of whom were keen on motocross. Mann says, "There were some real benefits for AHRMA coming to motocross relatively late. Other organizations had made all the mistakes and found solutions, and we learned from them and wrote a rule book that was pretty much right from the beginning." The result was that motocross became AHRMA's fastest growing and largest program, greatly increasing the membership and revenue of the organization.

Fred Mork, another Bay-area motorcyclist who learned to ride on the hills of Richmond, has a similar opinion. Mork has been AHRMA's chairman of the board for 13 years. He says, "Dick Mann is solely responsible for the vintage motocross movement. He has also brought to AHRMA a lifetime of good will and the ability to network through many influential people. Not only did he help develop the philosophy and a successful rule book, but he has supported the program with his presence and enthusiasm." In support of his claim, Mork points out that fully half of AHRMA's members name vintage motocross as their primary area of interest. Jeff Smith agrees, stating, "Dick Mann was the spur for the whole off-road side of AHRMA," and AHRMA trustee Beno Rodi adds, "Dick's presence and his name alone are 25 percent of AHRMA."

Mann, however, shrinks from this kind of exclusive praise, and is quick to point out that Marsh Runyon, Wayne Sumner, and Ron Clawson have been tireless volunteer leaders from the very beginning of the vintage motocross movement. In addition to these, he credits also Mork, Jim and Bill McClinton, John McCoy, Mike Green, Ernie Stair, John and Peter Ford, Butch Cochran, Mike Lightfoot, Frank Conley, Steve Martin, Mike Atkins, John Geer and Peter Cruttenden, and adds that it is quite impossible to overstate the importance of the depth of volunteer labor and leadership that has brought AHRMA its growth and current level of success.

Dick Mann has also been instrumental in the development of vintage trials. Mann learned that Adrian Moss and others were hosting trials the day before their vintage motocross races in England. Noting also in 1983 that Frank Conley was successfully hosting play days for British trials bikes at Kettelman Hills in central California, Mann incorporated a trials in his Sandhill Ranch program, and built a couple of vintage trials machines. The trials bikes sold quickly, suggesting a growing interest in the sport. Consequently, Mann, Steve Martin, and Peter Cruttenden started organizing events at several California venues, including the ranch of *On Any Sunday* film maker Bruce Brown. The movement got a big boost when modern trials specialists Derek Belvoir and Mike Fenner brought their expertise to vintage trials. Soon the sport was springing up in the Midwest and the East, supported by the BSA Owners Club of Ohio and leaders like Stan Jakubaszek and Bowie Pearre. Other spark plugs for the vintage trials movement were Bob Ginder in the South, Don Smutzler in the Midwest, and Jim Cameron in Southern California. Mann says with obvious satisfaction, "This aspect of the sport has grown to the point that vintage trials are attracting entrants in numbers equivalent to modern trials events."

Dick Mann sometimes became disappointed with the motorcycle press because in the beginning the editors didn't seem to understand the vintage movement. He says, "Many of them seemed to think it is about jalopy racing. They are so wrapped up in technical innovation and the latest thing, they think anything not new is junk." Vintage bikes, he points out, are not junk. They are beautiful machines from a bygone era, and they did their job as well then as modern bikes do today. Vintage racing, Mann explains, is about having fun and taking pride in riding a motorcycle well at your level of expertise. He feels that many more people would extend their racing careers indefinitely—just as he has—if they will give vintage racing a try, rather than continue with taller and more powerful bikes until they hurt themselves or drop out through

AHRMA stalwarts, twice world champion Jeff Smith and twice AMA champion Dick Mann, at Mid-Ohio in 1997. *Rick Kocks photo.*

discouragement. He says, "As we get older, none of us can continue to achieve higher performance forever, and at some point we need to figure out what about motorcycling is still fun, then go with it." He adds, "There's no point in buying a really expensive gun if you can't shoot straight!"

Mann may be right, because AHRMA is not just about nostalgia and old guys racing what they used to race. It is attracting a whole new crop of younger riders who are not nostalgic about vintage racing, but have come to it as a new experience that gives pleasure in its own right. A perfect example is Allen Wenzel, who, at 35, is the youngest member of AHRMA's board of trustees. Wenzel recalls, "I was home on leave from the Army, and my father took me to Dick Mann's vintage event at Sandhill Ranch in 1986. I was hooked. My father still had his last motorcycle—a 1973 Husky—sitting in the garage, and when I got out of the Army I got right into it." Wenzel organized vintage motocross races at Carnegie, California in 1994 and 1995. He was recruited to serve on the AHRMA rider grading committee, and in 1995 ran for the AHRMA board of directors. Wenzel was only six years old when his father's Husqvarna was built. Vintage racing may be a nostalgia trip for people his father's age, but he is too young to have the same memories. In vintage competition, he sees a form of motorcycling that is economical, enjoyable, and sensible. Wenzel says, "Vintage is not about innovation. And it is not about returning to the past. It is about maintaining the status quo at a certain point in time. You can run a bike just as long as you can keep it running, and it will continue to be fun and always be competitive in its class."

There have been motorcycle dealers who have fought the vintage movement, wrongly believing that racing vintage motorcycles detracts from new motorcycle sales. Nothing could be farther from the truth. Vintage and modern motorcycles are totally separate market segments, and vintage significantly

One of Dick Mann's favorite vintage motocrossers is the big Swedish four-stroke Monark. This photo was taken in October, 2001. *Ed Youngblood photo.*

expands aftermarket sales. Mann offers an example: "One day Mike Atkins was in his local dealership buying some oil and gloves, and the dealer quipped, 'You still messing with that old stuff?' to which Mike responded, 'If I were not still messing with this old stuff, I wouldn't even be here spending my money.' " Mann says, "The dealer never made another crack about vintage. Suddenly it dawned on him how he and other dealers benefit from the vintage movement."

While he remains deeply involved in AHRMA's vintage motocross program, Dick Mann has moved on to yet another area of vintage development. One of Dick's great dreams was to ride the International Six Days Trial. He did it only once, and he never earned a gold medal, but Mann has continued to live out his dream by becoming a guiding light in a relatively young vintage enduro movement in America. Officially, the movement began in the autumn of 1997 in Ozark, Arkansas, where the late Leroy Winters hosted the first ISDT Reunion, planned by Winters and Mann. The purpose of the event was to honor America's great Six Days riders, showcase their aging enduro bikes, and give people—old and young—an opportunity to experience and enjoy a classic Six Days-type competition of a bygone era. Mann says, "We wanted to celebrate and honor an event that is gone and will never come again. The ISDE is not the ISDT. It is totally changed in so many ways. The ISDT was an event that recognized team competition and team performance. It did not glorify the individual rider."

As with vintage motocross, Mann feels that the relationship between the course and the bike is equally important to a successful vintage off-road event, and he has devoted a lot of time and effort to the format of the ISDTR, the quality of the trail, and the planning of special events, believing that the emphasis should be on fun rather than achievement. In an article on the AHRMA web site in 1991 he wrote, "We want the entrants of the ISDTR to know how tough the real event was, but we do not want them to experience that part of it. This will be a laid-back, fun event with an enjoyable trail ride and the emphasis on special tests and the reunion dinner."

Mann's age-old philosophy of "do it and they will come" appears to be working again, as evidenced by steady annual growth for the ISDTR. By 2001 the event drew 150 entrants, including more than 40 of the nation's most famous Six Days veterans. In fact, America's most successful team was on hand, including Husky riders Malcolm Smith, Dick Burleson, Ed Schmidt, and Ron Bohn, who won the prestigious Silver Vase in 1973. The ISDTR has spawned a new community of vintage enduro enthusiasts who are actively locating, retrieving, and restoring classic enduro motorcycles, facilitated by worldwide Internet communication.

While the vintage motorcycling movement may be largely ignored or misunderstood by the motorcycle press and the industry's marketing experts, AHRMA's systematic and well-thought-out program probably has a more powerful influence on a vital and healthy modern motorcycle market than anyone realizes, simply because a longer, more enjoyable, low pressure competition career keeps an entire family involved in motorcycling. When mom and dad continue to ride and enjoy motorcycles into their middle years and beyond, a new generation of motorcyclists—their kids—are exposed to motorcycling as a joyous and satisfying experience that cuts across all generations.

In 1992 AHRMA named Dick Mann its Sportsman of the Year, and in 1994 the American Motorcyclist Association bestowed on Dick Mann the AMA Dud Perkins Award, which is the Association's highest honor for service to the sport of motorcycling. While these awards certainly embody recognition of his remarkable and versatile racing career as well as his tireless and dedicated service to AHRMA and the rule-making bodies of the AMA, one might make a strong argument that Dick Mann's greatest contribution to motorcycling had to wait until he stepped away from his own career to become mentor, visionary, and elder statesman of America's vintage motorcycle movement.

19

Dick Mann, Through His Friends

Dick Mann was and is the Michael Jordan of our sport.
– Jim Odom, friend and racer.

Dick Mann has lived a long and fruitful career as a professional motorcyclist. He has excelled in nearly every aspect imaginable of a hard and competitive sport. Throughout, he has adhered unflaggingly to a set of personal values that include persistence, determination, self-reliance, honesty, and a love of hard work and learning. It is not possible to count the lives he has touched and influenced in a positive way, and it is remarkable that within a profession driven by ego, passion, and competitive spirit, he has developed so few enemies. It seems that everyone in American motorcycling, and many at the international level, knows Dick Mann, and the vast majority consider him a friend. He is a complex personality that perhaps few really understand in its depth and entirety. Neil Keen, who met Dick Mann at the old Gardena Stadium short track in 1955 and likely knows Mann as well as any living person, says, "He is a private and mysterious person. I have known him all my adult life, but I don't really know him at all." Perhaps it is not possible for one person to fully understand Dick Mann; however, a fuller picture begins to emerge when we view him through the words of his many friends.

Rivals, competitors, champions, and friends: Gene Romero and Dick Mann, October 1971. *Photo courtesy of the Mert Lawwill collection.*

Humility and Self-Effacement

Carl Donelson, a successful motorcycle dealer in Missouri, first met Dick Mann at a BSA dealer meeting in 1971, just after he had won his second Grand National Championship. He says, "Dick was a lot better rider than he ever thought he was, and he probably never realized how big his following was. When he was staying in the Midwest, he would sometimes ride at Granite City, Illinois. I have seen people come to the ticket window and ask if Dick Mann is there, then get back in their cars and leave if he was not. Yet he always seems shocked that anyone would want to talk to him."

Among his friends, Mann's shyness is legendary. His long-time racing companion Neil Keen says, "He is almost reclusively shy. He is a reluctant hero who never became comfortable with his celebrity status." Chris Draayer says, "Humble is the word I think of when I think of Dick Mann." Allen Wenzel, who was a youthful Dick Mann fan and now works with him as a colleague on the AHRMA board, says about his low-key style, "It's not like you're meeting a rock star. He's just another guy who drove up in his pickup."

Dave Mungenast, who competed ten times at the ISDT, says, "He is one of these people you hold in awe, and you hesitate to go up and bother him. But he dislikes anyone treating him special. He never boasts about himself, but always praises the accomplishments of others. He is a special guy who does not act like a special guy."

Journalist, television commentator, and founder of the Dirt-Track Hall of Fame, Dave Despain says, "Dick Mann was the ultimate privateer. He is a pragmatist, a very practical guy, and a make-do person. The fact that he won Nationals on so many different brands is proof that he ran his own program."

Role Model and Mentor

Because he had such a long career, Dick Mann performed before at least two generations of fans, and over three decades had the opportunity to meet and influence many upcoming riders. Mann does not offer his opinions and advice when they are not solicited, but he is available to those who want to learn, and has much to teach those who choose to listen. Bob Hicks, who met Mann on the scrambles tracks of New England in the 1960s, says, "He is the ideal role model of a professional racer. He earned widespread affection throughout the country, and it had nothing to do with the brand he was riding." Hicks' friend Joe Bolger adds, "He always behaves like a gentleman. Other riders speak well of him. He is always pleasant. He is patient, respectable, quiet, and dignified." Chris Draayer says, "Dick is unselfish. He is an educator, and is always willing to help."

Jim Odom says, "I learned focus and seriousness from Dick Mann, and I respected him for his knowledge and experience. Dick didn't reject anybody; he was there for everyone. Dick supported the sport at every level." Two-times Grand National Champion Gary Nixon says, "Bugs was kind of like my mentor and big brother. I had no money and just a bike, and he helped take me around. I learned so many things from Bugs. He taught me how to be a racer." Dave Aldana says, "He was the guy I wanted to be like, because he could do anything." Gene Romero says, "I always looked up to Dick Mann. He and Neil Keen were kind of the elder statesmen of motorcycle racing."

Jim Rice states, "Dick Mann was my hero. I wanted to be like him. As I got to know Bugs on a personal level, I found that he would say things that were so perfect, so well thought out. Just about everything he said was substantial and important. The guy is a genius."

Twice Grand National Champion and three-time road-racing world champion Kenny Roberts says, "Dick was very helpful. I met him when I was a junior and he was winding down his career. He shared his experience and taught me how to set goals. One time he said, 'Kenny, you have to decide if you want to party or want to race.' We talked about chassis and bike setup, and Dick was always right. He didn't have a lot to say, but when he did you listened."

Work Ethic and Self-Reliance

Neil Keen says, "Dick worked at racing. He worked like a dog at racing. He could make it look so easy, but I know how hard he worked at it." Motorsports photographer Dan Mahony says, "Dick had a lot of natural talent, but he worked very hard at learning how to race." Dick Hammer says, "Bugs was a superman. He could ride anything. He was independent and did all his own work. He could tear an engine down and fix it between the heat and the final." Walt Fulton says, "Maybe Dick would have gotten more sponsorship and support if he had done things someone else's way, but he always ran his own program and did things his way."

Character

Tom Clark, who met Mann at Daytona in 1959 and rode with him on the BSA factory team in 1960, says, "Bugs was a person driven from within, but he never had an attitude. If he ever made an enemy, I don't know who it was." Motorsports photographer Dan Mahony says, "I've never seen Dick Mann get mad at anybody, and I don't recall anyone ever saying anything bad about Dick Mann." Friend and Six Days rider Charlie Vincent concurs, "He is a man of good will. I've never known anyone who could say something bad about him."

Claude McElvain, who sometimes worked as Dick Mann's pit man, recalls, "At Santa Fe one year he jammed his thumb so

Mann, flanked by friends Mert Lawwill and Jimmy Odom at the Houston short track in 1970. *Mahony Photo Archive.*

bad, he couldn't even push the button on the truck door. But we went on to Peoria and he set fast time and won his heat race. We were set to win, then he broke a chain. He just calmly changed into his street clothes and watched the races like the rest of the fans. I was amazed that this kind of disappointment didn't make him angry." Bill Tuman said, "Bugs is a good guy. He gets along with anyone, in any situation. If the bike fell apart, he would smile and say that was just part of racing."

John Taylor, who hired Dick Mann to develop frames for OSSAs and his Yankee project, says, "He is very determined, but mild-mannered. He is very fair, and never a quitter. He is a special guy." Ed Kretz, Jr. says, "Bugs is always a good sport. You can go into a corner with him and not worry about him running you off the track." Four-time Grand National Champion Carroll Resweber says, "Bugs is quiet, and such a nice guy. If you ever need any help, he will help you."

Dick Mann and Mert Lawwill at the Charity Newsies in 1971. *Rick Kocks photo.*

Professionalism

Babe DeMay, who raced with Dick Mann on the Kansas circuit, says, "Dick Mann was very easy going. He never gave anything away on the racetrack, but he was always fair and clean and in control." Daytona winner Ralph White echoes, "He was a fierce competitor, but never rode dirty. He always knew what he was doing."

Nineteen-sixty-nine road-racing world champion Kel Carruthers, who battled furiously with Dick Mann during the 1971 season, says, "I could trust riding with Bugs. He was not beyond giving me a little shove in the turns, but he always knew what he was doing and never put us in danger. My problem was that he had that big BSA and I had a little Yamaha, and I couldn't shove back!"

Gunnar Lindstrom, who competed with Mann at the AMA's first professional motocross race, says, "I thought Dick Mann was one of the most ambitious and dedicated riders. He was one of the few who made a living at it. There were other riders in the States who had more talent than ambition. I really respected Dick. He could race motocross with me, then he would go off into the dirt-track world and do things I didn't even understand." World champion Torsten Hallman concurs: "Dick Mann is a really nice guy, friendly, and helpful and fair, but he was really serious about his racing."

John Taylor, who sponsored Mann on an OSSA at the 1975 ISDT, says, "He was the most accomplished professional rider this country ever produced. Even Kenny Roberts did not excel at motocross and enduro."

Intellect and Dedication to Learning

Claude McElvain says, "Dick was not a naturally talented guy. He was an observer and a learner. He would walk a motocross track backwards in practice to observe what the better riders were doing." AHRMA director Brian Slark says, "He has an uncanny understanding of chassis dynamics. He is a thinker and a mechanical engineer. When you get a Dick Mann motorcycle, you get a whole lifetime of experience of a Number One rider."

Lindstrom says, "I met other riders in the States who had more talent, but Dick had ambition and dedication. He was a dedicated professional and constantly worked to learn more and become better. I had the ultimate respect for this guy."

AHRMA chairman Fred Mork says, "He has an inquisitive and soul-searching intellect. He always has a different way of looking at things, and will defend his point of view with the courage of his convictions. But he is also a team player and will support the board when a decision has been made." Long-time friend Jim Cameron says, "Dick Mann is smart and has a wide range of knowledge. He is a Civil War expert and a student of history, in addition to knowing practically everything there is to know about motorcycles." Grand National Champion Mert Lawwill says, "Bugs is one of the smartest people I've ever known."

Humor

Most people know Dick Mann from his professional racing environment, where he was businesslike and often serious. However, he has a sharp wit and a dry sense of humor. He is a master of the quip and the one-liner. Often, he uses his sense of humor to poke fun at himself. For example, once a star-struck fan said, "Are you really Dick Mann?"and Mann replied, "I'm all that's left of him."

Ohio motorcycle dealer and former racer Glenn Jordan recalls, "One day I watched Dick at an AHRMA event just ride and ride and ride. It was hot as hell and he was in his 60s, and he was still practicing when the younger guys were quitting. When I finally came in I said, 'Dick, don't you ever get tired?' He replied, 'I think you have to have muscles to get tired. I don't have any muscles!' "

At one time the AMA distributed national championship entry blanks, which included information on the purse structure, to the promoters to publish in their programs. Dick Mann once asked the AMA's public relations officer, "Why do you do that? The public already thinks motorcyclists are stupid or crazy. Is there any better way to prove we are stupid or crazy than to tell the public how little money we are willing to race for?!"

Kathy Donelson once introduced Dick to someone and said, "This guy can walk on water," to which Dick quickly replied, "Only if it isn't very deep."

Don Emde recalls the time Dick Mann got some new racing Dunlops while the rest of the BSA/Triumph team stayed with Goodyears: "I asked Dick, 'How are those new Dunlops?' and he said, 'I don't think I'm going fast enough to tell.' "

Paul Dean, who was a colleague of Dick's at Yankee Corporation, was visiting Dick at his shop one day. He describes it as a typical shop with parts everywhere and pipes and frames hanging from the rafters, but he noticed an expansion chamber that was cut off in the middle with a metal plate welded over the end. Dean took it down and said, "Dick, how does this work?" Mann took the pipe from him and replied, "Pretty good, except every few miles you have to unbolt it and let the noise out." He then shook the pipe like he was dumping something out of it, while making roaring engine noises. Dean says, "I knew I had been had. Dick made up that pipe and hung it there, just waiting for suckers like me to come along."

Dick Mann, Mert Lawwill, and their wives would sometimes visit movie producer Bruce Brown at his ranch north of Santa Barbara. Brown says, "We would usually sit around and eat and talk about what we could do and places we could go, but we would just talk and never go anywhere. One day Dick said, 'We're always talking about dumb places to go that we never go to. How about today we talk about someplace really neat like Tahiti, then not go there either.' "

One day Dick Mann was visiting John Sawazhki and looking at his motorcycle collection, which included a rare Swedish four-stroke Lito. Dick was crazy about the bike, and asked Sawazhki how it handled, and Sawazhki confessed he had never ridden it. Sawazhki says Dick was silent for a moment, then he said, "That's okay. When you're dead and gone, someone else will ride that motorcycle." Sawazhki adds, "I couldn't quit thinking about that remark, so the next day I rolled it out and rode the damned thing."

Joe Leonard is big and tall, unlike the diminutive Dick Mann. Leonard says, "Bugs called me Big Joe, and he would say, 'Big Joe, I like to ride against you, because that gives me three more horsepower in my back pocket.' "

Skip Van Leeuwen says, "Dick was always so quiet and reserved, you never knew he had a sense of humor. He would come to the bar after the races at Ascot, but he never imbibed. One night he was there with his buddy Dick Dorresteyn, and we had this north/south thing going, always arguing over who was better, the Bay Area riders or the Los Angeles riders. Dorresteyn and Bob Bailey got into tossing down shots and arguing about who was the better man. They had tossed down 12 or 13 shots, then suddenly, without any warning, Bailey just fell over like a tree and hit the floor out cold. I have never seen Dick Mann laugh so hard about anything. He thought it was so funny he could hardly breathe."

Dick Mann's sense of humor is characteristically good-spirited, but Joe Bolger recalls one time when Dick employed a one-line comeback in justified irritation. Bolger says, "I was talking with Dick, who was sitting on the back of his truck at Laconia. He had just set a very fast time. It was very hot, and

Old partners in crime, Dick Mann and Bob Hansen, back together at AMA Vintage Motorcycle Days in 1997. *Rick Kocks photo.*

he was sweating and exhausted. Some character with about sixteen cameras around his neck came by and said, "Hey, that was a pretty good time for an old man," and Bugs shot back, "That was a pretty good time for a young man!"

Leadership

World champion Jeff Smith, who has served with Dick on the AHRMA board, says, "He is quite a diplomat, but he is an iron fist in a velvet glove. He is very faithful to his ideas and willing to follow through and work hard to make them work. He is stubborn, but always listens to the ideas of others." Gary Winn, who was AHRMA's first executive director, says, "Dick has very good insight into how an organization should be run. He always sticks to his principles, but is tactful and firm. He is a gentleman, and always kept his word."

Motorcycle enthusiast and AHRMA legal counsel Ted Bendelow says, "He has made a substantial contribution to the AHRMA board. He is analytical and approaches problems differently from others. He is a mature thinker with a broad sense of perspective. He has a global understanding, but always takes the point of view of the enthusiast. He sees the big picture."

20

Dick Mann Today

I don't relax. I go to sleep at night, that's it. I don't like to relax. I'll have plenty of that . . . someday.

– Dick Mann, 1983

Dick Mann stopped chasing AMA championship points in 1974, but he did not stop racing professionally. In fact, he broadened his program, racing selected Class C events, professional motocross races, and the IDST qualifiers. At Class C events he rode his Triumph or a 750cc Yamaha twin sponsored by Champion Frames, and he used one of his BSA thumpers to race motocross. He raced in the Midwest, winning the non-national June TT at Peoria and several half-mile events. Then at San Jose a rider crashed in front of him, and Mann, seeing that there was no choice but to hit the fallen motorcycle, yanked back on the handlebars to try to ride over it rather than have it flip him forward for a header. Mann says, "It launched my motorcycle about 50 feet through the air and right through the fence. I stepped off the flying bike, landed on my heel and broke it, and went tumbling through the hole in the fence right behind the motorcycle." The injury put Mann on crutches and ended his professional season, so he and Paul Hunt went to Italy to be spectators at the ISDT. While in Italy Mann visited the SiDi boot factory, and for a time became an American importer for the company. At that time, he and Jeff Hammond

Dick Mann and some of his cow-trailing companions Mike Atkins, John Geer, and Bill McClinton. Every motorcycle in the photo is a Dick Mann creation. *Ed Youngblood photo.*

partnered to build a high-quality boot, but realized that a high priced product would not survive in a market where the Japanese manufacturers had begun to dump their boot inventory at fire-sale prices.

At the Six Days at the Isle of Man in 1975, Mann got a look at a new Yamaha four-stroke prototype, the bike that went into production as the TT500. Mann was happy to see a new, big four-stroke single come onto the market, so he bought one. He liked the engine and many features of the bike, but did not like the way it handled. Ever the innovator, Mann designed a new frame for the motorcycle and rode it in the 1976 ISDT qualifiers. The frame was very successful, and people started buying them. They were designed so an average mechanic could retain and install all of the parts from his production Yamaha, converting over to the new frame in less than a day. Between 1976 and 1981 Mann produced over 200 frames for the TT500, plus high-performance frames for the 370 Suzuki and the Honda RX500, expanding from his production of BSA B25 and B50 frames that he had been manufacturing since 1972.

As the manufacturers began to improve their chassis and the business of aftermarket frames for Japanese motorcycles played out, Mann got into the gray-market automobile business in 1981, converting European-spec cars to U.S. specifications. As always, his innovative mind prevailed, and he developed a way to install safety door guards without dismantling the doors. This saved a lot of time and increased profits, but Dick Mann did not like working on cars. He says, "The work sustained me, but it simply was no fun. I think I have enjoyed almost every motorcycle project I've ever started, but working on exotic and expensive cars was just boring." However, it was at this time that Mann became involved in the old-timer's motocross program, and began, in 1983, to promote his vintage event at Sandhill Ranch. He says, "I had begun to build vintage motocross bikes for my own use. I really enjoyed it, because it was just like when I was building my own professional racing equipment thirty years ago. I built a really nice Gold Star, and someone wanted it really bad and was willing to pay more than I had in it. So I sold it and built me another one. Then the same thing happened, and I sold it, too." Soon Dick Mann was working as many hours a day as he chose to, building vintage racing motorcycles, mostly big British singles. For the past 15 years he has consistently cranked out six to eight motorcycles a year, and is always about a year and a half behind in his orders. His bikes are so prized that he has no need to advertise, but relies simply on word of mouth.

John Sawazhki says, "You might as well get in line if you want a Dick Mann racer, because you just don't see used ones come onto the market. People who have them like them so much, they rarely get rid of them, even if they stop racing them." Sawazhki adds, "They're put together just like Dick put together his racing machines in the 1960s. The gearboxes work so well, the engines are so carefully assembled, and everything works so smoothly, there is just nothing else like them available." Mann hastens to point out that these bikes are not, and are not intended to be, faithful restorations. They are built strictly for racing just as they were in their day, assembled from various bits that work well, including fabricated parts. If a certain bracket off a Triumph or a Norton makes a BSA work better, then that's what it gets. Mann says, "I have done a few true restorations for people, and I don't enjoy it. They take so much time, it is almost impossible to charge enough." On his AHRMA-legal racers Mann spends as much as 200 hours each, but charges a price equivalent to about 100 hours at modest shop rates. It is estimated that today there are more than 70 Dick Mann bikes in the country, about half of which are trials bikes. Mann laughs, "Thanks to AHRMA, today we have more British four-stroke racers in the United States than were ever sold here in the first place."

In 1978 Mann was contacted by Gene Hartline, an old midwestern racing buddy, asking him to do some stunt work on the movie "Deathsport," starring David Carridine and Claudia Jennings. Dick says, "It was a futuristic movie and we were riding motorcycles all decked out in futuristic body work. I was one of the bad guys chasing the hero, and John Hateley was Carridine's stunt double." The plot called for Carridine (Hateley) to escape the villains by leaping his motorcycle off a cliff. Of course, being lowlifes and cowards, the villains were

Dick Mann and his Tririel hybrid (Ariel frame with Triumph engine), photographed in October, 2001. *Ed Youngblood photo.*

afraid to follow. Hartline tells an amusing story about working on another movie with Mic Rogers, one of the best stunt coordinators in the business. Rogers did all the stunt work for *Braveheart* and is a friend of Mel Gibson and other top stars. Hartline says, "We were taking a break, sitting around talking about motorcycles, and someone started talking about how Dick Mann was building vintage motocross bikes." Rogers mentioned that he would love to have a Dick Mann BSA Gold Star motocrosser, and Hartline said, "Call him up. He's probably in his shop right now." Hartline continues, "Rogers said, 'I can't do that! I can't just pick up the phone and call Dick Mann!' We really got a kick out of that. Here's a guy who has private numbers for Gibson and Spielberg and all kinds of famous people, and he's afraid to call up Dick Mann!" As it turns out, they called Mann and Mic Rogers placed an order for a vintage racer.

Dick and his wife Kay met in the 1960s when Dick was on the professional racing circuit and Kay was married to professional racer Jim Corpe. Mann also worked with Corpe at Yankee Motors, where he was production manager. Both Dick and Kay became divorced in 1968 and began to see each other when they could, although Kay lived in Illinois and Dick was in California. In 1976 Kay moved to Pinole with her job, and she and Dick began to see each other more often. After both of their mothers died in 1981, they decided to get married. Kay facetiously refers to their 13 years of dating as "their engagement." Dick says, "We each had two kids, and they were all out of the nest. When our mothers died in 1981 we were both on our own, and we couldn't see any reason not to get married." He smiles, "I guess we decided we were both old enough and had learned enough by then that we might not screw it up!" Kay is also a motorcycle enthusiast, and rides vintage motocross, using a beautiful little 350 BSA named Beatrice. Beatrice is, of course, one of Dick's creations.

Richmond, which had always been a rough town, turned outright dangerous in the 1980s with the emergence of a drug culture. Violence was rampant and at one point the National

Dick and Kay Mann with Kay's 350 BSA called Beatrice. *Ed Youngblood photo.*

Guard was brought in just to help keep Richmond High School open and functioning. Dick's shop, on Ohio Street, was in a particularly nasty part of town. He says, "I started carrying a sidearm to work, and I kept a shotgun propped by the door. Kay and I finally got enough of it. That was just no way to live, and we started looking for a place to relocate." The Manns considered several locations, including Oregon, but settled on Gardnerville, Nevada, just south of Reno at the base of the Sierra Nevada mountains, where they moved in 1993. Rising up 10,000 feet from their back yard is Job's Peek, and looking eastward from their front porch and garden is the 15-mile-wide fertile plain of the Carson River valley, bounded by the Pine Nut mountain range. Just 50 yards down the drive toward the road is Dick's shop, containing his racing bikes, machining tools, and several big singles in various states of assembly. It is a good life, a life that both Dick and Kay have earned and thoroughly enjoy.

All of the children and grandchildren live in the Bay Area where Dick and Kay can visit them frequently. Dick's children are Viann, 43, with three sons: Jeff, Danny, and Matthew; and Scott, 39. Kay's children are Ken, 42, with a son, Joseph; and Katie, 40, with a son and daughter, Spencer and Sarah.

Except among the AHRMA community where he was actively involved in developing vintage activity, Dick Mann somewhat fell from public view during the decade and a half following his retirement from the AMA Grand National series. This, however, began to change in the 1990s with a growing interest in America's motorcycling history and traditions. To a certain extent, this trend was stimulated by the opening of the Motorcycle Hall of Fame Museum (at that time called the Motorcycle Heritage Museum) in August of 1990, and the activities fostered by the American Motorcycle Heritage Foundation. The AMHF began to host a breakfast at Daytona every year to honor the great personalities of the motorcycle sport. In 1992, it also initiated an event called Vintage Motorcycle Days that has grown to a summer festival where 50,000 people gather to watch vintage racing and see rare and historic motorcycles. Each year Vintage Motorcycle Days is built around a commemorative marque and a historical hero, who is designated its Grand Marshal.

In 1997 the commemorative marque for Vintage Motorcycle Days was Honda, and Dick Mann was named its Grand Marshal in recognition of his remarkable career in general, and specifically his legendary ride at Daytona in 1970 that took Honda into the winner's circle. Replicas of the Hansen-tuned Honda Four were on display. In addition, between 1992 and 1997, BMW of North America sponsored a promotional campaign called The BMW Legends. BMW brought to key events—including Vintage Motorcycle Days—an eighteen-wheeler filled with motorcycles, and hired many of the great personalities in American racing to ride them. These included riders like Yvon DuHamel, Don Emde, Bart Markel, Roger Reiman, Gary Nixon, Chris Draayer, Don Vesco, and of course, Dick Mann. The BMW Legends series was enormously popular with the fans, and did much to bring great riders back into the limelight and give them the public recognition they deserved. For Dick Mann, the BMW Legends series put him back in touch with his adoring fans, but it was also a bit of an eye-opener for him and several other riders. Mann explains, "Getting on a road racer again brought back my vision problem in the worst way. The BMW was equipped with a standard street muffler, and I could not ride it by ear. I kept having to look down at the tachometer, then back up at the track, then back at the tachometer, and I just couldn't do it. Bart was also struggling with getting back up to speed on a road course, and one day we came in from a race and I said, 'Bart, we don't need to be out there. I think we're just getting too old for this kind of nonsense.' It really made me feel bad to admit it was time to quit, but I think Bart was relieved to learn that someone else felt the same way. We had our fun, thanked BMW, and turned in our Legends rides so BMW could give them to some other worthy champions."

In addition to the establishment of a motorcycle museum, the American Motorcycle Heritage Foundation established the Motorcycle Hall of Fame, into which Dick Mann was inducted in 1998. Then, in July 1999, Mann was diagnosed with cancer of the throat, and underwent surgery on August 22nd. He says, "It was centered in the mechanism that allows you to swallow, and they removed a portion of my voice box, some of the base of my tongue, and the lymph nodes on both sides of my neck. Kay and I agreed we would allow the doctors to pursue the most aggressive approach possible. In addition to the surgery, I got chemo for 24 hours a day for a full week. I went through two rounds of chemo like that, and got radiation treatment at the same time." Because the surgery limited his ability to swallow, Mann was given a feeding tube in his stomach and a tracheotomy. He was out of commission and unable to work on his motorcycles for six months, then slowly began to return to his bike building business and his work for AHRMA.

Mann says, "This cancer has been one of the most frustrating experiences in my life. I have always rebounded quickly from injuries, but not this. It has been very slow going." In fact, Mann's surgery was life-threatening. He remained in intensive

Dick Mann today, in his shop in Gardnerville, Nevada. Dick still builds eight to ten AHRMA-legal motocrossers and trials bikes per year. *Ed Youngblood photo.*

care for a week, then even after returning home, the prognosis remained very uncertain. Kay took leave from work and remained at Dick's side continuously for a month. Dick explains, "I had to learn a new way to swallow. I could choke at any time, and Kay had to be with me constantly to help keep the trach and my air passage clear." Mann adds, "The help and good wishes we received from others was tremendous. We got hundreds of cards, more than we could ever respond to; and people sent us money. The donations we received helped us through a very rough time when I couldn't work and Kay had to take leave from her own job. It was very humbling to see such an outpouring of moral and financial support. We will never be able to appropriately say thanks for all the help we got."

Mann has dealt with his bout with cancer just as he dealt with adversity during his racing career. He has remained philosophical and uncomplaining. And, somewhat amusingly to his friends, it brought out his need to innovate and make bad things better. The plastic trach installed in the hole in his

Dick Mann, relaxing at home in 1994. *John Gola photo.*

throat proved an irritation. He told his doctors, but they said that's just how it was. The little trach, they explained, was a one-size-fits-all item, and was bothersome to a lot of patients. Mann was just astonished at their attitude that bad was good enough. Kay reports, "One day I came home from work, and there was Dick at the kitchen table, working away at the trach with a piece of emery paper. He had shortened it and was polishing off any remaining rough edges." When Dick's doctors learned about his "Mann-made" trach, they were amazed and asked him if he could do the same work for other patients who were having a problem.

By December 2000, Dick Mann was back aboard a motorcycle, cow trailing with his friends and riding vintage trials. However, the knee that he had broken on the Kansas circuit in 1955 began to bother him to the point that he could not work or sleep. He toughed it out until his AHRMA responsibilities at AMA Vintage Motorcycles Days West were behind him in April, then submitted to surgery to replace the knee. Mann says, "I studied the situation, and I was very impressed with some of the technology that had come along. A new kind of ceramic prosthetic knee was available, and I decided it was time to get it done." Mann came through the knee surgery well, and as he had in the past, astonished the medical personnel with his ability to heal. He recalls, "They couldn't believe their eyes when I walked into my first physical therapy session, rather than arrive in a wheel chair."

However, shortly after the knee surgery, Mann experienced a serious setback in his recovery from cancer. He explains, "The doctors were baffled, and still can't explain it. At first they thought it was somehow connected with the knee surgery, but that didn't make sense. It was not a recurrence of cancer, but it was some kind of regression in my efforts to recover from the radiation treatments." Badly weakened, and back into slow recovery mode from his cancer experience, Mann again had to stop riding motorcycles. Although Dick Mann's life has been significantly altered by cancer, he has gradually returned to a lifestyle far more productive and active than most men his age. He rises at 5:30 each morning and puts in up to ten hours a day in his shop, building AHRMA legal motocross and trials machines. Then he spends his evenings doing AHRMA business with Kay. His AHRMA duties and motocross track design work have him traveling again, and he is back riding. Kay also puts in long hours. In addition to her volunteer work for AHRMA, she rises at 4:30 each morning to go to work at Carson-Tahoe Hospital where she is a clerk in the X-Ray department.

On December 10, 2001, Dick Mann was up before dawn, looking at the Weather Channel, trying to figure out what was going on in the mountains rising between his back door and the California Central Valley. A vintage trials machine was already loaded in the back of his pickup, and he had a big urge to go riding. This would be the first time he had ridden a motorcycle in eleven months. He tried the weekend before, but the snow above 5,000 feet made the Sierras impassable. Looking eastward through the glass doors of his living room, Mann could see the Pine Nut Range as an irregular black silhouette, bounded above by the soft dawn and below by the line of lights that were Gardnerville, Nevada. Outside it was practically shirt-sleeve warm, but that meant nothing about what might be happening on the mountain. The house had been battered by winds throughout the night, and that meant there would be fresh snow on the Sierras. Today's plan—if the Sierras permitted—was to drive four hours across the mountains to Stockton, rendezvous with some buddies, ride motorcycles for three hours at the Frank Raines ORV Park, then drive four hours back across the mountains, hoping that in the meantime they had not become impassable from additional snow. Kay usually went along on such outings, but today she would stay behind to go shopping and finish some AHRMA paperwork.

It seems like a bit of an ordeal for a few hours of riding, but it's not just about the riding. It is also about old friends on old vintage British motorcycles, and at the end of the day's experience, the bikes, the riding, and the friends are essential and equally important parts of the whole. Yet, for Dick Mann there is something more. He is testing himself against his own high standards, discovering where he stands these days for stamina, skill, and attitude after battling cancer and being off a motorcycle for nearly a year. He is testing his mettle to see where he stands for another upcoming AHRMA season. Illness has added a new dimension to the test, but testing himself is what he has always done every time he threw his leg over a motorcycle, be it the intense and gritty job of earning a living, or the easy joy of cow trailing for fun. As Frank Conner wrote in *Cycle* in 1972, "In Dick's way of thinking, you race against yourself. You might be in the company of motorcycling's toughest competitors, but, at the end of the day, you always raced against yourself."

This morning Mann decided to head north, up the Kingsbury Grade and across the mountains on the old Pony Express route, Highway 50, through Tahoe, and over Echo Summit. It is farther in distance, but less susceptible to the snow than Route 88 to the south. By the time he reached 4,000 feet he was halted by a safety patrol, turning back anyone who did not have tire chains or four wheel drive. Snow this low indicated it might get rough toward the summit, and as he continued up the mountain he saw several cars and SUVs in the ditch. At one point a black Pontiac Grand Prix running an eighth of a mile ahead suddenly yawed into a big, looping slide, crossing two lanes and heading toward the low side ditch. Dick gently touched his brake pedal, and began to evaluate his escape routes. But before he had to make that critical decision to go right, left, or up the middle past the careening Pontiac, it suddenly realigned itself in the lane and continued on. Mann muttered, "Nice save!" and shortly thereafter the Pontiac driver, yielding to Dick's four-wheel-drive and his own jangled nerves, pulled over toward the berm to let Mann by. The pines were so heavily laden with snow there seemed to be no colors in the overcast morning light. Everything was black or stark white, with almost no shades of gray between.

Coming out of the snow on the California side, Mann headed down into the Central Valley, and by the time he got to Stockton, it wasn't even raining. Mike Atkins and John Geer were waiting at John's place. Geer's garage is like a small AHRMA museum, containing a couple of Dick Mann-built

Dick Mann, photographed at AMA Vintage Motorcycle Days in 1997. *Rick Kocks photo.*

Dick Mann, Grand Marshal at AMA Vintage Motorcycle Days, 1997. At that event Mann was reunited with Bob Hansen and had the opportunity to ride laps of honor on restored Honda road racers. *Rick Kocks photo.*

BSAs, a banana-frame Six Days Jawa, a couple of Greeves, a beautifully restored CZ motocrosser, and several other vintage racing bikes in various stages of repair and restoration. The men transferred Dick's bike into John's trailer, and headed south on I-5 for Frank Raines Park, where they planned to meet Bill McClinton. By the time they arrived, McClinton was already unloaded and riding his 441 BSA single. He had obviously been at it for a while, because he was still wearing a rain suit from the morning. The others quickly unloaded Mann's Tririel (a 500cc Triumph twin in an Ariel frame), Geer's Greeves, and Atkins Norial (a 500cc Norton ES2 single in an Ariel frame). As the men suited up in serviceable and battered gear (Dick Mann reckoned his boots were about 15 years old), a couple of young motocrossers circled around in their fancy color-coordinated Fox riding outfits, eying the collection of strange British motorcycles. "Are them things four-strokes?" one Honda CR-mounted rider asked. "All of them except the Greeves," someone replied. Studying the collection until he spotted the bike with "Greeves" on its side cover, the young man asked, "How come it's got two shifting levers?" Someone answered, "It doesn't. That's just a heel/tow shifter so you can shift up or down while you're standing up." Anticipating the next question, he quickly added, "It's an observed trials bike." All four machines, each possessing a kind of simple, functional beauty, were Dick Mann creations.

After three hours of negotiating the rugged terrain of the coastal mountain range, the four riders decided to call it a day. Discussing the ride, Mann seemed a little exasperated, stating, "I fell off three times." Atkins replied, "No you didn't. All you did was step off the bike a couple of times. At least we didn't have to lift the bike off of you, like last time." Geer and Mann both laughed. Looking at his Noriel, Atkins said, "This thing will be idling along in a slow section, then all of a sudden it will make a big cough and backfire through the carb. It doesn't stall, it just kind of burps. What makes it do that?" Mann replied, "What makes it do that is the part called 'Norton.' " As the others laughed, Mann added. "They've always done that. Jeff Smith used to ride one of these in trials, and they tried their best to make it quit doing it, but nobody could figure it out. It's just a Norton!" On the way back to Geer's place, the men talked about Tommyville, a vintage Grand Prix scheduled to take place the following weekend. It was the last event of the season—the last hurrah for vintage die-hards who wanted one more ride before Christmas.

Arriving back in Gardnerville late that night, Dick found Kay waiting up for him. "How did it go?" she asked. "Ah, okay, I guess. I still just don't feel like I've got it. My timing is off," he replied. "Did you fall down?" "No, not really." "Well, that's good!" Kay knows how important it is to Dick to rise to his self-imposed standards. She knows how important it is for Dick to believe he is coming back on form after his illness. Then Kay began to recount the phone calls she received during the day from people calling about the 2002 AHRMA rules and schedule. AHRMA has become such an important part of their lives. It is what Dick's life work in motorcycling has evolved into. Dick Mann does not want to rest, and AHRMA enables him to continue to work hard, almost as hard as he did nearly five decades ago when he mounted tire after tire under the blazing Kansas sun while other riders tried to catch a fitful nap in a spot of shade under the trailer. As then, much of life today is still on the road. Dick Mann travels over 50,000 miles a year attending AHRMA board meetings, going to races, inspecting tracks, designing tracks, and carrying out other services for the growing American vintage motorcycle movement. Kay accompanies him on many of those trips, serving as one of the countless volunteers who energize the organization.

And though it is something he never intended, AHRMA has brought him a higher level of recognition than ever before. The whole American motorcycling community has begun to recognize and appreciate the remarkable contribution of this shy and quiet man. His fans come from every segment of the sport, and this alone is a tribute to his versatility of achievement. The Japanese have a special recognition for such people. Those who have contributed immeasurably to their culture, who have achieved vast and useful knowledge, who have contributed a lifetime of work to the betterment of all, who have performed feats that bring honor to the nation, they call Living National Treasures. In America we do not have such a title, but Dick Mann is just such a person, whether he likes it or not.

While Dick Mann is uncomfortable with fame and cringes from adulation, he cannot hide from the fact that to America's motorcycling community he is a hero, albeit, as his old buddy Neil Keen says, "a reluctant hero." As with all things, in response to such adulation Dick Mann refuses to let praise turn his head, but continues to measure himself by his own tough standards. When a British journalist recently asked him what it is like to be a hero, Dick Mann replied, "If you think that's what I am, then I am flattered. But if you think I think that's what I am, then I'm embarrassed."

Author's postscript: Just as this book was going to press in the Spring of 2002, Dick Mann resumed competitive riding, entering the AHRMA 60+ class at AMA Vintage Motorcycle Days West at Sears Point Raceway. He won!

A

A Dick Mann Chronology

1934 Born June 13th, in Salt Lake City.

1942 Moves with family to Richmond, California.

1946 Gets San Francisco Examiner newspaper route and Cushman scooter.

1949 Buys first motorcycle, a 125cc BSA Bantam, from Hap Alzina.

1950 Finishes third in turkey run, wins a goose.

1951 Trades Bantam in for a 350cc BSA. Enters first scrambles race, in Fairfield, California.

1952 Graduates from Richmond High School, goes to work at Standard Oil, takes a pay cut to work as a gopher for Hap Alzina in Oakland for $1.00 an hour.

Begins to race at Belmont Speedway. Sells 350 BSA and gets a Gold Star dirt-track racing bike. Continues racing at Belmont until 1954.

1953 Begins to race at Tulare and Hollister.

1954 Earns AMA Amateur status, begins to race at Vallejo.

Meets Vido Durante and is offered sponsorship to race the Kansas fair circuit.

Wins the ten-mile AMA Amateur championship at Bay Meadows aboard a borrowed BSA, setting an Amateur track record.

Gets sponsorship from Louie Thomas and embarks on pro tour with Albert Gunter.

Is ranked second Amateur in the nation, behind Brad Andres.

1955 First year to ride Daytona. Runs 4th, falls off, finishes 7th.

Rides the Catalina Grand Prix, officially finishing 4th.

Gets ride from Ang Rossi. Rides local races and travels to Kansas, Nebraska, Colorado, Iowa, and South Dakota with Donnie Smith. Crashes at Stockton, Kansas, breaking left leg.

Gets fired from Alzina's for missing too much work due to racing and injury.

Goes to work at Carl & Walt's, a local BSA dealership.

Finishes 29th in the AMA standings. Joe Leonard is Grand National Champion.

1956 Along with Gunter, gets a factory BSA for Daytona; leads the race until his clutch fails on the 36th lap.

Finishes 15th in the AMA standings. Brad Andres is Grand National Champion.

1957 Gets arrested with Al Gunter at Daytona for testing bikes on a public road.

Breaks into the AMA top ten standings, finishing 6th. Joe Leonard is Grand National Champion.

1958 Rides a factory Harley-Davidson at Daytona, finishes 2nd to Joe Leonard.

Is suspended by the AMA for promoting a rider boycott over purse and racing conditions at Fresno.

Finishes 8th in AMA standings. Carroll Resweber is Grand National Champion.

1959 Rides a Charlie West-tuned Harley at Daytona, finishes 2nd to Brad Andres.

Wins 25-Lap TT at Peoria, Illinois on borrowed BSA owned by Ray Hendershot.

Finishes 2nd in AMA standings. Carroll Resweber is Grand National Champion.

1960 Wins 100-Mile Road Race at Laconia, New Hampshire on a BSA, setting a new track record and lapping all of the field except Carroll Resweber.

Finishes 5th in AMA standings. Carroll Resweber is Grand National Champion.

Wins all three motos at the AMA District 36 motocross championship.

1961 Qualifies 3rd at Daytona, but finishes 39th due to clutch trouble.

Wins 15-Mile Dirt-Track National at Heidelberg, Pennsylvania on a BSA.

Finishes second at Springfield in an official dead heat with Bart Markel, riding with a flat front tire.

Finishes 3rd in AMA standings. Carroll Resweber is Grand National Champion.

1962 Obtains sponsorship from Indian Sales Company on G50 Matchless. Finishes second at Daytona behind the factory Triumph of Don Burnett.

Wins 100-Mile Road Race on Matchless at Laconia, New Hampshire.

AMA bans modified BSA dirt-track frame for G50, Mann continues to race dirt tracks with stock swingarm frame.

Breaks hand at Springfield; returns to racing six weeks later.

Appears with Al Gunter and Neil Keen before the AMA Competition Committee to seek rule changes leading to reduced injuries and fatalities.

Finishes 3rd in AMA standings. Bart Markel is Grand National Champion.

1963 AMA bans G50 from road racing. Mann is not allowed to compete at Daytona.

Mann is seriously injured at a non-National at Freeport, Illinois. Enters and wins the Ascot 50 lap TT aboard Matchless three weeks later.

Wins AMA Grand National Championship by one point over George Roeder.

District 36 dedicates annual Christmas Seals Benefit to local hero, Dick Mann.

1964 Following Dick Klamforth's retirement, Mann's national number is changed from 64 to 2.

Wins 50-Mile Road Race at Windber, Pennsylvania aboard Matchless.

Wins 175-Mile Road Race at Greenwood, Iowa aboard Matchless.

Wins 150-Mile Road Race at Meadowdale, Illinois aboard Matchless.

Wins 25-Lap TT at Peoria, Illinois aboard Matchless.

Crashes into the fence at Sacramento, breaking ribs.

Finishes 2nd in AMA standings. Roger Reiman is Grand National Champion.

Appears with Gary Nixon before the AMA Competition Committee to seek better purses, better officiating standards, and rider representation on the committee.

1965 Wins the lightweight 100-miler at Daytona riding a Yamaha, beating the previous track record by over 3 miles per hour.

Wins 120-Mile Road Race at Wentzville, Missouri aboard Matchless.

Wins 80-Mile Road Race at Nelson Ledges, Ohio aboard Yamaha.

Wins 150-Mile Road Race at Meadowdale, Illinois aboard Matchless.

Withdraws from the road race at Marlboro, Maryland, due to vision problems.

Finishes 2nd in AMA standings. Bart Markel is Grand National Champion.

1966 Takes job at a motorcycle dealership in Hawaii, goes into semi-retirement and decides to race only selected Nationals.

Breaks collarbone at a non-national road race at Carlsbad, California.

Is voted Most Popular Rider by AMA clubs.

Returns to racing by July.

Starts custom frame business.

Becomes a rider representative on the AMA Competition Committee.

Finishes 12th in the AMA standings. Bart Markel is Grand National Champion.

Races against world champion Torsten Hallman at a hare scrambles at Wilseyville, California and finishes second.

1967 Becomes sponsored by Hap Jones Distributing Company.

Wins 12-Mile Dirt Track at Reading, Pennsylvania aboard BSA.

Wins 25-Lap TT at Peoria, Illinois aboard BSA.

Takes a job with Yankee Motor Company in Schenectady, New York to consult and design frames for OSSA and Yankee motorcycles.

Finishes 5th in AMA standings. Gary Nixon is Grand National Champion.

1968 Finishes first American in the 250cc class at the Inter-Am international motocross races at Pepperell, Massachusetts, and at New Philadelphia, Ohio.

Suspended by the AMA for racing an unsanctioned motocross.

Leaves full-time employment with Yankee Motor Company, but continues to provide consultation from west coast.

Does not win a national championship, but finishes 8th in AMA Standings. Gary Nixon is Grand National Champion.

Becomes a delegate to the AMA Competition Congress.

1969 Wins Daytona short track on an OSSA of his own design.

Rides on BSA speed and endurance record team at Daytona, setting speed records for distances of 100 and 150 miles.

Wins 20-Lap Short Track at Hinsdale, Illinois aboard OSSA.

Wins 25-Lap TT at Peoria, Illinois aboard BSA.

Finishes 6th in AMA standings. Mert Lawwill is Grand National Champion.

1970 Wins Daytona 200 aboard Honda.

Wins 25-Lap TT at Castle Rock, Washington aboard BSA.

Crashes with Jim Rice at Sedalia while running 2nd in the AMA point standings, breaks leg.

Finishes 4th in AMA standings. Gene Romero is Grand National Champion.

Defeats Gunnar Lindstrom in the 250cc class at the first AMA sanctioned professional motocross at Croton, Ohio.

1971 Is signed to BSA factory team with Jim Rice, Dave Aldana, and Don Emde.

National Number is changed from 2 to 4.

Wins 20-Lap TT at Houston, Texas, aboard BSA.

Wins Daytona 200 aboard BSA.

Attends the Trans-Atlantic Match Races in England with the BSA team; is designated American Team Captain. Sets fast time at Oulton Park.

Wins 100-Mile Road Race at Kent, Washington, aboard BSA.

Wins 100-Mile Road Race at Pocono, Pennsylvania, aboard BSA.

Wins AMA Grand National Championship.

Honda asks Mann to pilot the Honda Hawk streamliner at Bonneville, but he must decline due to contract with BSA.

Named *Cycle* magazine Man of the Year.

Elected *Motorcycle Weekly* Man of the Year.

Named AMA's most popular rider for second time.

1972 Is chosen for the Trans-Atlantic Match Race Team along with Rayborn, Emde, Baumann, and Nicholas.

Wins Mile National at Homewood, Illinois, aboard a BSA, thus becoming the first rider to complete the Grand National Grand Slam by winning each of the five categories of championships.

Wins his last National at the Peoria TT aboard a BSA.

Ties with Jim Rice for 6th in the AMA standings. Mark Brelsford is Grand National Champion.

Publishes *Motorcycle Ace: The Dick Mann Story,* co-written with Joe Scalzo.

1973 Finishes 10th in the AMA standings. Kenny Roberts is Grand National Champion.

Qualifies to ride on the American team at the International Six Days Trial.

1974 Retires from the AMA Grand National Series, but continues to race professionally.

Wins the Peoria June TT.

Qualifies to ride on the American team at the International Six Days Trial.

1975 Qualifies for the ISDT and earns a bronze medal at the Isle of Man.

1976 Begins a business building high-performance frames for Japanese four-stroke, single-cylinder motorcycles; continues through 1981

1981 Begins business modifying gray-market automobiles to U.S. specifications.

Marries Kay Corpe.

1983 Promotes the Dick Mann Vintage Dirt-Bike Rally at Sandhill Ranch, continues to promote the event through 1988.

1985 Travels to England with Team Obsolete, meets British vintage scrambles organizer Adrian Moss.

Organizes AHRMA vintage motocross race at Steamboat Springs, Colorado.

1989 Joins the AHRMA board of trustees.

1992 Named AHRMA Sportsman of the Year.

1993 Moves from Richmond to Gardnerville, Nevada.

1994 Receives the AMA Dud Perkins Award, the AMA's highest honor for service to motorcycling.

Named by *American Motorcyclist* among top ten dirt-track racers of all time.

1997 Named Grand Marshal at AMA Vintage Motorcycle Days.
Selected to ride for the BMW Legends.

1998 Inducted into the Motorcycle Hall of Fame.
With LeRoy Winters, organizes the International Six Days Trial Reunion.

1999 Is diagnosed with cancer and undergoes surgery on August 22nd.

2002 Returns to competition, winning the AHRMA 60+ motocross at AMA Vintage Motorcycle Days West.

B

Dick Mann's Championship Victories

August 30, 1959	Peoria, Illinois; TT	BSA
June 19, 1960	Laconia, New Hampshire; Road Race	BSA
June 11, 1961	Heidelberg, Pennsylvania; Half Mile	BSA
June 17, 1962	Laconia, New Hampshire; Road Race	Matchless
September 21, 1963	Gardena, California; TT	Matchless
August 2, 1964	Windber, Pennsylvania; Road Race	Matchless
August 9, 1964	Indianola, Iowa; Road Race	Matchless
August 16, 1964	Carpentersville, Illinois; Road Race	Matchless
August 30, 1964	Peoria, Illinois; TT	Matchless
July 4, 1965	Wentzville, Missouri; Road Race	Matchless
July 11, 1965	Nelson Ledges, Ohio; Road Race	Yamaha
August 15, 1965	Carpentersville, Illinois Road Race	Matchless

May 12, 1967	Reading, Pennsylvania; Half Mile	BSA
August 13, 1967	Peoria, Illinois; TT	BSA
August 15, 1969	Hinsdale, Illinois; Short Track	OSSA
August 17, 1969	Peoria, Illinois; TT	BSA
March 15, 1970	Daytona Beach, Florida; Road Race	Honda
July 11, 1970	Castle Rock, Washington; TT	BSA
January 29, 1971	Houston, Texas; TT	BSA
March 14, 1971	Daytona Beach, Florida; Road Race	BSA
July 11, 1971	Kent, Washington; Road Race	BSA
August 22, 1971	Pocono, Pennsylvania; Road Race	BSA
August 5, 1972	Homewood, Illinois; Mile	BSA
August 13, 1972	Peoria, Illinois; TT	BSA

C

Dick Mann's Championship Standings

Year	**Place**	**Champions**
1954	2nd	Amateur in the Nation; Brad Andres Top Amateur
1955	29th	Joe Leonard, Grand National Champion
1956	15th	Brad Andres, Grand National Champion
1957	6th	Joe Leonard, Grand National Champion
1958	8th	Carroll Resweber, Grand National Champion
1959	2nd	Carroll Resweber, Grand National Champion
1960	5th	Carroll Resweber, Grand National Champion
1961	3rd	Carroll Resweber, Grand National Champion
1962	3rd	Bart Markel, Grand National Champion
1963	***1st***	***Dick Mann, Grand National Champion***
1964	2nd	Roger Reiman, Grand National Champion
1965	2nd	Bart Markel, Grand National Champion
1966	12th	Bart Markel, Grand National Champion
1967	5th	Gary Nixon, Grand National Champion
1968	8th	Gary Nixon, Grand National Champion
1969	6th	Mert Lawwill, Grand National Champion
1970	4th	Gene Romero, Grand National Champion

Year	Place	Champions
1971	***1st***	***Dick Mann, Grand National Champion***
1972	6th	Mark Brelsford, Grand National Champion
1973	10th	Kenny Roberts, Grand National Champion

D

About Dick Mann, A Bibliography

Anonymous, "Dick Mann: 1963 Grand National Champion," *American Motorcyclist,* November, 1963.

Anonymous, "Dick Mann Has His Day at the Championships," *American Motorcyclist,* October, 1969.

Anonymous, "Dick Mann," *Cycle Racing Annual,* 1970.

Anonymous, "Dick Mann: 1971 Champ," *AMA News,* November, 1971.

Anonymous, "Dick Mann: *Cycle* magazine Rider of the Year for 1972," *Cycle,* March, 1972.

Anonymous, "Dick Mann: Two Time Grand National Champion," *Motor Cycle Weekly,* August 20, 1977.

Anonymous, "American Heroes: Who's The Best Dirt-Tracker of All Time?" *American Motorcyclist,* January, 1994.

Anonymous, "Dick Mann," www.amadirectlink.com/museum/halloffame/members/mann/mann.htm, September, 2001.

Bagnall, William, "Mann Makes it at Daytona," *Motorcyclist,* June, 1970.

Carruthers, Paul, "Still At It After All These Years," *Cycle News,* February 19, 1986.

Clifford, Peter, "Bugs," *The World of Motorcycles,* Volume 9 (of 22). Orbis Publishing, Ltd., London, 1979.

Coleman, Barry, "Bugsy and His Passion for the Past," *Kenny Roberts: Okie, Racer, Philosopher, King,* Arthur Barker Limited, London, 1982.

Conner, Frank, "Bugs," *Cycle,* February, 1972.

Dean, Paul, "The Mann Plan," *Cycle Guide,* November, 1977.

Hicks, Bob, "Dick Mann Singled Out for Suspension by AMA," *Cycle Sport,* December, 1968.

Hicks, Bob, "Dick Mann Honored," *Cycle Sport,* April, 1972.

Jennings, Gordon, "BSA Sets Speed Records at Daytona," *Cycle,* July, 1969.

Mann, Dick, "The Right Way Up in Class C Flat-Tracking," *Cycle Racing Annual,* 1968.

Mann, Dick, and Joe Scalzo, *Motorcycle Ace: The Dick Mann Story,* Henry Regnery Company, Chicago, 1972.

Mann, Dick, "The ISDT Reunion: A Unique Event," http://ahrma.org/previews/isdt_reunion.htm, September, 2001.

Martin, George, "Meet Dick Mann," *Cycle World,* August, 1964.

Parsons, Grant, "Dick Mann: Reflections of a Racer's Life," *American Motorcyclist,* January, 1998.

Reynolds, Boyd, "Mann Wins 50-Mile Road-Race," *American Motorcycling,* October, 1964.

Rockwood, Roxy, "Mann Wins Demanding 175-Mile Road-Race," *American Motorcycling,* October, 1964.

Rockwood, Roxy, "Mann's Third Win in a Row," *American Motorcycling,* October, 1964.

Rockwood, Roxy, "The Only Mann in Racing is Dick," *Daytona 200 Program,* 1973.

Rousseau, Scott, "Utility Mann," *Cycle News,* August 10, 1994.

Sims, Carol, "Dick Mann," *Motorcycle Sport Quarterly,* Summer, 1970.

Swift, David, "Dick Mann: The Complete Racer," *Cycle News West,* August 24, 1971; August 31, 1971; September 7, 1971.

Tarbox, Brian, "70s Super Heroes: Dick Mann," *Classic and Motorcycle Mechanics,* May, June, and July, 2001.

Weed, Len, "Mr. Motorcycle Explains it All to You," *Dirt Rider,* June, 1983.

E

Acknowledgments

With sincere gratitude, the following are acknowledged for their time, support, advice, and contribution to the research for this project. "MHF" indicates that the individual is a member of the Motorcycle Hall of Fame.

Cary Agajanian, promoter and motor-sports attorney.

Dave Aldana (MHF), professional motorcycle racer.

AMA and FIM vice president **Bill Amick.**

Three-time Daytona winner and 1955 Grand National Champion **Brad Andres** (MHF).

Motorcycle enthusiast and AHRMA legal counsel **Ted Bendelow.**

Motorcycle journalist **Matt Benson.**

Joe Bolger, racer and motorcycle designer.

Motorcycle racer and businessman **Everett Brashear** (MHF).

Bruce Brown (MHF), motion picture producer.

Motorcycle marketing consultant **Don Brown** (MHF).

Al Burke, professional racer.

Professional racer **Sid Carlson.**

Jim Cameron, friend of Dick Mann.

Kel Carruthers (MHF), 1969 road-racing world champion.

Professional racer and businessman **Tom Cates.**

Professional racer and former AMA official **Tom Clark.**

Racer and motorcycle industry leader **Pete Colman** (MHF).

Frank Conner, motorcycle journalist.

Six Days rider **Don Cutler.**

Motorcycle dealer and professional racer **Ted Davis.**

Paul Dean, journalist.

Professional racer and tuner **Babe DeMay** (MHF).

Journalist and television commentator **Dave Despain** (MHF).

Motorcycle dealer **Carl Donelson** and spouse **Kay Donelson.**

Engineer and friend of Dick Mann, **Jim Dour.**

Darrel Dovel, professional racer and former AMA official.

Chris Draayer, professional racer.

Promoter and former Bultaco importer **Bill Dutcher.**

Edison Dye (MHF), motorcycle importer and the father of American motocross.

AHRMA co-founder **Jeff Elghanayan.**

Professional racer and Daytona winner **Don Emde** (MHF).

Professional racer **Walt Fulton.**

Photographer and Dick Mann fan **John Gola.**

Paul Goldsmith (MHF), professional racer.

Four times motocross world champion **Torsten Hallman** (MHF).

Johnny Hall, friend of Dick Mann.

Dick Hammer (MHF), professional racer.

Tuner and team owner **Bob Hansen** (MHF).

Motorcycle collector and Vincent expert **Herb Harris.**

Movie stunt coordinator and racer **Gene Hartline.**

Professional racer **John Hateley.**

ISDT veteran **Harry Hellerman.**

Marshall Digger Helm, professional racer.

New England Sports Committee leader and Inter-Am promoter **Bob Hicks.**

Six Days rider and motocrosser **Barry Higgins** (MHF).

Bobby Hill (MHF), professional motorcycle racer.

Millie Horky, spouse of AMA official Jules Horky (MHF).

ISDT veteran **Fred Hunter.**

AHRMA co-founder and Team Obsolete owner **Rob Iannucci.**

John Indelicato, Dick Mann fan.

Dick Mann highschool class mate **Kay Indelicato.**

Mike Jackson, Norton and AJS motorcycle importer.

Motorcycle dealer and professional racer **Glenn Jordan.**

Racer and philosopher **Neil Keen** (MHF).

Three-time Daytona winner **Dick Klamfoth** (MHF).

Rick Kocks, photographer.

Motorcycle racer **Ed Kretz, Jr.**

Motocross world champion **Brad Lackey** (MHF).

AHRMA executive director **Dave Lamberth.**

Motocross pioneer **Lars Larsson** (MHF).

Six Days rider **Dave Latham.**

Grand National Champion **Mert Lawwill** (MHF) and spouse **June Lawwill.**

Three-time Grand National Champion **Joe Leonard** (MHF).

Engineer and motocross racer **Gunnar Lindstrom** (MHF).

John Lund, motorcycle dealer.

Marcia Macdonald, photographer and Six Days team manager.

Motorcycle racer, dealer, and Six Days rider **Tommy McDermott** (MHF).

Claude McElvain, motorcycle mechanic.

Professional racer **Jim McMurren.**

Dan Mahony, motor-sports photographer.

Twice Grand National Champion **Dick Mann** (MHF) and his spouse **Kay Mann.**

Vintage enduro enthusiast **Andre Ming.**

AHRMA chairman **Fred Mork.**

United Kingdom vintage racing organizer **Adrian Moss.**

Professional racer **Eddie Mulder** (MHF).

Dave Mungenast (MHF), Six Days rider and motorcycle businessman.

Professional racer **Jody Nicholas** (MHF).

Road-racing frame builder **Rob North.**

Twice Grand National Champion **Gary Nixon** (MHF).

Jim Odom, professional racer.

Chuck Palmgren, professional racer.

American Enduro Grand National Champion and Six Days rider **John Penton** (MHF).

Barbara Phillips, spouse of the late Jimmy Phillips (MHF), professional racer.

Professional racer **Ronnie Rall** (MHF).

Four-time Grand National Champion **Carroll Resweber** (MHF).

Jim Rice (MHF), professional racer.

Three-time road-racing world champion **Kenny Roberts** (MHF).

Vintage road racer and AHRMA trustee **Beno Rodi.**

Professional racer **George Roeder** (MHF).

Grand National Champion **Gene Romero** (MHF).

Motorcycle collector and AHRMA volunteer leader **John Sawazhki.**

Motorcycle journalist **Carol Sims.**

Brian Slark, AHRMA trustee.

Jeff Smith (MHF), two-time motocross world champion and AHRMA executive director.

Off-road champion **Malcolm Smith** (MHF).

Bill Stewart, Dick Mann fan.

AMA special events manager **Will Stoner.**

Sammy Tanner (MHF), professional motorcycle racer.

Motorcycle businessman **John Taylor.**

Bill Tuman (MHF), professional motorcycle racer.

AHRMA official **Jack Turner.**

Mann's friend and fan **Red Underhill.**

Motorcycle racer **Howard Utsey.**

Professional racer **Skip VanLeeuwen** (MHF).

Don Vesco (MHF), tuner and land speed record holder.

Six Days rider **Charlie Vincent.**

AHRMA trustee **Allen Wenzel.**

Photographer **Jerry West.**

Professional racer **Ralph White** (MHF).

Tom White, motorcycle businessman.

Former AHRMA executive director **Dr. Gary Winn.**

Index

Y

About the Author

Ed Youngblood has been riding motorcycles for more than 40 years, and has spent 30 years earning his living in the motorcycle industry. Following completion of a Master of Arts degree in English Literature in 1968, he became an editor for *Cycle News East,* then joined the staff of the American Motorcyclist Association in 1970, where he served as an editor, director of government relations, and its president and CEO from 1981 through 1999. In addition to his 28-year tenure at the AMA, he served for 20 years on the management counsel of the Federation Internationale de Motocyclisme, retiring in 1996 with the title of Honorary Deputy President.

Youngblood is a member of the Motorcycle Hall of Fame, he was named Man of the Year by the Women's Motocross League in April, 1999, and in

September, 1999, received the John Farmer Eggers Award, the highest honor bestowed by the Motorcycle Riders Foundation.

Youngblood is a management consultant to non-profit organizations, and has been a curatorial advisor for both the Motorcycle Hall of Fame Museum and the Guggenheim Museum's "The Art of the Motorcycle" exhibition. His exhibits at the Motorcycle Hall of Fame Museum include "Women & Motorcycling" and "A Century of Indian, Presented by Progressive Motorcycle Insurance." In addition to writing dozens of articles for motorcycling and association management publications, his previous books include a series of remedial reading texts for Capstone Press (1999), *John Penton and the Off-Road Motorcycle Revolution* (Whitehorse Press, 2000), and *A Century of Indian* (Motorbooks International, 2001). His scholarly paper, "The Birth of the Dirt-Bike: Technology and the Shift in Attitude Toward American Motorcyclists in the 1970s" was selected for presentation at the Southwest Pop Culture Conference in February, 2002.

About *Mann of His Time* Youngblood says, "I don't have many motorcycling memories that predate Dick Mann. When I attended my first professional race in the 1960s, Dick Mann was there. As an officer of the AMA, I frequently felt his influence. After we created a museum, it was Dick who convinced me we needed to place a higher priority on the establishment of the Motorcycle Hall of Fame. He is a man who understands the importance of knowing our history and honoring our traditions, and among current living motorcyclists, Dick Mann has had more influence than perhaps any other person in creating that history and forming those traditions. It has been a welcome challenge and an honor to attempt to tell his remarkable story."